OF PRIVACY AND POWER

Of Privacy and Power

The Transatlantic Struggle over Freedom and Security

Henry Farrell

Abraham L. Newman

PRINCETON UNIVERSITY PRESS

PRINCETON AND OXFORD

Copyright © 2019 by Princeton University Press

Published by Princeton University Press
41 William Street, Princeton, New Jersey 08540
6 Oxford Street, Woodstock, Oxfordshire OX20 1TR

press.princeton.edu

All Rights Reserved

Library of Congress Control Number: 2018967494
ISBN 9780691183640

British Library Cataloging-in-Publication Data is available

Editorial: Eric Crahan, Bridget Flannery-McCoy, Alena Chekanov, and Pamela Weidman
Production Editorial: Karen Carter
Jacket Art and Design: Amanda Weiss
Production: Erin Suydam
Publicity: James Schneider and Caroline Priday
Copyeditor: Cindy Milstein

This book has been composed in Adobe Text Pro.

Printed on acid-free paper. ∞

Printed in the United States of America

10 9 8 7 6 5 4 3 2 1

To Jack, Kieran, Micah, and Sadie

CONTENTS

LIST OF ILLUSTRATIONS

Figures

Table

LIST OF ABBREVIATIONS

ACLU	American Civil Liberties Union
CAPPS	Computer-Assisted Passenger Prescreening System
CIA	Central Intelligence Agency
CRS	Computerized Reservation System
DG	Directorate-General
DHS	Department of Homeland Security
DPAs	Data Privacy Authorities
EDRi	European Digital Rights Initiative
FBI	Federal Bureau of Investigation
FISA	Foreign Intelligence Surveillance Act
FTC	Federal Trade Commission
GAO	Government Accountability Office
GCHQ	Government Communications Headquarters
GDPR	General Data Protection Regulation
IATA	International Air Transport Association
Interpol	International Criminal Police Organization
ISIS	Islamic State of Iraq and Syria
MEPs	Members of European Parliament
MLATs	Mutual Legal Assistance Treaties
NGOs	Nongovernmental Organizations
NIA	New Interdependence Approach
NSA	National Security Agency
NSC	National Security Council
OECD	Organization for Economic Cooperation and Development
PIU	Passenger Information Units
PNR	Passenger Name Record
PPD	Presidential Policy Directive
SEPA	Single Euro Payments Area
SWIFT	Society for Worldwide Interbank Financial Telecommunication
TEU	Treaty on European Union

TFTP	Terrorist Financial Tracking Program
TFTS	Terrorist Financial Tracking System
TSA	Transportation Security Administration
WTO	World Trade Organization

PREFACE

At the turn of the millennium, privacy and terrorism seemed nearly irrelevant to international affairs. The big questions were obvious. What explained states' openness to trade? What were the sources of war and peace among the great powers? Privacy was at best an afterthought and at worst irrelevant. Terrorism was admittedly a problem for some countries, but it was a problem that could be tackled through better policing.

Now we live in a different world. The attacks of September 11, 2001, the rise of the Islamic State of Iraq and Syria, the Edward Snowden revelations, and the dominance of the platform companies have reshaped our politics and economy. New problems—such as competition over artificial intelligence and the disinformation campaign conducted as part of the 2016 US election—are coming to the forefront of international policy debate. Yet the international relations academy still has to catch up. In international political economy, there is little research on the politics of privacy and data rights, even though they are fundamental to the global information economy and the conflicts that plague it. Mainstream international security scholars have devoted great attention to understanding terrorist networks and their tactics, but have mostly ignored government responses to such threats.

This book begins to remedy these problems. We have carried out research over a period of nearly two decades, examining how governments have built an intricate web of connections across the Atlantic, sharing information (often gleaned from private companies) and quietly cooperating to manage emerging security risks. These new relationships have altered the preexisting balance between privacy and security, causing a decades-long counterreaction in which privacy and civil liberties advocates have looked to protect what they have as well as restore what they can.

The book recasts these policy debates so that they can be seen where they belong: at the heart of the global politics of information. Our investigation of privacy and security in the transatlantic relationship allows us to understand both their implications for world politics and their origins in broader changes. Globalization has led to economic openness and interdependence, which in turn have generated political opportunities for actors to transform policy domestically and internationally.

Three observations motivated us to write this book. First, we were frustrated by overly simplistic depictions of global politics in general and the transatlantic relationship in particular. Most inquiry into global politics starts from a convenient shorthand in which international relations is reduced to deals and disagreements between discrete states. Over time, this has become a misleading caricature; the map has been mistaken for the territory. Regular complaints about "state-centric" models have not produced many systematic nonstate alternatives.

Thus, for example, scholars and policy makers have seen clashes between the United States and European Union over domestic security issues as battles between a warmongering United States and rule-loving European Union, with each trying to impose its preferred approach on the other. This was not what we saw when we conducted interviews or read primary documents. Instead, we found a host of nonconventional actors directly involved in the conduct of international affairs. While foreign ministers and ambassadors continue to matter, they no longer enjoy a monopoly over global negotiations. Firms, privacy regulators, nongovernmental organizations (NGOs), interior and finance ministries, and intelligence agencies set agendas, propose solutions, and create the political coalitions that underpin international deals on privacy and security.

When one considers this wider set of players, the monolith of the state shatters into a myriad of individual pieces. Rather than a "US" or "EU" position, the transatlantic relationship is shaped by quarreling societies of actors, which often have one faction pushing for greater leeway to pursue security concerns, and another arguing for greater attention to privacy issues. Once internal disputes have been transformed by globalization, these competing factions are no longer bound to fight their battles within domestic politics. Instead, some players have access to global political opportunities, allowing them to forge alliances across societies as opposed to within them.

Second, we were struck by how EU-US negotiations over privacy and security were plagued by repeated disagreements rather than convergence on a single solution. Each deal seemed no more and no less than the platform for the next stage of institutional struggle, so that true equilibrium was never reached. Formal modelers are adept at forcing such square pegs into round holes—sometimes with surprising and usefully counterintuitive results. We took a different path, moving away from the rationalist models of negotiation that are usually employed in international relations to incorporate insights from sociology, comparative politics, and law. This body of work depicts contentious politics that does not necessarily conduct toward a stable outcome. By thinking of the transatlantic relationship as an ongoing struggle between competing factions hoping to promote privacy or security, we turned our attention from trying to understand the success or failure of actors in bargaining over a specific "deal" to the strategies that these actors deployed as they sought to bolster their cause in partially unpredictable processes of institutional change. When one is not as focused on discrete, time-limited outcomes, it becomes easier to characterize the longer-term dynamic processes in which the losers of a first round often come back to fight another day.

Third and finally, we were impressed by the far-reaching consequences that transatlantic politics had for the balance between civil liberties and surveillance. This was not simply a process of technocratic adjustment or shared approaches to governance. It was politics, and often bitter politics at that, involving sharp disagreements between actors who strongly disagreed. Much of the work on globalization emphasizes the frictions and problems that it generates, and the solutions that international institutions provide for those frictions. We saw the opposite: instead of fixing political problems, international institutions opened up old domestic bargains and new topics of contention. International institutions are not just quick fixes to coordination or cooperation problems. We also found that these institutions generate opportunity structures that some actors, but not others, use to further their political objectives.

In other words, transatlantic interactions and institutions generate distributional consequences and power asymmetries among competing factions. These transnational interactions have real implications for the relationship between the state and its citizens, and for the extent to which individuals enjoy a reasonable expectation of privacy. Therefore, *Of Privacy and Power* offers an alternative vision of global politics that is much less centered on purportedly functional solutions, and much more concerned with enduring forms of political contention and how global politics transforms them. In this vision, a range of actors—firms, interior ministers, and NGOs—seek to deploy the transatlantic relationship to transform their own societies as well as the interaction between them.

To write this book, we drew heavily on our scholarly community. We thank Karen Alter, Jeff Anderson, David Bach, Tim Bartley, Ralf Bendrath,

Francesca Bignami, Marc Busch, Charlotte Cavaille, Pepper Culpepper, Daniel Drezner, David Edelstein, Michelle Egan, Rachel Epstein, Maria Farrell, Martha Finnemore, Orfeo Fioretos, Julia Gray, Adrienne Hèritier, Markus Jachtenfuchs, Tana Johnson, Miles Kahler, Orin Kerr, Susanne Lütz, Edward Mansfield, Kathleen McNamara, Manuella Moschella, Daniel Nexon, Elliot Posner, Tonya Putnam, Nita Rudra, Frank Schimmelfennig, Paul Schwartz, Katrin Seig, Susan Sell, Greg Shaffer, Spiros Simitis, Debora Spar, Sid Tarrow, Anna von der Goltz, James Vreeland, Steve Weber, Holger Wolf, Alasdair Young, and John Zysman. Caspar Bowden, who foresaw many of the crises of the Snowden era before they happened, died far too young; he offered valuable early encouragement. Nikhil Kalyanpur went above and beyond the call, providing invaluable research support, proofing and general criticism, and good conversation as well as common sense. We thank Filip Savatic for his assistance constructing the index.

We presented sections of the manuscript at the Free University of Berlin, Georgetown University, George Washington University, the Hertie School, Princeton University, the University of Denver, and the University of Pennsylvania, and at the annual meetings of the European Union Studies Association (2017), International Studies Association (2014), and American Political Science Association (2013 and 2016). In all these places, we received invaluable feedback and constructive criticism, and want to thank the audiences, participants, and discussants.

This book is the culmination of a decadelong collaboration. We are thus indebted to the many expert reviewers who closely engaged with our work over the years. This includes articles that appeared in the *Review of International Political Economy*, *World Politics*, and *Comparative Political Studies*.[1] We also want to thank Eric Crahan and Princeton University Press. We could not have imagined a more productive engagement with a press or editorial team.

The book benefited from substantial institutional support too. We are grateful to our home universities, both George Washington University and Georgetown University. Henry also thanks the Max-Planck Institut zur Erforschung von Gemeinschaftsgütern, where he first began working on this topic, the University of Toronto, where he continued, and the Woodrow Wilson Center for International Scholars, which provided him a home for a crucial year of research and writing. His contributions to the book were fueled by Quartermaine's coffee and the music of Burial. Abe thanks the faculty and staff at Georgetown including the BMW Center for German and European Studies, Mortara Center for International Studies, Government Department, and School of Foreign Service as well as Big Bear and Royal coffeehouses.

In many ways, we are intellectual doppelgängers. We first met in summer 2003 in Bonn, Germany, where Henry was on a postdoc studying EU-US privacy negotiations, and Abe was doing preliminary fieldwork on a related topic for his dissertation. We then spent the following years crossing paths at job talks, publishing on similar themes, and living in the same town. Rather than falling victim to the competitive dynamics that this might have produced, we found commonality and strength in our collective voice. We have now spent nearly ten years working together in a rare intellectual partnership. Such journeys are not without risk, as their success relies on sharing half-baked ideas and exposing personal limitations. They are successful—as this project was—when it becomes impossible for either collaborator to identify which ideas were originally whose. We are so lucky and grateful for that beer back in 2003 and look forward to the next decade of joint work.

Finally, we owe our deepest gratitude to our families. Far too many hours were spent at the computer and on the manuscript as our spouses and children waited patiently for us to finish up. To our spouses, Nicole and Craig, thank you for your endless support and love. To our children, Jack, Kieran, Micah, and Sadie, we dedicate this book to you.

OF PRIVACY AND POWER

Introduction

FREEDOM AND SECURITY
IN THE NEW INTERDEPENDENCE

In June 2013, a former intelligence contractor, Edward Snowden, released top-secret documents detailing the global surveillance activities of the US National Security Agency (NSA). Press reports emphasized the Orwellian implications of programs denoted by sinister-sounding acronyms like PRISM and MYSTIC. Many Europeans were outraged by the revelation that the United States had trampled on their freedoms and comprehensively gathered data on their communications. Less frequently noted was the fact that in addition to collecting massive amounts of internet data, the NSA provided help to its European partners, who themselves were busy spying. While Snowden himself, in his testimony to the European Parliament, highlighted the importance of data sharing between US and European intelligence agencies, most commentators focused instead on the easier stories about the United States and Europe's clash over privacy.

This is just one example of how scholars and policy makers overlook one of the most significant ongoing changes in global politics: the internationalization of domestic security. People think of homeland security, domestic security, counterterrorism, or interior policy as things that happen inside national borders. That is no longer the case. These issues have become far more internationalized, both in scope and intensity, over the last few decades. In turn, debates over civil liberties and privacy are no

1

longer confined behind national borders but have been internationalized as well.

States make considerable efforts to guarantee the safety of their citizens from domestic attack, and since the attacks of September 11, 2001, it is painfully clear that global politics have domestic security repercussions. As threats have become transnational, so too have policy responses to them. Interior ministry officials, like their counterparts in foreign affairs and defense ministries, travel the world to coordinate through bilateral exchanges and multilateral summits. Such meetings play an especially prominent role in the transatlantic relationship between the United States and European Union along with its member states. During the George W. Bush administration, Homeland secretary Michael Chertoff spoke directly to the European Parliament in spring 2007, and Obama administration Homeland Secretary Janet Napolitano traveled to Europe almost as frequently as Secretary of State Hillary Clinton. These interactions continue and have been regularized.[1] High-level ministerial meetings have been accompanied by a host of ongoing formal and informal agreements and dialogues among civil servants forging links among internal security bureaucrats on both sides of the Atlantic.

Europe and the United States play key roles in this area. They control the world's largest markets and thus enjoy enormous clout. They also have the most developed state agencies tasked with overseeing information sharing, policing, and counterterrorism. The transatlantic politics of domestic security, then, shape the policies, practices, and lived experience of security forces, firms, and citizens across the globe.

This tacit condominium belies the mythology, which depicts the politics of transatlantic domestic security in antagonistic terms, pitting the United States against Europe in battles over principle and practicality. Reporters and op-ed writers regularly suggest that the United States is "Mars" (to extend Robert Kagan's rather-loaded analogy), pushing for stronger security measures and more willing to relax executive constraints, while the European Union is "Venus," obsessed with the rule of law, privacy, and human rights.[2] Under this perspective, the United States has forced (and is forcing) the European Union to adopt much more extensive antiterrorism measures than anyone in Europe wants, eroding homegrown European privacy protections.

This emphasis on US demands and bullying as a driving force blinds observers to the intricate dynamic that has emerged between the transatlantic partners: demands repeatedly rebuffed, cooperation imperiled, and ad hoc work-around agreements that produce broader institutional changes in both jurisdictions. Behind apparent deadlock lies a burgeoning set of institutional arrangements for the transatlantic exchange of security information, which not only changes the parameters of potential surveillance globally but is also altering fundamental domestic bargains within the two jurisdictions about the proper balance between government control and individual liberty. This is neither stasis nor convergence; instead, it is an emerging space of political opportunity for nonstate and substate actors as well as governmental leaders, rife with ambivalence and contradictions to be harnessed for strategic purposes.

This book addresses these dynamics through a specific application of a broader account that we have previously described as the New Interdependence Approach (NIA).[3] The internationalization of domestic security offers a window into a more general transformation in world politics unleashed by globalization. Our approach emphasizes how globalization is creating new channels for a variety of actors, who are not always conventional diplomats or trade negotiators, to assert themselves. Increasing economic interdependence destabilizes existing national bargains over policies and institutions, catapulting seemingly domestic policy disputes into the international arena. It also generates political channels of cooperation, allowing actors from different jurisdictions to forge alliances with their peers in other countries, often with quite-dramatic consequences for how markets and societies are governed.

Rather than viewing transatlantic disputes over domestic security and privacy as a clash of systems between the United States and Europe, we analyze them as a set of political battles between alliances of those respectively oriented toward security and civil liberties that often span the two. Power rarely resides in brute coercion, but rather in the political opportunities generated by interaction. The book, then, describes the strategies of change— cross-national layering, insulation, and defend and extend—enabled by interdependence, which security agencies, interior ministries, privacy NGOs, bureaucrats, and others exploit in their struggle over freedom and security.

The Internationalization of Domestic Security: Moving beyond Systems Clash

As domestic security threats have been internationalized, policy interdependence between Europe and the United States has increased and expanded into global coordination as well as convergence across domestic surveillance and policing policies. Such cooperation expands far beyond early minimal efforts at information sharing such as Interpol. Ongoing dialogues at the subministerial level exist side by side with greater ministerial contact.[4] The transatlantic High Level Contact Group on Information Sharing, for example, offers a forum for internal security and civil liberties bureaucrats in the European Union and United States to discuss emerging issues, develop cooperative templates, and build a common agenda.[5] Interior ministers share information on topics such as financial transactions, biometric data, and airline travel. Domestic security officials have been deputized to pursue criminals across borders, and countries have agreed to far-reaching (albeit ungainly) arrangements covering mutual legal assistance.[6] From surveillance to arrest, cross-border collaboration has proliferated.[7]

This transformation, in turn, spurs debates over the increase in interdependence, which often carry an intense normative charge.[8] The internationalization of domestic security provokes bitter arguments between those who demand action to protect populations from transnational threats and those who fear that outsourced police functions threaten individual freedom.[9]

Some see the EU-US relationship as involving the effective subordination of the European Union to the US national security state, and so believe that transatlantic interdependence challenges basic civil liberties.[10] From the 1990s on, the European Union developed extensive rules to protect privacy through managing the collection and exchange of personal information.[11] This has led human rights and privacy rights activists to point to the critical problems of accountability and legitimacy that the EU-US homeland security relationship raises. If states delegate internal policing activities to other states, citizens quickly find themselves subject to another government's authority. This threatens to attenuate local civil liberties such as due process, privacy, and fair trial. Moreover, as many of these cooperative efforts skirt formal international legal institutions and rely on administrative agreements between ministries, they lack even the indirect democratic legitimacy typical of traditional treaty documents. Although some scholars identify this as part of a growing trend across the advanced industrial democracies, many critics blame US hegemony more or less directly.[12] Privacy International, a leading nonprofit organization based in the United Kingdom, identifies EU decisions to weaken protection on airline passenger data as the product of Europe's "capitulation" to a US security agenda driven by the US Department of Homeland Security (DHS).[13] Members of the European Parliament (MEPs) frequently describe the United States as intent on trampling civil liberties in pursuit of self-defeating security objectives.

Others view the EU-US relationship in just the opposite terms, arguing that the European Union is holding the United States back from protecting its security. US conservatives and some US liberals maintain that September 11 demonstrated the dangers of a new kind of terrorist attack, and suggest that broad civil liberty concerns are outmoded, if not positively dangerous.[14] They contend that US deference to certain aspects of international law, and the sensibilities of traditional US allies in Europe and elsewhere, hinders the US ability to prosecute the war against terror. Here, policy interdependence is threatening because it requires the United States to rely on the whims of feckless foreign officials to implement policies necessary to the integrity and security of the US homeland.[15] As the United States becomes more open and more dependent on others to achieve domestic interests (e.g., to secure borders or cut off terrorists' access to the financial system), it is simultaneously exposed to new vulnerabilities.

This has led to a small industry in conservative commentary, depicting European officials as imperiling the safety of US citizens because of their mindless attachment to abstract principles of privacy protection. For instance, Stewart Baker, former assistant secretary for policy at the DHS, writes that the European Union's response to US security concerns is that it "sure sucks to be you," claiming that the European Union seeks to "cripple US antiterror intelligence programs," and adding that the European Union's "institutionalized hostility to the United States" threatens to get US citizens killed.[16]

These two perspectives on transatlantic domestic security relations draw opposite lessons about the policy problem posed by EU-US interactions. Both see the transatlantic relationship on domestic security issues as resulting from a clash between political systems inspired by antithetical sets of values.[17] Europeans are purportedly motivated by their fundamental faith in law, civil liberties, and peaceful relations as a means of securing long-term stability, whereas Americans are more belligerent and inclined toward muscular responses to evildoers. This understanding of what is at stake is nearly entirely pervasive among commentators. Both journalists and policy analysts emphasize the basic incompatibility of European and US values along with the conflict that this generates. Regardless of whether the winners are warmongering Americans or lily-livered Europeans, the battle is being fought between profoundly different systems, with profoundly different internal norms.

The problem is that neither of these accounts provides a good explanation of the ambivalences at the heart of the EU-US security relationship.

Those who condemn the United States as a hegemonic bully, using its out-size power to force security measures down the throat of the European Union, fail to explain the timing and character of cooperation, which is by no means always correlated with US threats, and the key moments of resistance. Nor do those blaming the intransigence of Europeans have a better grasp of the truth. Europeans sometimes oppose US demands, but often go further than US negotiators either expect or ask. Neither of these accounts explain why the European Union and United States have created a framework for domestic security cooperation over the last several years, nor yet how resistance to this framework has spread across the Atlantic. This framework is neither a capitulation by the European Union to the United States, nor an acknowledgment by the United States of European unwill-ingness to take security seriously, nor a simple compromise between the two positions. Instead, it is something new: a set of cross-national relation-ships that differs in important ways from the domestic institutions governing freedom and security on both sides of the Atlantic, but that is increasingly coming to structure both.

A New Way of Understanding Interdependence

One cannot explain these relationships by looking to system clash. Rather, one has to go a level deeper to understand how interdependence is reshaping power relations between actors—interior ministries, civil liberties NGOs, privacy regulators, and others—both in the European Union and United States, and most important, *across* the two jurisdictions. When we use the term *interdependence*, we are referring to the growth in exchange of goods, services, and communication across borders.[18] Such interactions create a situation in which the actions and/or policies of actors in one jurisdiction have significant consequences for the actions and/or policies of actors in other jurisdictions.[19] Interdependence sets in motion three powerful dynam-ics, which transform domestic institutions and in turn global governance.

First, it produces a situation of rule overlap in which the stability and credibility of domestic rules and laws become increasingly uncertain. As firms and citizens engage in market and political activities that span multi-ple jurisdictions, they face overlapping regulatory claims made by multiple sources of authority (often with incongruous rules covering a specific activ-ity), thereby creating cross-national tensions. Groups that are dissatisfied with their domestic rules now have opportunities to exploit these conflicts in order to destabilize their domestic legal status quo. In the absence of concerted policy action by policy makers, existing policies may be undermined. This suggests that interdependence substantially affects the bargaining weight of national authorities. Where there is conflict between actions and policies in different jurisdictions, public officials cannot simply assume a reversion point under which the policy will continue to apply if it is not changed.[20] In other words, interdependence destabilizes the status quo so that policy makers find their policies being eroded by cross-national pressures if they do not take specific actions to defend them.

Second, interdependence expands the number and type of actors who engage in global politics.[21] To be clear, we do not claim that the state or chief executive is irrelevant. We argue instead that it no longer enjoys a diplomatic monopoly. Revolutions in communication technology and travel mean that many more actors conduct transborder politics. Bureaucrats, firms, and NGO activists, meeting their peers at conferences (or through videoconferencing) develop policy proposals that resolve the uncertainty raised by rule overlap.

Third, interdependence provides these actors with new platforms for cooperation. As more and more political institutions transcend national borders, political actors use alternative channels to redefine the global rules, not only by lobbying their home state, but also by creating cross-national alliances with other actors in other jurisdictions.

As we discuss at greater length in chapter 1, these dynamics of openness and globalization allow actors to use transnational strategies to undermine or defend domestic institutions. We specifically draw on the historical institutionalist literature within comparative politics and the literature on American political development to understand how different relationships to the transnational context lead actors to adopt strategies of action, such as cross-national layering, insulation, and defend and extend.[22] Cross-national layering involves actors using transnational interactions to generate policy proposals that over time erode domestic rules. They do this by providing an international alternative to domestic policy bargains, which themselves have been unsettled by rule overlap. Insulation, by contrast, occurs when actors deploy domestic institutions to defend against transnational policy proposals, limiting the reach and consequences of these efforts. Finally, defend and extend describes efforts by domestic actors to externalize their domestic policy environment globally through transnational means. More generally, we build our historical institutionalist account up from comparative politics to international relations and then down again, as we show how the international context shapes domestic policies and institutions. Not only does the book demonstrate how theories more commonly employed in comparative politics have purchase on international relations; it also shows how comparativists, if they want to understand the consequences of globalization, need to pay serious and sustained attention to international and transnational politics.[23]

Interdependence empowers actors with opportunities—but it does not empower all actors equally, and some actors may not be empowered at all. As a result, interdependence generates winners and losers with varying consequences for the influence of different actors; ceteris paribus, those with access to transnational channels are likely to do better than before, and those without such access are likely to do worse. More specifically in the context of the transatlantic domestic security relationship, we argue that the dynamic is less a simple story of US hegemony than a matter of interactions within and across the two jurisdictions between an alliance of more security-minded officials and an alliance oriented more toward civil liberties. The political battlefield is shifting as both groups must consider transatlantic as well as domestic institutional strategies. These two groups are engaged in an ongoing struggle over freedom and security made possible by the new politics of interdependence.

New Interdependence and Transatlantic Domestic Security Relations

The main reason that we are interested in the internationalization of domestic security is its substantive importance. From the response to the attacks of September 11 to the Snowden affair to cyberattacks surrounding the 2016 US elections, domestic security plays a critical role in how the two largest global powers define the relationship between their citizens and emerging threats such as terrorism, organized crime, cybersecurity, hybrid warfare, and drug or human trafficking.[24] It has been neglected by nonspecialist international relations scholars, despite its importance both to policy makers and the present-day conduct of international politics.

The EU-US relationship is perhaps the best-developed example of global interdependence between separate jurisdictions.[25] It is also one of the best-studied international regulatory relationships in the world; EU-US interactions are central for core existing theories of international politics.[26] It therefore allows us to assess the relative benefits and drawbacks of the NIA and other major theories of international politics. The latter propose to explain this relationship too, without reference to the causal relationships emphasized by the NIA. In particular, we contrast our argument stressing cross-national alliances and interactions with the standard accounts focusing on clashes between different jurisdictional systems. We thus meet the challenge raised by scholars like Robert Keohane (2017) who pushes historical institutionalists to test their assertions against plausible alternatives.

The book's methodology rests on detailed analytic narratives, which use process tracing to assay the merits of the competing causal stories through careful examination of the empirical evidence.[27] In particular, we exploit substantial variation in the character of cooperation or conflict across time and specific policy area to scrutinize our claims about actor strategies. Empirically, the book focuses on three interlinked disputes (related to airline passenger data, financial sector information, and commercial data) over security, information, and interdependence between the European Union and United States over the last two decades. Each of the three disputes examined contains useful points of internal variation across time, with periods of deadlock followed by agreements that sometimes produce institutional change and sometimes are undermined. We employ a range of evidence drawing on a large data set of original interviews, primary documents, and secondary literature, compiled over nearly two decades of research. In addition, we exploit a novel contemporaneous source of data—the Wikileaks cables archive—to uncover both the US approach to negotiations and US perceptions of the political positions of European negotiators and politicians. As well as contributing to theoretical debates concerning globalization and interdependence, we make a more straightforward empirical contribution by offering detailed accounts of highly consequential interlinked negotiations. As such, we hope to inform those interested in studying global cooperation on domestic security issues, surveillance, and privacy in the post 9/11 period.

The Implications of the NIA for Global Politics

The NIA shifts the study of global politics away from traditional perspectives that underscore interactions between jurisdictions toward perspectives that emphasize interactions across them. We hope to use it to push scholars from both comparative politics and international relations to reconsider overly simplistic models of the intersection between domestic and international politics that sidestep transnational causal relationships.[28]

Rather than viewing globalization or interdependence as an exogenous shock that is filtered through domestic institutions, we see global politics as ongoing dynamic processes in which the domestic and international shape each other. As we discuss at greater length in chapter 1, our way of cutting into these complex dynamics and rendering them intelligible is to emphasize the interaction of rule overlap, opportunity structures, and asymmetrical access to these structures. This provides an alternative to the semiubiquitous metaphor of two-level games—a metaphor that has drawn attention away from dynamics between levels that do not flow through the positions adopted by formal negotiators.[29] This has led researchers to detach transnational forces from the domestic contestation that they structure, and instead build models that emphasize domestic interest groups or cleavages. Promising early work in the two-level games tradition, which noted the possibility of "reverberations" between different systems, has not generated a self-sustaining research agenda.[30] Standard models now focus almost exclusively on national interests and the domestic institutions that aggregate them rather than the ways in which international interactions transform domestic political struggles, and vice versa.

Equally, we look to move away from the standard diplomatic channels of global governance depicted in the two-level game metaphor, in which chief executives negotiate and then ratify agreements through domestic legislatures. Executive-legislative relations continue to matter in a world of globalization, but so too do a host of alternative channels through which actors engage in global politics.[31] As we show in chapters 3 and 4, negotiators can build less formal transnational institutions, sidestepping the direct oversight of executive leadership and legislative ratification, which in turn influence domestic institutions.[32] At the same time, as we demonstrate in chapter 5, nonstate actors who do not have access to the channels of formal negotiation may employ unconventional tactics to seize the initiative back from more traditional diplomatic actors.

This is not a world in which national executives—responding either to the median voter or interest groups, or some amalgam—build agreements that neatly fall into a policy space determined by the preferences of all the relevant actors. It is instead a world in which negotiators, regulators, firms, and NGOs jostle with each other as they each look in their different ways to protect their interests. National institutions themselves are often up for grabs, and national executives and legislatures have limited capacity to monitor or rein in the behavior of alternative initiatives. Thus, our perspective calls into question the faith placed in principal-agent models of delegation, which emphasize the ability of political principals to monitor and discipline unwanted political entrepreneurship by agents. Instead, it accords with empirical evidence demonstrating the limits of state control in a world of complex governance arrangements.[33]

We hope not only to contribute to debates on the interaction between domestic and international politics but also to shift how researchers view institutional change in the international arena. The majority of studies in international relations today focus on discrete institutional outcomes, such as ratification of a treaty, negotiation outcome, domestic legal change, or compliance. Such snapshots are important, and there is much we can learn from examining them. That said, we believe that this work tends to reinforce the perception that such snapshots represent stable equilibrium outcomes. In actuality, institutional stability is at best the provisional outcome of forces that themselves deserve sustained investigation, and at worst an unrealistic analytic convenience.

In contrast, our approach views politics as a process of ongoing contestation, where institutional outcomes are not static but instead platforms for efforts aimed at changing, building on, or undermining them.[34] Here, we emphasize two claims. First, political losers will seek over time to undermine political outcomes that are uncongenial to their interests, which means that we need to understand the strategies that they employ. Second, and in contrast to many common analyses, institutional change is not a succession of leaps, whether modest or extravagant, from one equilibrium to another. Institutions are not saltations; they are processes over time. An apparent win by one coalition of actors in $t = 1$ may be thwarted by a seemingly innocuous reform in $t = 2$ that then grows to supplant the institutions in $t = 3$.[35] For sure, at every moment in the sequence there are winners and losers as well as important power asymmetries generated by the process. Winning, however, often involves little more than cementing a temporary advantage that may in turn be undermined unexpectedly in a later round of play. By taking the long view, we eschew scoreboard assessments in which one coalition can be said to have definitively won or lost, and instead look at how apparent outcomes tend to fold back into processes similar to the ones that gave rise to them.

Finally, the book makes an important empirical contribution to research on the internationalization of domestic security and personal freedom.[36] In particular, we provide the most comprehensive study to date of EU-US interactions over information sharing, surveillance, and privacy. As we emphasize throughout, this narrative reveals that the conflict is not primarily between a United States focused on security and a European Union focused on the rule of law. Rather, there are political factions within each jurisdiction, which variously privilege security interests or civil liberties, and work together and against each other to alter the rules that govern domestic security. The book, then, reframes the conflicts between the United States and Europe on these issues, and reconsiders how transnational interactions unsettle the balance between civil liberties and surveillance. It furthermore shows how important domestic security, privacy, and information are for the global affairs studied by scholars of international politics.

The Book's Chapter Plan

Of Privacy and Power is intended for two related but also distinct audiences. On the one hand, it speaks to academics who want to understand how globalization is transforming world politics. These readers should begin with chapter 1, which presents our theoretical approach in detail. Chapters 3, 4, and 5 provide empirical demonstrations of the mechanisms—cross-national layering, defend and extend, and insulation—developed in the theoretical chapter. On the other hand, the book offers a comprehensive account for policy specialists concerned with transatlantic domestic security and privacy negotiations. Readers more interested in the substantive debate over freedom and security may prefer to skim or skip chapter 1, and start instead with chapter 2, which provides the factual background for the later account. They can then focus their attention on the empirical sections of chapters 3, 4, and 5, which detail, respectively, the negotiations over airline, financial, and commercial data. Some readers may be interested in both, in which case we commend their enthusiasm and promise that at least the book is not too long. In what follows, we offer a quick summary of each individual chapter.

Chapter 1 elaborates the fundamental theoretical argument of the book. Here we present the basic assumptions of the NIA, highlighting how economic interdependence creates conditions of rule overlap and opportunity structures for cross-national cooperation. The second half of the chapter develops a more specific set of claims about the strategies—cross-national layering, insulation, and defend and extend—that actors employ to leverage interdependence for their political ends.

Chapter 2 provides a comprehensive account of the origins and implications of EU and US policy positions as well as the evolution of global cooperation over domestic security. It maps out the diverse actors in each region, identifies their interests and perspectives, and lays out the sources of potential transnational coalitions. In particular, it identifies those groups at the domestic and international levels most focused on security, civil liberties, or economic concerns. The chapter charts the relative strength and preferences of the different actors within their respective political systems in the status quo ante before September 11, when domestic security issues were largely handled within national borders. It then systematically examines how preferences and institutional strength changed after September 11. In short, the chapter offers the essential background needed to understand the internationalization of domestic security issues, with a particular focus on the transatlantic relationship.

Chapter 3 examines how the alliances of actors fought over the issue of airline passenger data. It shows how a transnational alliance of security-minded officials used transatlantic cooperation to expand their discretion beyond what was possible under their own domestic rules and ultimately changed them. After the terrorist attacks of September 11, the US Congress passed a law that required foreign air carriers to transfer data concerning their passengers to the Bureau of Customs or risk significant fines. This transfer of information was in direct conflict with European privacy laws, and put European air carriers in the awkward position of trying to satisfy both US security requirements and EU rules. What followed was a series of contentious and volatile negotiations over how to regulate the sharing of airline passenger data across the Atlantic. Despite court challenges and active lobbying by civil liberties groups, the European Union ratified an agreement that now allows unprecedented amounts of individual data to flow to the United States. Additionally, the European Union reformed its own internal legislation to permit similar data flows internally. These kinds of domestic transformations are not what current theories of comparative and international politics would have predicted. The chapter concludes by identifying the lessons of the airline passenger debate for future transatlantic negotiations.

Chapter 4 offers a more in-depth examination of a particular strategy—cross-national layering—and how it was deployed by the security community to transform the debate over financial transactions data. In 2006, the *New York Times* published an article detailing a secret US Department of the Treasury program in which it obtained personal financial transactions from a banking consortium in Europe to track suspected terrorist activity. Once again, US demands came in conflict with European civil liberties rules. This led to a five-year period of negotiations, which swung from pledges of quick cooperation to complete breakdown to the culmination of a final agreement.

In contrast to the dispute over airline passenger data negotiations, the United States and European Union did not immediately make significant changes to their domestic laws. Instead, they constructed a transatlantic agreement intended to work around domestic opposition. This agreement used the principle of reciprocity to provide security actors in Europe with access to data on financial transactions that they had previously been denied under domestic institutions via an international cooperative arrangement. That arrangement is in turn giving rise to institutional change, and the likely creation of new rules within the European Union that would have been highly unlikely or even impossible without the EU-US interaction. Far from a standard international agreement on a technical issue area, the transatlantic bargain on financial data sharing underscores how global cooperation circumvents and undermines domestic political bargains. The chapter outlines the mechanisms of cross-national layering through which these changes took place.

Chapter 5 examines the urgent political transatlantic controversies over surveillance in the wake of Snowden's revelations. These have reshaped transatlantic arguments over security and privacy, allowing a coalition of privacy-friendly actors to undermine the Safe Harbor Agreement, which allowed the transatlantic sharing of commercial data, effectively holding e-commerce firms hostage for changes in US (and over the longer term, European) privacy practices. When the Safe Harbor Agreement was initially built in 2000, bureaucratic actors in the European Union and United States sought to use it to defend their respective domestic systems and promote commercial data exchange. After the Snowden revelations, a different set of actors that was motivated by civil liberties sought to undermine the agreement in the European Union so as to insulate their domestic system from transnational pressures. Again, this illustrates how actors seek to protect existing domestic arrangements as they come under pressure from coalitions of actors empowered by interdependence. In contrast to airline passenger data, civil-liberties-oriented actors were able to leverage domestic political arrangements at home so as to win real power abroad.

The book concludes by setting out a broader international agenda for the study of privacy and power. It first considers the policy implications of the findings for those interested in debates surrounding privacy and freedom. The conclusion discusses both the importance of transnational data flows and the blurring between public and private sector surveillance. Second, the chapter reconsiders the role of power in world politics, highlighting the insights of the NIA, demonstrating the fundamental importance of information in world politics. It ends by emphasizing how transatlantic conflict and cooperation on the intersection between domestic security and civil liberties not only produces important global agreements but also provides actors with crucial institutional resources to transform basic rights and security policies on both sides of the Atlantic.

1

Politics in an Age of Interdependence

What is the relationship between globalization and world politics? As we observed in the opening chapter, this is an urgent real-world question. The global economy has rapidly changed from one based on the simple exchange of goods and Ricardian comparative advantage to a more complex system involving a host of economic activities that are organized across borders—transnational services, data flows, global production chains, and investment—to name just a few.[1]

Politically, we have moved from a world market based around trade between actors located in discrete national systems to the world that trade built—a world in which the rules and principles that govern the behavior of market actors are no longer developed and enforced purely at the level of the nation-state. Instead, firms, citizens, and NGOs face multiple political demands—and opportunities—stemming from the overlapping of domestic and global authorities.[2] In many cases, these actors are both setting rules and responding to them. Internet firms including Google and Facebook find themselves in the crosshairs of both European privacy authorities and US national security agencies, while at the same time Apple, Nike, and Volkswagen shape labor practices in countries ranging from China to South Africa.[3] The politics of globalization is marked, then, by policy interdependence: the ways in which rules developed by one authority (a state, international organization, or private regulator) spill over so that they affect the rules and regulations of another authority.[4]

These shifts have consequences for the politics of globalization, which have expanded from struggles over free trade and protectionism to a much broader and more complicated fight over the regulations and principles that affect how the economic as well as political benefits of globalization are distributed.[5] These battles have become even more heated because economic and security issues are increasingly intertwined. Data, for example, serve simultaneously as an essential basis for economic exchange for the largest and most valuable companies in the world, including Amazon, Facebook, and Microsoft, and a potent source of control for government agencies, including the US Department of the Treasury, the NSA, and the United Kingdom's Government Communications Headquarters.

This poses important theoretical questions for international politics. Scholars like to draw sharp differences between jurisdictions, whether they be "Mars versus Venus" or "liberal versus coordinated economies."[6] But these distinctions blur into confusion in a world where financial, informational, and trade flows have increased dramatically so that the effective ambit of different countries' national authority overlaps.[7] New actors are emerging and engaging in forms of contestation that weaken the traditional divide between the domestic and international.[8]

This is certainly not to suggest that a single world market, society, or government has emerged. Rather, regulators, civil society, and firms that were once cast in domestic roles now play on other stages too. These actors forge alliances across jurisdictions and policy arenas to alter international as well as domestic public policy.[9] As policy makers realize that their choices are interdependent with the choices of policy makers in other jurisdictions, they not only try to mitigate the problems that this imposes and reduce clashes with other regulatory systems but also attempt to take full advantage of the opportunities. Those actors who are dissatisfied with their domestic political status quo may use the politics of interdependence to unsettle national or global rules.

This chapter moves beyond describing this new world order. It provides a theoretically grounded model of global politics within it: the New Interdependence Approach (NIA). We do this by reviving an older strain of scholarship on interdependence that emphasizes the opportunity structures forged by globalization, and coupling that tradition with more recent historical institutionalist work in comparative political economy and American political development.

This allows us to explain actor strategies and how they feed into trajectories of institutional change. We examine variation in the policy environment across domestic and international settings to identify the conditions under which strategies familiar to international relations scholars predominate, such as seeking to defend and extend one's domestic rules. We better specify the conditions under which actors will turn to novel strategies such as *cross-national layering* and *insulation*. Our arguments move away from an approach that takes snapshots of world politics, examining the factors that led to a given equilibrium outcome, and toward one that looks at processes in train, emphasizing how even apparent moments of stasis contain the opportunities that allow actors to transform them. From a longer historical perspective, a negotiation that looks like a failure at one moment in time may turn out later to provide the seeds of a regime shift.

The primary objective of this chapter is to present the theoretical framework for the book's later arguments and situate it in political science debates. Readers who are primarily interested in policy debates concerning privacy and security in the transatlantic space may want to skim this chapter to identify key themes that we return to throughout the book and then proceed to chapter 2. Alternatively, they can skip it for the moment and only return as necessary to explain necessary concepts.

In the next section, we review the dominant accounts that have been used to explain the politics of globalization and policy interdependence. These accounts surely helped spark debate over how globalization can be managed, but have done so at a cost. They systematically emphasize the state level at the expense of other important vectors of causation and tend toward static rather than process-driven explanations. The succeeding section provides the foundations for our proposed alternative. We emphasize how *rule overlap* and changing *opportunity structures* reshape actor strategies. Then we go on to identify how the intersection between actors' orientations toward existing domestic institutions (do they wish to protect these institutions or overturn them?) and their level of access to cross-national institutional structures (high or low?) predispose them toward specific strategies (defend and extend, cross-national layering, insulation, and challenge).

We briefly summarize our empirical expectations, and show how the theoretical approach outlined in this chapter offers insights into the ongoing transatlantic struggle over freedom and security. Finally, we lay out the general implications of our alternative understanding of globalization and policy interdependence.

The Shock of Globalization

The simple economic account of globalization sees it as involving the increasing of goods, services, information, and people across borders.[10] The dominant literatures in international relations have tended to view such movements as causing four kinds of external shocks to the international political economy: shocks of exit, openness, cooperation problems, and market power. Scholars espousing these different approaches have sometimes tried, with limited success, to construct nomothetic accounts of international economic politics. They have been rather more successful in identifying broad causal relationships linking domestic and international politics that explain the openness or closure of particular economies.

The exit approach emphasizes *business power vis-à-vis states*. Falling capital controls and transportation costs mean that some firms find exit opportunities. These firms use the threat of relocating their investments and jobs to pressure states into converging on liberal policies that favor economic exchange. The resulting scholarly debate has focused on the extent to which the threat of exit constrains (or does not constrain) government behavior.[11]

Here, the posited causal relationship runs from increased opportunities for economic mobility in the international environment, through increased bargaining power for private actors (especially firms) able to take advantage of these opportunities, to changes in domestic institutions. Governments find that the costs of some institutional configurations (specifically, configurations that mobile businesses find unpalatable) are much higher than they used to be. This may cause them either to abandon these institutions where they already exist, in favor of ones that are more congenial to business, or to decline to adopt such institutions where they are not present. Crude versions of this argument posit a generic "race to the bottom."[12] More subtle and defensible versions examine how some institutions (such as training institutions) may be valuable to businesses that hope to compete in the global economy, and how business power varies from sector to sector or country to country.[13]

The openness approach sees globalization as *reshuffling the coalitions* that either support or oppose continued openness. As economic exchange across borders increases, the benefits of such exchange are unequally distributed within jurisdictions. Scholars have used a range of models, focusing either on sectoral or asset differences, to explain variation in preferences over open or closed exchange. These preferences are then filtered through various domestic institutions such as presidential or parliamentary systems, or different electoral rules within either, to determine the ultimate level of political support for economic openness or protectionism.[14] Such arguments frequently use some version of the two-level game framework in which the domestic-level preferences and institutions define the win-set for the legislature. This win-set then constrains the negotiating flexibility of the executive as they seek to win agreement for potential international trade deals.[15]

Here, the posited causal relationship runs from the ways in which international trade shapes the preferences of different sectoral groups or collective actors, through institutionalized preference aggregation mechanisms at the national level, to shifts in national bargaining positions (and hence in the likely final forms of international agreements). The international shock affects domestic politics through its consequences for primitive group preferences, while national-level institutions remain constant. These assumptions lead the literature to emphasize traditional, formal interstate agreements, where the institutional mechanisms aggregating preferences are straightforward and easy to capture using formal or informal models.

The cooperation problem approach focuses on the *difficulties resulting from increased economic exchange*. Global markets produce various externalities such as environmental degradation that spill across borders. They also throw up governance challenges that require coordination across markets to prevent rule fragmentation. The rational design literature, in particular, has discussed how international organizations or agreements mitigate such cooperation problems.[16] International organizations monitor or enforce, helping governments resolve information asymmetries and the threat of shirking as well as signaling the extent of government commitment to a given regime.[17]

Here, the posited causal relationship runs from exogenous changes in the problems faced by states, through changing state preferences over international institutions, to the creation of international institutions designed to mitigate or solve these problems. While these accounts often center on formal institutions, recent work on "regime complexes" has sought to incorporate some less formal and/or more voluntary arrangements within this approach.[18]

Finally, the power-based approach emphasizes the role of *market power*. Jurisdictions leverage their market clout to shape others' policies.[19] Both the United States and European Union, for example, employ equivalency clauses to condition market access on the adoption of compatible rules in other jurisdictions or work within international organizations to dominate policy debates. This can be reinforced indirectly by processes like "trading up."[20] These approaches see interdependence between different national systems as causing regulatory clashes, but maintain that these clashes are resolved primarily through state-to-state bargaining based on market size.

Daniel Drezner (2007) argues that market size puts the United States and European Union at the center of most global regulatory debates.[21] When the two great powers share preferences, global standards emerge, and when they disagree, rival standards are more likely. Drezner contends that states want to replicate their domestic rule structures globally. Subsequent work operationalizes these preferences by identifying differences in varieties of capitalism that make switching cheaper or more expensive.[22] Here, the relevant causal channels run from state preferences through state bargaining power (which reflect market size, internal institutions, or some combination) to deals or stalemates that reflect the interests of powerful states.

Each one of these debates has produced a thriving scholarly literature. At the same time, they focus on a narrow subset of the causal relationships through which globalization shapes international politics.[23] For both methodological and theoretical reasons, these accounts tend to view globalization as an exogenous shock that disrupts domestic or international politics.[24] In so doing, they reemphasize distinctions between the national and the global.[25] The pressures of globalization filter through domestic institutions, which then shape state preferences over the policies of international organizations or agreements, leading to international agreements that vary according to the problem to be solved, market power, or other relevant variables.[26]

These accounts tend to view institutions at both the domestic and international levels as equilibrium outcomes or "rules of the game" rather than sites of active contention and change. Hence they ignore how such institutions themselves disrupt the political process and serve to transform it.[27] The current literature emphasizes a limited number of empirical questions, most prominently including the extent of national commitment to openness and free trade, or the degree of national policy convergence/divergence around liberal policies.[28]

The World That Trade Built

The approaches described above made a lot of sense empirically and theoretically during the postwar era, as the key actors in the global political economy grappled with extending trade in goods. The Bretton Woods system severely restricted the movement of capital across borders, and the exchange of information and services was limited by technology. Instead, nations focused on lowering tariff barriers so as to promote trade (primarily in commodities and manufactured goods). During the greater part of this period, most political contestation was contained within the nation-state. As liberalization processes really got under way, theory assumed the primacy of domestic politics while looking to understand the international politics of the complex trade regime including the World Trade Organization as well as bilateral and regional trade agreements.

Yet by focusing on the question of what explains globalization, these approaches discount what globalization explains. Specifically, they do not take account of how globalization has transformed the world since the oil crisis and the end of the gold standard—changes that have recently accelerated.[29] Trade in oil and other commodities opened up large flows of money that passed through the hands of smaller nations as well as international banks. The end of capital controls spurred foreign investment and the transformation of the firm, both through the creation of multinational affiliate systems and global production chains. Banks, manufacturers, and producers of consumer products have investments and suppliers that span borders. Apple's iPhone, for example, carries the insignia "Designed in California. Assembled in China." These changes in the flows of investment and firm behavior have been accompanied by similarly dramatic transformations in the movement of information. Thanks to the rise of the internet in the 1990s and 2000s, and a dramatic decline in transportation costs, data and people increasingly interact on a global scale. While such mobility offers tremendous economic opportunity, it also opens the door to new security threats as malicious actors from hackers through drug traffickers to terrorists exploit the openness of globalization.[30] Economic transformations in the world economy have unleashed a host of unpredictable (and unpredicted) political dynamics. Investigating these dynamics is at the heart of this book and the research agenda that it lays out.

We are not, of course, the first scholars to study this rise in interdependence and its political consequences. Modern debates on the sources and consequences of interdependence begin in the 1970s.[31] We argue that these debates leave crucial questions—questions that we hope to explore—systematically understudied. Despite a sizable literature demonstrating the importance of "other actors" in world politics, most work still sees the unitary state as the key actor, and treats interdependence as an exogenous shock to either international or domestic politics. We, in contrast, hope to revive earlier debates in international relations that emphasized both the significance of intersocietal interactions above and below the state, and the structural political implications of interdependence.

The first body of modern scholarship to concern itself closely with interdependence was the transnationalism literature pioneered by Robert Keohane, Joseph Nye, and their collaborators in the early 1970s.[32] These scholars wanted to challenge traditional international relations' preoccupation with the state. They argued that modern states had no unique status in international politics, but instead found themselves enmeshed in a web of transnational relations. Many nonstate actors—such as businesses, multilateral organizations, and the Catholic Church—played an important role in international politics. Moreover, states were not unitary actors but rather composed of both bureaucratic units and individual decision makers.[33] By analyzing these more complex dynamics, transnationalists hoped to provide a more textured and realistic account of international politics.

For better or worse, this literature foundered. Statists such as Stephen Krasner (1976) pointed to the inability of transnationalism to explain enduring features of international politics. Although transnationalism shed light on international economic politics, it was notably better at describing than at predicting. Most corrosively, Kenneth Waltz's (1979) *Theory of International Politics* radically reshaped how international relations scholars thought of their discipline. It promised a properly "scientific" account of world politics based on abstract and starkly simplified assumptions about states and structures, rather than an inductive approach based on description. By these criteria, transnationalism appeared to be flabby and atheoretical.

Other work continued to try to provide a more supple account of how globalization led to increasing entanglements between different national systems. A second-wave literature on transnational politics, for example, suggested that a broader set of actors engaged in global politics than Open Economy Politics models or realist accounts might expect. James Rosenau (1990) argued that domestic and international politics are increasingly hard to distinguish from each other. He used sometimes-ungainly terms such as "fragmegration" to capture the complex dynamics that result from this interpenetration. These concepts were sketched out in broad strokes rather than tightly specified and testable arguments. Liesbet Hooghe and Gary Marks's (2003) work on "multi-level governance" provided a useful and intriguing way of thinking about how political imperatives have led in some cases to endemic jurisdictional overlap. Most recently, a number of scholars have challenged the domestic/international distinction, emphasizing the importance of transgovernmental and transnational politics.[34] While concepts such as multilevel governance or transnational pluralism remain useful descriptive heuristics, drawing attention to particular features of emerging global politics, they do not yet offer a developed theory of institutional change.

There is a different emerging body of articles and books that study the importance of relations between different domestic political spaces in more particular contexts.[35] For example, Tim Büthe and Walter Mattli argue that governments and firms are pushing for private rule-making processes that straddle domestic and international politics.[36] Elliot Posner (2009b) looks at how regulatory shifts led to the creation of new stock markets in Europe. David Vogel (1995, 13) identifies the ways in which protective regulations "[blur] the distinction between domestic and international regulatory policies." Marie-Laure Djelic and Sigrid Quack (2007, 2010) examine the deep interaction between US and German regulatory politics over accounting as financial services became intertwined.

Most recently, work on diffusion brings interdependence to the fore in a way that standard international political economy does not.[37] It is precisely because we live in an interdependent world that policies diffuse from one national system to another. Here, the fundamental intuition is that states (or other political units) are embedded in networks of relationships, across which influence operates through something like a process of contagion. Thus, for example, privacy policies spread internationally as states that are linked through networks of privacy activists and officials begin to copy each other's policies, and converge on roughly shared underlying privacy principles. Shared religious ties, crosscutting economic relations, membership of international organizations, or informal networks of government officials serve as channels of diffusion through which the policies of one state percolate and move to others.[38]

This literature clearly demonstrates the importance of policy interdependence. It is, however, better at explaining patterns of policy adoption than the complex politics that such interdependence produces. Policy interactions in an interdependent world will not be limited to decisions by states to adopt or not adopt another state's policies.[39] States seek to take advantage of other states' strong regulations to create new markets by weakening their own regulatory apparatus. States with strong regulations and market clout try to use their influence to force states with weaker regulations to strengthen them. Most interesting, substate actors take advantage of the opportunities of interdependence to create alliances across jurisdictions in order to pursue change in one or more jurisdictions, but not necessarily convergence.

In short, globalization opens up political channels for other actors beside the state to engage in international politics. It has at the same time created a host of political interactions at the transnational level, where these actors participate.[40] Standard accounts in the Open Economy Politics tradition or power-based approaches will be systematically blind to most of these mechanisms because they assume by fiat that the primary channel of cross-national influence is direct state-to-state communication. As states become increasingly interconnected as a result of the push toward globalization during the 1990s and after, we expect these deficiencies to become ever-more glaring. Correcting the deficiencies requires a new conceptual language and new theoretical tools.

The NIA

In what follows, we develop an alternative analytic framework—the NIA—to explain the dynamics of world politics in an age of globalization. Our approach draws on existing research traditions that emphasize the dynamic relationship between domestic and international politics. This includes earlier work on interdependence from the 1970s as well as the more recent literature on transnational politics. In contrast to standard arguments, which frame global politics as a product of system clash, we emphasize the importance of *intersocietal* interactions, in which globalization creates opportunities for "transnational actors" to shape international politics.[41]

Within most jurisdictions, there is lingering disagreement among actors over status quo institutional bargains. This is unsurprising since such bargains are the result of political fights that generated winners and losers.[42] Interdependence reopens these bargains, eroding the certainty of national rules as they are exposed to overlapping regulatory claims, thereby allowing some collective actors with shared interests and access to the transnational arena to create alliances *across jurisdictions*. The politics of interdependence revolves around struggles between alliances of actors who hope to leverage global interactions to turn their policy positions into institutional change, and alternative coalitions that seek to protect themselves and their preferred institutions from such pressure. In the following section, we first lay out the basic assumptions that underpin the NIA, and then develop an analytic typology to better understand the strategies of actors hoping either to transform or protect a set of policies in a globalized world.

RULE OVERLAP

We reject the usual assumption that the most fundamental condition of international politics is the ruleless space of anarchy. Instead, we begin from the assumption that increasing globalization (which we think of as increased flows of capital, goods, and information) creates a condition of *rule overlap* in international markets. Cross-national interactions mean that domestic rules of different regulatory systems come to interfere with and influence each other.[43]

Standard approaches typically assume a two-level game in which domestic preferences are aggregated internally through some process that may or may not be explicitly theorized, and form the basis of negotiation between states in an anarchic system.[44] In that account, states are discrete and nonoverlapping, suspended within a thin interconnected web of economic and diplomatic relations. The NIA, in contrast, argues that as national markets become interpenetrated, the rules and principles of markets (especially large ones) and global regimes clash with each other. As market actors such as firms and individuals engage in economic activities that span territorial borders, they face requirements from multiple authorities including state regulators, private actor governance, and international institutions, to name a few.[45]

This also generates second-level problems as large markets like the United States, the European Union, and increasingly Japan and China make extraterritorial claims to influence the behavior of actors outside their own jurisdiction. Extraterritoriality extends the reach of domestic rules outside geographic borders. In the United States and Europe, regulators often rely on a presence standard; the specific regulatory violation does not have to occur in the specific jurisdiction so long as a firm has an economic or legal presence in it. Domestic anticorruption policies, financial rules, and environmental standards, among others, penalize company's global behavior by conditioning market access. The complex affiliate structures of international firms means that business exposes itself to the regulatory hand of multiple governments. Firms not only have to play by different rules in different markets but also find that compliance with the rules that apply to them in one jurisdiction open them up to punishment for having violated rules in others.[46]

Globalization is not characterized primarily by an absence of rules or norms. Rather, the process of creating openness—in trade, finance, production, and information—creates a series of overlapping authority claims made by domestic and international actors. The importance of rule overlap is demonstrated by continuing global controversies in policy areas as diverse as antitrust, taxation, bank supervision, and data privacy.[47]

Rule overlap exposes actors to mounting levels of uncertainty as to the actual rules that govern global markets. Where those rules are incompatible, they impose extraordinary pressures on actors, especially multinational firms, which need to work under the rules of different systems. Because these actors are politically important, they put pressure on public authorities to resolve these contradictions. While large firms have preferences over which regulator's rules should obtain, these preferences are often subordinated to the more urgent need to create regulatory certainty. In the face of rule overlap, businesses typically generate strong political pressures to reach *some kind* of arrangement and thus destabilize existing domestic regulatory bargains. They urgently want certainty, and may defect from politically supporting their home market rules or status quo international regimes in return for a common rulebook. Rule overlap destabilizes the domestic and global regulatory status quo as the reversion point minus policy change is uncertainty rather than the previous policy equilibrium.[48]

This has consequences both for *change actors*—actors who would like to change their domestic institutions in significant ways—and *status quo actors*—actors who would prefer to keep them as they are. The former have new opportunities to disrupt the institutions that they dislike, in a world where those institutions clash with other countries' domestic rules and thus are open to cross-national challenge. They are likely to seek out opportunities to press any advantages they have. The latter find that institutions that they like, and that were previously well entrenched, are now open to attack from unexpected directions. They are likely to use whatever opportunities they have to protect and shore up these institutions.

OPPORTUNITY STRUCTURES

Where will both change actors and status quo actors look for such opportunities? At the same time that globalization creates a condition of rule overlap, it offers channels for political cooperation and contestation. In the early days of globalization, political contention was still largely contained by the borders of the nation-state. Actors who were dissatisfied with their policy status quo had to look primarily to domestic policy reform strategies.

The politics of the NIA allow collective actors—especially civil society actors, national regulators, and international organizations—below and above the level of the nation-state to participate directly in global politics. The nation-state is not gone or irrelevant but it nonetheless faces competition in its efforts to set agendas and make rules. Both states and other actors are now embedded in transnational institutions such as free trade agreements, regional economic associations, and investment treaties. These institutions have turned from simple rules of the game into sites of contention for a variety of collective actors apart from national executives.[49] Both change actors and status quo actors use these institutions to press their interests, and generate their own transnational bodies in order to shape agendas. In short, collective actors who seek to upset or defend their policy status quo—if they have the right opportunities—build transnational alliances with partners from other countries, international organizations, and private actors.

Globalization creates *opportunity structures* for these groups.[50] It does this both by increasing the number and types of actors that engage global politics, and by expanding the platform for such interactions through formal as well as informal international institutions. Actors work together to develop alternative rule sets, which may then be used to resolve the uncertainty posed by rule overlap, and transform domestic institutions and global rules.[51] This means that globalization is no longer an exogenous shock but instead an endogenous process in which some collective actors leverage institutions to alter the terms of global markets.

In this world, international institutions are potentially important—but in rather specific ways. Rather than seeing international institutions as collective instruments through which states solve their common problems, the NIA treats these institutions as opportunity structures that facilitate cross-national coordination between collective actors (whether regulators, interest groups, international organization secretariats, or others). They serve to distribute power between groups, generating winners and losers.[52]

In short, political contestation now takes place in multiple and overlapping venues, providing opportunity structures for collective actors that are not necessarily controlled by national governments.

How Does Overlap and Opportunity Affect Actors' Strategies?

A core insight of the NIA is that the combination of rule overlap and opportunity structures has asymmetrical consequences for political power. As we have just discussed, one key factor determining whether actors or change influence global standards is their respective degree of access to transnational forums, where regulatory disputes are addressed through hard agreements (rarely), or soft law or memorandums of understanding and the like (frequently).[53] Recommendations for legal reforms that are backed by the collective actors in the appropriate transnational network are more likely to succeed. Those who are in direct contact with each other will have far better information about what other jurisdictions are or are not prepared to countenance than other national-level actors. Such networks will enjoy the legitimacy benefits accrued from their joint membership.[54] Most important, other actors seeking certainty, including multinational business, often support such efforts so as to end regulatory clash. If change actors have access to channels of global cooperation, then, they will be better positioned to forge domestic and global rules. The collective actors involved in building these initiatives (because they have access to the relevant transnational forums) will have opportunities to reshape existing national bargains, both in their home jurisdictions and elsewhere, that would be unavailable in a world without interdependence. Alternatively, if status quo actors retain control over the relevant opportunity structures, they will be able to impede change or perhaps even block it entirely.

Hence, the "solutions" favored by different actors will not be driven by functional imperatives of, for example, achieving efficient and mutually satisfactory outcomes but instead by varying objectives and varying abilities to prosecute those objectives cross-nationally.[55] The key political struggles in an interdependent world are between those who seek to use opportunity structures to transform policy and those who seek to insulate themselves from such transnational pressures.

While the interdependence literature suggests how clashing regulatory systems will both undermine existing domestic institutional arrangements and offer an opportunity structure for actors, historical institutionalism points to the strategies that collective actors, such as regulators, civil society, business organizations, and others, will employ. Building on this work from comparative politics, we develop an analytic typology of four change strategies that collective actors use in an interdependent world: defend and extend, cross-national layering, insulation, and challenge.

TABLE 1.1. Transnational Strategies: Relative Cross-National Access versus Orientation toward Existing Domestic Institutions

	Favors existing domestic institutions	Wishes to overturn existing domestic institutions
Transnational access high	Defend and extend	Cross-national layering
Transnational access low	Insulate	Challenge

This simple framework starts from the basic assumption that domestic institutional bargains are liable to external disruption, and institutional politics is dominated by struggles between collective actors who favor the institutional status quo and those who wish to overturn it.[56] These actors will have different degrees of relative access to the transnational forums where negotiations and semiformal discussions over regulatory clash take place. Where they have high relative access to and influence in the relevant forums—that is, they are better able to shape these cross-national solutions than their opponents—they will use their access to pursue their goals. Where, in contrast, they have little access in relative terms, they will pursue their interests at the national level. This allows us to make clear predictions about the strategies that actors will pursue in the context of policy interdependence.

DEFEND AND EXTEND

Collective actors who have high access to transnational forums yet prefer the domestic institutional status quo will use these forums to defend (and where possible, extend) their domestic institutional arrangements. Where they can, these actors employ transnational networks and international organizations to remake other jurisdictions in the image of their own systems, along the lines suggested by Drezner (2007). This ensures that actors in their home jurisdiction do not have to bear adjustment costs (which will instead be borne by actors in other jurisdictions). Where this is not possible (for reasons that go beyond this simple framework, such as insufficient bargaining power or institutional capacity), they will look to build hybrid arrangements with other jurisdictions that mitigate policy spillovers.

These efforts help underpin the international influence of US regulators in areas like financial regulation or pharmaceuticals, where regulators use their privileged position in international networks both to disseminate their domestic regulatory model and to defend it.[57] David Bach and Abraham Newman (2010), for example, demonstrate how the US Securities and Exchange Commission worked through the International Organization of Securities Commissions to export US rules regarding insider trading. Equally, transnational networks support the efforts of EU regulators to extend rules in areas such as airline carbon emissions, good governance, food quality, and product standards.[58] Research on vote buying shows how states large and small use international organizations to dampen global criticism on domestic political practices ranging from human rights to whaling.[59]

For much of the 1990s, in the area of privacy, bureaucratic actors within the European Union used regional and international cross-border trans-actions to defend and extend European rules.[60] Most notably, the European Commission understood that data privacy rules in Europe might ultimately conflict with trade regulations developed through the General Agreement on Tariffs and Trade process. In order to prevent the trade regime from affecting European privacy rules, the European Commission negotiated a privacy exemption from the General Agreement on Trade in Services, which entered into force in the mid-1990s. This exemption, in turn, stymied future US efforts to challenge EU privacy rules as a protectionist barrier to services trade.[61]

Chapter 5 examines the case of the Safe Harbor Agreement, which the European Union and United States signed in 2000 to defend and extend their respective approaches to privacy rules. The agreement set out to buffer each jurisdiction from the domestic privacy rules of the other, but also allowed each to bet that the other would eventually succumb to its own preferred approach. It created a hybrid agreement in which global US firms complied with the basic principles laid out in European law. As a result, these global firms presented less of a threat to EU rules while also limiting the political need to revisit US domestic law more generally.

CROSS-NATIONAL LAYERING

Collective actors who wish to undermine the domestic institutional status quo and have high levels of access to the relevant transnational forums can use these forums to create arrangements that fundamentally alter their own domestic institutional structures. Such transnational agreements create a layer of cross-national institutions, whether formal or informal, that overlay domestic institutions, and over time, may subsume or replace them. This logic is clearly identifiable as a cross-national variant of the national-level mechanism of "layering" discussed by Kathleen Thelen and others.[62] For example, Jacob Hacker (2004) argues that it was extremely difficult for US conservatives to directly attack the Social Security system, which had built up a considerable base of support. Instead, they fostered parallel institutions, based around favorable tax treatment for various private retirement accounts, thereby hoping that it would fracture the pro–Social Security coalition over time.

Building on this work in historical institutionalism in comparative politics, we consider such transnational institutions as a source of endogenous change *within* national jurisdictions. We term this process "cross-national layering." Once such a layer has been established, it can have powerful consequences for other rules and institutions. Actors like international firms, which face rule overlap and mounting uncertainty, will have an incentive to look to the transnational agreement so as to mediate contradictory demands. Such transnational agreements create a cross-national informal institution that overlays domestic rules. At a minimum, such rule overlap generates uncertainty and legal fragmentation, which allows actors dissatisfied with status quo rules to qualify their compliance with those rules or even defect altogether.

Over time, the transnational agreement subsumes or replaces the domestic rule by making it less and less relevant to the actual behavior of key actors (e.g., businesses with cross-national exposure). Support for (and compliance with) transnational agreements reshapes the incentives of domestic collective actors who were previously inclined to block change. Where it is possible to craft a transnational layer, typical resistance strategies, such as maintaining the status quo through blocking alternative policies, lose their bite.[63] The existence of the layer means that the status quo is up for grabs. At the same time, the presence of a transnational layer delimits the options available for the reform agenda, constraining institutional choices to those that are compatible with the cross-national arrangement. Given the context of rule overlap, blocking actors find that their best-available strategy is to engage the transnational rule-making process rather than suffer further losses in influence. As support leaches away from status quo domestic institutions, actors who had once defended them find themselves obliged to get the best deal that they can in the transnational arena that is increasingly coming to dominate.

This helps explain actors' strategies in a range of policy disputes. Alasdair Young documents how both the US Trade Representative and a specific directorate-general of the European Commission worked together to create a transatlantic genetically modified organism regime that reshaped European regulations, circumventing opposition from other domestic actors in both jurisdictions.[64] Sigrid Quack and Sebastian Botzem show how coalitions of actors were able to use cross-national accounting standards as a tool to reshape domestic standards.[65] Abraham Newman and Elliot Posner (2018) demonstrate that international soft law erodes support for "homegrown" European standards, increasing the likelihood of transatlantic preference alignment in finance. Far from simply providing a focal point for cooperation, these cross-national policy layers transform the policy status quo in powerful jurisdictions and thus in turn alter the global governance of an issue area.

Chapters 3 and 4 illustrate how cross-national layering strategies have worked in the transatlantic struggle over freedom and security. The attacks of September 11 accelerated the internationalization of domestic security, generating a series of conflicts over overlapping rules. Globally oriented firms, ranging from United Airlines to Deutsche Bank, found themselves trapped between new security obligations and privacy laws, undermining the stability of existing national legislative frameworks. The security community in the United States and Europe, which had long been constrained by domestic privacy rules, exploited transnational interactions to develop an alternative policy layer while excluding civil-liberties-oriented actors. Transnational agreements on airline passenger and financial data sharing eroded domestic privacy restrictions or circumvented their constraints. Civil-liberties-oriented actors found the pre-9/11 policy status quo evanescing into nothingness around them and were forced to contend with transnational rules that were presented to them as faits accomplis.

INSULATION

Actors who wish to preserve existing national institutional bargains but have little access to the relevant transnational forums will be actively hostile to cross-national efforts to resolve jurisdictional clashes. Instead of using international forums to prosecute their aims, they will seek to *insulate* domestic institutions against outside pressures. They do this by adopting domestic rules to promote resistance, weakening the linkages between cross-national proposals and domestic processes of institutional change, proposing their own initiatives (aimed at surreptitiously or openly strengthening existing domestic institutions), and challenging the impact of cross-national alliances in domestic courts. They use blocking statutes, equivalency clauses, or other threats of limited market access to externalize their own arrangements.[66] Moreover, they look to domestic veto points as well as other legal and regulatory tools to blunt the effect of international pressures.

As we demonstrate in chapters 3 and 5, civil-liberties-oriented actors in the European Union have adopted insulation strategies as an important response to transnational policy pressures. Since they were systematically excluded from many transnational forums, they had little opportunity to shape cross-national layering institutions. Instead, they worked through European courts to challenge the legitimacy of the layering arrangements.

Their efforts initially failed: the European Court of Justice was disinclined to back a privacy-rights-based approach.

As we discuss in chapter 5, privacy activists like Max Schrems had later success. Schrems, an Austrian lawyer, brought a case against Facebook, arguing that new security agreements between the transatlantic partners violated the terms of the Safe Harbor Agreement, which allowed commercial data exchanges between the regions. Ultimately, the European Court of Justice ruled in his favor, defending European privacy rules and weakening the pressure of cross-national layers on existing European privacy policies. In the concluding chapter of the book, we discuss how a European data privacy reform from 2016, known as the General Data Protection Regulation (GDPR), is providing new tools for the civil liberties coalition as it attempts to leverage the European single market to promote privacy protections globally.

CHALLENGE

Finally, collective actors who have low relative access to the relevant transnational forums yet wish to overturn existing domestic institutions will challenge these institutions more or less as the comparativist historical institutionalists expect them to. They will choose between domestically focused strategies of change, such as (domestic) layering, drift, and conversion, depending on their relative degree of access to domestic institutions. While it is possible for actors in the other three cells to combine these domestic strategies with those that leverage (or seek to break) the relationship between domestic and cross-national politics, actors in this cell will have no recourse to cross-national politics. Hence their strategies can be described using the concepts developed in the comparativist literature.

This book focuses on how interdependence and international interactions transform the politics of freedom and security. Purely domestic dynamics hence do not go to the heart of the central case studies. That said, chapter 2 provides many examples of such conflicts prior to the internationalization of domestic security. In both the United States and European Union, security- and civil-liberties-oriented actors clashed domestically in their efforts to shape national politics. Our argument implies that as interdependence increases, purely domestic forms of challenge become less relevant than they used to be.

Conclusion

This chapter offers an analytic framework that connects transnational politics to domestic institutional change. Political science has good theories of domestic politics and international politics, but remarkably little to say about how they intersect as domestic political systems increasingly interpenetrate one another. Standard accounts tend to emphasize the separation between the two levels, confining domestic and international actors to their respective domains. Increased globalization has made these assumptions unsustainable. Firms, NGOs, security agencies, and regulators both work across multiple domestic political settings and craft global agreements. Our alternative model explores how the interaction between the domestic and international levels of politics reshape institutions in both.

At the same time, we move past heuristic descriptions of this new world order. While a number of scholars have identified a general trend toward transnational politics, these accounts frequently lack clear empirical expectations. Building on the literature on transgovernmental politics and multilevel governance, we offer a causal typology, linking actor change strategies to the international and domestic policy environment that actors find themselves in.

This provides a different understanding of power than competing accounts in international relations. Of course, other approaches to international relations than the NIA stress the importance of power asymmetries. What is novel about the NIA is the specific set of asymmetries that it identifies. Much existing work tends to assume that cross-national disputes will necessarily be resolved in favor of the interests of the most powerful states in terms of market size, or international bargaining heft.[67] The NIA, in contrast, invites scholars to focus on specific collective actors rather than states and incorporate differences in their power resources. In short, we shift the focus of explanation from clashes between different national systems to clashes between alliances of substate actors that span across these systems. Regulators or other public officials, even if they operate within the largest states, will lose if they do not have sufficient resources and access to exert influence through the relevant transnational as well as domestic opportunity structures.

Our model highlights the importance of long-term change processes for global politics, emphasizing *actor strategies* instead of *outcomes*. Standard rationalist models imply that one can identify end points in institutional change: stable self-sustaining institutional states. By analyzing the distributional implications of these end states, they arrive at clear conclusions about who has won and who has lost. Where they face extraordinary difficulties is in explaining how these equilibriums break down so that changes are possible, or to the extent that they model breakdown, what institutions might arise to replace old ones.[68]

Rather than treating institutional change as having a determinate end point with absolute winners and losers, we regard it as an ongoing process of contestation and seek to explain the strategies that actors employ. We certainly say that some actors' preferences are more consequential than others at any given point in time and even that some actors' preferences prevail over long periods of time when they have had substantial influence in helping set long-term stable paths of institutional change. Over the course of the book, we discuss moments of asymmetry in which one coalition succeeds in deploying a powerful change strategy to the discomfiture of its rivals and opponents. We also expect that actors will respond to one another's strategies, both when they seek to counteract others' influence in struggles over institutional change and when they seek to respond to institutional changes that others have successfully carried through. At any point in time, we make plausible predictions as to the kinds of strategies actors employ given the structural circumstances that they face.[69] We cannot, however, predict which actors win or lose over the longer run, in part because there is no point at which we finally assign wins and losses to different actors, and in part because each moment of institutional change creates (some ex ante unpredictable) institutional circumstances that actors will seek to respond to and in turn change.[70]

Finally, our model offers a synthetic argument explaining potential variation in various modes of global governance. Separate literatures have emerged examining international negotiations, diffusion, trading up, and harmonization, to name a few. Our approach seeks to bring these different processes into one causal model. In doing so, we force a broad range of literatures to engage with one another and hope to shed light on their interrelationships. Additional work will therefore be needed to connect work on the power resources of actors to our more structural account of opportunities and constraints. That said, our model offers a way to bridge work, for example, on formal international institutions with the scholarship on diffusion.

In the next four chapters, we apply the framework to a set of interrelated disputes between the European Union and United States. As we will see, at different moments the configurations of available opportunity structures along with wishes to undermine or strengthen institutions induce actors to adopt strategies of cross-national layering, defense and extension, and insulation. Before engaging in the analytic narratives, we describe the background conditions to these disputes: How is it that domestic security, personal privacy, and economic interdependence became entwined on both sides of the Atlantic?

2

Domestic Security and Privacy in the Transatlantic Space

Interdependence changes the international system in ways that generate political opportunities for those seeking to upend their domestic policies. Even if globalization does not create a single global market, it vastly increases the interconnections between societies, and thus actions taken in one jurisdiction have consequences in others. The key to understanding how interdependence transforms politics is to look at how it allows actors within countries to forge alliances across them.

In this chapter, we provide the necessary historical background to understand how these interconnections arose between the European Union and United States in the area of domestic security and privacy. We argue that these policy domains initially developed along different trajectories in the two jurisdictions we study—the European Union and United States—and were shielded from each other for the first four decades after World War II.[1] During the 1990s, economic interdependence began to reshape domestic security understandings within the European Union, pushing the European Union to build its own transnational institutions, although it never came close to emulating the more wide-reaching federal law enforcement and information-sharing arrangements seen in the United States. The United States, for its part, began to manage international problems such as drug trafficking that had domestic security implications without engaging in any major international institutional transformations. Despite burgeoning trade and economic exchange, the European Union and United States had extremely limited interaction over domestic security questions.[2]

This changed drastically after September 11, 2001, when security actors within the two systems, and especially the United States, came to perceive their interdependence with other countries as a source of grave weakness.[3] Security-oriented actors in both the European Union and United States faced varying barriers to enhanced cooperation. Many of these resulted from the two jurisdictions' different privacy architectures, which had been built before interdependence really took hold. This led security-oriented actors in the United States to push for the European Union to make substantial concessions on transatlantic cooperation as well as its own internal security and information practices. Security actors in the European Union, in turn, sought increased cooperation on some forms of information exchange. As we discuss in succeeding chapters, they had many potential levers to employ; as the two systems became interconnected, it became easier for such actors to press for institutional change.[4] Still, they faced resistance from a diverse civil liberties community in both the European Union and United States—including NGOs, European privacy regulators, and activists—that sought to resist such encroachments.[5]

This chapter identifies the historical conditions under which domestic security, privacy, and economic interdependence became intertwined in the European Union and United States. It does this by providing a detailed chronology of how the EU and US systems of domestic security initially developed in isolation from each other, following quite-different paths of institutional development on each side of the Atlantic, and then became imbricated so that their paths came to influence each other.

The European Union and United States are not monoliths. Instead, they are jointly and separately complex governance systems in which privacy advocates, security officials, and politicians struggle to achieve their distinct and often-conflicting policy goals. This chapter's central aim is to describe the various factions within each jurisdiction along with their institutional and political resources so as to better help the reader understand how these factions forge or fail to forge alliances transnationally in the controversies covered in the remainder of the book.

The chapter proceeds in four parts. The first three sections examine efforts to address domestic security and privacy at the international level, within the European Union and within the United States prior to the terrorist attacks of September 11. The fourth section covers the rapid development of policy and institutions after these attacks.

International Domestic Security Cooperation before September 11

Domestic security centers on the protection of civilian populations against security threats that do not involve direct military attack by other states. Typically, two broad kinds of institutions or agencies are involved in domestic security: police and justice officials, who operate through the criminal justice system with some degree of public oversight, and intelligence agencies, which operate through clandestine activities and in practice usually have far more limited oversight.[6]

For much of the postwar period, domestic security was conceived of as primarily an internal matter.[7] Militant organizations such as the Black Panthers in the United States or the Red Army Faction in Germany were largely homegrown, although there were loose patterns of attachment and resource sharing between some terrorist organizations.[8] This led to a minimal global infrastructure for international information sharing and cooperation, in sharp contrast to many other postwar international regimes like those centered on trade or finance.

In the area of police cooperation, the International Criminal Police Organization (Interpol) is the most formal effort to coordinate issues concerning transnational crime.[9] It had its origins in the International Criminal Police Commission, which was created in 1923 and renamed Interpol in 1956. With 170 member countries, it is among the largest international organizations by membership, although not by staffing. Its main objective is to support mutual assistance among criminal police organizations. Cold War disagreements ensured that the organization's mandate restricts it to facilitating cross-border investigations rather than engaging in extensive activities on its own behalf.[10]

Having no police powers, Interpol serves as a liaison between national police officials in cases of transnational crime. It focuses on standards for extradition, mutual legal assistance, and the sharing of cross-border arrest warrants, explicitly rejecting cooperation on political crimes and in turn limiting cooperation on terrorism. It only has a limited internal institutional infrastructure, which is dedicated primarily to information networking.[11] In practical terms, this involves Interpol's I-24/7 system, which allows national police access to data concerning arrest warrants or international investigations.[12]

At the end of the Cold War, transnational threats to the homeland began to capture the imagination of policy makers, who had previously focused on broader geopolitical questions. This started with the war on drugs inspired by the United States and its corresponding emphasis on fighting transnational organized crime.[13] The 1990s saw the beginnings of a security agenda pushed by the United States, which had no strong geopolitical rivals. Both George H. W. Bush's New World Order and Bill Clinton's stress on "new security" threats reflected a shift in focus from great power conflict to emerging challenges posed by weak states and illicit activity.[14]

A new policy domain—homeland security—emerged in US debates. The rising political importance of drug trafficking as well as a series of terrorist attempts on US targets including the World Trade Center in 1993 and the Oklahoma City bombing in 1995 increased the policy salience of such threats.[15] The 1995 Presidential Decision Directive 39 on "US Policy on Counterterrorism," the 1998 Presidential Decision Directive 62 on "Protection against Unconventional Threats to the Homeland and Americans Overseas," and the 2001 findings of the Hart-Rudman Commission on National Security/21st Century all highlighted the need for a robust homeland security apparatus.[16]

The final report of the Hart-Rudman Commission was particularly influential. One of its central findings was that "a direct attack against American citizens on American soil is likely over the next quarter century. . . . [W]e therefore recommend the creation of an independent National Homeland Security Agency with responsibility for planning, coordinating, and integrating various US government activities involved in homeland security."[17] Importantly, these efforts explicitly recognized the transnational nature of the problem. Even prior to the September 11 attacks, US officials explored expanding transnational cooperation. The Federal Bureau of Investigation (FBI), for example, had a limited number of overseas legal attaché offices (known as legats), which assisted in criminal investigations connected to simmering Cold War tensions.[18] It steadily expanded the number of overseas legats during the 1990s, nearly tripling the number of offices between 1992 and 2001 to 44 total, and locating them in a broader array of countries and continents.[19]

This recognition of transnational threats did not result in any major organizational shift, which might either have been marked by the creation of an executive branch office for homeland security or a major change of priorities within the relevant agencies.[20] It did provide limited opportunities for organizations to build competences. For example, Interpol developed incident response teams to help in investigations of terrorist attacks or organized crime.[21] The UN Financial Action Task Force was created in 1989 to co-ordinate action against money laundering.[22] Within the United States, the FBI and the Drug Enforcement Agency expanded their global cooperative efforts, focusing on mutual legal assistance and information sharing.

It became increasingly apparent to policy makers and security officials that as domestic threats transcended domestic borders, policy responses needed to as well. Police, who had local or national jurisdiction, confronted criminals, who spanned the globe. Most important, this change led to a focus on bilateral and multilateral agreements, particularly mutual legal assistance treaties (MLATs) to plug holes in the international infrastructure and tackle the cross-border aspects of domestic security issues. The primary function of MLATs is to facilitate the exchange of legal evidence between different national systems, ranging from witness testimony to bank records used for criminal prosecutions.[23]

MLATS replaced the earlier approach of letters rogatory—in which a legal team in one jurisdiction could make a nonbinding request to a foreign court to share legal evidence—which often led to frustration. Foreign courts were reluctant to share evidence or adjust their regular procedures to meet the constitutional and evidentiary requirements of other legal systems.[24] MLATs, by contrast, establish an obligation to provide assistance, and aim to reconcile the differences between the common law and civil law's procedures and demands. The spread of MLATs was facilitated by the adoption of the UN Model Treaty on Mutual Assistance in Criminal Matters in 1990 along with the provisions on mutual legal assistance in the 1988 UN Convention against Illicit Traffic in Narcotic Drugs and Psychotropic Substances.

While exact data on the use of MLATs is difficult to obtain, we know that between 1981 and 1999, the US government processed thousands of requests. Ethan Nadelmann (1993, 340) reports that evidence obtained through the US-Swiss MLAT between 1980 and 1990 was used to successfully prosecute hundreds of state and federal cases, including major figures in organized crime syndicates. Swiss global cooperation on such evidence sharing was also essential for bringing cases against a number of former dictators ranging from Ferdinand Marcos from the Philippines to Jean-Claude Duvalier from Haiti.

Figure 2.1 uses an original data set to document the spread of MLATs signed by seventy countries worldwide, including all major powers, between 1980 and 2015. As the figure shows, the number of MLATs has been steadily rising since the 1980s, with an especially precipitous increase in the 1990s.[25]

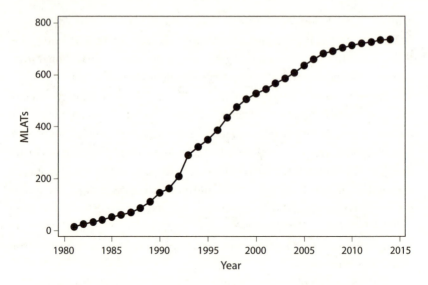

FIGURE 2.1. Spread of MLATs, 1981–2014

Despite this spread, MLATs have many inbuilt checks and frustrations for law enforcement officials. Countries such as the United States still demand a relatively high level of evidence before cooperating under an MLAT, and the process can be quite cumbersome and slow.

The burgeoning of e-commerce and the internet in the 1990s led to supplementary efforts to improve cooperation among states over criminal matters connected to new technologies. Most prominently, the Council of Europe, a body that involves all major European states as well as the United States, Canada, South Africa, and Japan as observers, negotiated a draft Convention on Cybercrime, which was concluded in November 2001.[26]

In addition to seeking to harmonize cybercrime legislation, the convention was supposed to complement MLATs by providing for mutual legal assistance under circumstances that existing MLATs did not cover. For example, Russia's MLAT with the United States did not cover computer-related crimes—an obvious problem after the rise of Russian hacker collectives linked to organized crime. The convention too has had a checkered history; states were slow to sign on, and the treaty is widely regarded as cumbersome and ineffective.[27] Jack Goldsmith and Tim Wu (2006) argue that this led states to turn instead to informal arrangements fostered by clubs such as the G8 and G20 to cooperate on information sharing. Evidence suggests that systems such as the G8's 24/7 Network for Data Preservation have themselves seen relatively little use.[28]

Before September 11, there were also international agreements for sharing classified data among intelligence agencies. The sensitivity of such data (and the fear that it might leak and reveal sources) has always been a brake on wide cooperation among states. Nonetheless, agreements, including the UK-USA Agreement more popularly known as Five Eyes, have had important consequences.

Concluded between the United States and United Kingdom in 1946, and then expanded to include the intelligence community of Australia, Canada, and New Zealand, the Five Eyes agreement focuses on intelligence sharing between the signal, defense, and human intelligence services of the five members while excluding those members from targeting each other. This agreement anchored UK-US intelligence sharing so strongly that according to one authority, "consumers [of intelligence] in both capitals seldom know which country generated either the access or the product itself."[29] Once one of the intelligence community's best-kept secrets, it is said that the prime minister of Australia did not know of the agreement until the 1970s, and the text of the agreement was not made publicly available until 2010.

It is difficult to know how much of this intelligence cooperation involved the sharing of information on nation-state adversaries, and how much intelligence on allies and friendly actors. For sure, the exclusion of other Western European states such as Germany and France from the Five Eyes system generated resentment, which helped fuel repeated political concerns that Five Eyes capabilities were turned against ordinary Europeans. This became a public issue after revelations about the Echelon system, a critical asset of Five Eyes cooperation, which was created in the early 1960s, and targets signal information via, for example, satellite and fiber-optic communication. The system uses software to analyze traffic on most of the major public and commercial communications networks. It first came to public attention in the late 1980s, when news reports emerged that shed light on the existence and extent of monitoring.[30] This led to a series of hearings held by the European Parliament concerning the system in 2000 and 2001, but produced few results.[31]

Thus before September 11, there was little formal cooperation between states on domestic security issues. Police and justice cooperation relied on institutions with inbuilt limitations such as Interpol, or cumbersome bilateral or multilateral agreements such as MLATs. Efforts to produce more sophisticated instruments such as the Convention on Cybercrime did not prove successful. While only limited data are available on intelligence cooperation, what there are suggests intense cooperation between a small number of states with a strong culture and tradition of cooperation, and moderate-to-minimal sharing with others.[32] It is unclear how much intelligence cooperation involved information on domestic security issues (such as terrorism) as opposed to information on geopolitical threats, such as the Soviet Union.

These initial institutions and arrangements did have consequences. Earlier arguments about "homeland security" provided the basis for a new agency in the United States after September 11. When US and EU officials began to think about building an architecture, they turned, where possible, to the structures at hand and sought to extend them.[33] This follows a broader pattern in postwar international governance in which domestic regulatory legacies and initial international efforts often leave important imprints on global cooperation, shaping later efforts even as the demands and problems facing policy makers change over time.[34] The sparseness of the international structure also provided space for domestic systems within both the European Union (considered as a nascent polity following the changes of the 1990s) and United States to grow up in relative isolation from each other. We detail each before examining how the international setting changed after September 11.

Domestic Security within the European Union before September 11

In this section, we chart the internal European governance of domestic security and privacy prior to the attacks of September 11. Well through the 1980s, national governments dominated internal security conversations and regional efforts took place outside EU institutions.[35] It was not until the 1990s that European countries gradually gave the regional organization greater institutional capacity to manage domestic security as well as privacy. Terrorism prevention, in particular, only received significant European attention in 1999 (foreshadowing the attacks of the new millennium). Earlier club-like arrangements gradually became more formalized, as arguments arose about how European integration created the need for new forms of domestic security provision and disagreements emerged about the consequences of cooperation for civil rights (especially privacy).

Transnational internal security cooperation within Europe was extremely limited for much of the postwar period.[36] Starting in the 1970s, as a number of European countries experienced frequent terrorist incidents, student protests, and rising Cold War tensions, national governments began an ongoing transnational conversation about domestic security.

A plethora of informal club-type organizations were created; they were intended to promote dialogue and coordination as well as address transnational threats.[37] The Club of Berne, formed in 1971, including representatives from European security and intelligence agencies, met on an ongoing basis to discuss shared policy concerns and to coordinate its intelligence activities. These discussions were perhaps more notable for the personal relationships that they forged than for the substantive transfers of intelligence that they produced.[38] The Police Working Group on Terrorism, created in 1979, provides an informal space for cooperation and information exchange among midlevel police officials heading counterterrorism policy.[39] The TREVI group, named after the fountain in Rome where the first meeting was held, was established in late 1975 as an intergovernmental forum of national ministers of justice and interior.[40] Integrated within the European Political Cooperation process, the TREVI group allowed EU members to begin a political conversation about homeland security issues before the European Union had competencies in the area.[41] The three groups, then, laid the foundation for a more robust European domestic security policy by fostering a security community built of pan-European links between high-level elites as well as everyday civil servants.[42] That said, they had little independent direct effect on European policy.

Everything started to change in the 1990s as the European project underwent a dramatic transformation. For much of the postwar period, the European Union was conceived primarily as an economic union focused on the common external trade policy and the European internal market. Member states began to experiment with increasing the free movement of people through policies such as the Schengen Agreement, which was first signed in 1985. Originally this agreement allowed the Benelux countries, Germany and France, to eliminate border controls between the countries and establish a common customs entry-and-exit system.[43] This quickly raised concerns over homeland security questions such as immigration and cross-border policing.[44] While increases in free movement provided immediate impetus for policy change, this change, as others described in this book, was crucially shaped by the previous experience of informal arrangements such as the TREVI group.[45]

This helped security-focused actors within the European Union to press for measures that would meet the security challenges posed by greater cross-border movement. Two important treaties—Maastricht and

Amsterdam—radically expanded the organization's mission. These treaties mark the entry and consolidation of EU efforts in the domain of domestic security.[46] The 1992 Treaty of Maastricht expanded EU policy competences substantially and divided them into three functional policy pillars. The first pillar represented the traditional activities associated with the internal market. The second pillar dealt with foreign policy, and has become known as the Common Foreign and Security Policy. The third and final pillar incorporated home and justice affairs.

Each pillar laid out distinct institutional rules regarding law and rule making, and allocated decision-making responsibilities in different ways among the various European institutions. In the area of home and justice affairs, the Council of the European Union, effectively composed of justice and interior ministers, held the most authority over policy development and passage. The European Parliament, by contrast, initially had little formal authority in the domain. As the Council had no institutional apparatus in home and justice affairs prior to Maastricht, the TREVI group served as the basis for much of the initial operational and coordination activities within the newly broadened European Union.

The Treaty of Amsterdam, which was signed in 1997 and entered into force in 1999, instituted important changes that implicated transatlantic relations.[47] Most critically, the treaty explicitly delegated an external dimension of home and justice affairs to the European Union.[48] As border controls within Europe were relaxed and asylum pressure from non-EU countries mounted, European officials argued for an EU dimension to domestic security policy.[49] The treaty thus created the Area of Freedom, Justice, and Security within the European Union, and as part of this institutional transformation pooled internal competencies, offering the European Union and outside actors a coherent institutional framework with which to conduct transnational homeland security diplomacy.

In 1999, justice and interior ministers met in Tampere, Finland, as part of the Council to discuss the operational objectives of the newly created Area of Freedom, Security, and Justice. In addition to highlighting the European Union's policy priorities, the Tampere Agreement explicitly called on the European Union to develop an external dimension to home and justice affairs.[50]

The Treaty of Maastricht and the negotiation of the Treaty of Amsterdam helped prompt interior ministers and security officials to build the institutional foundations for pan-European cooperation on domestic intelligence (externally oriented intelligence activities remained outside the competences of the European Union, including controversial activities aimed by one member state against another). These two treaties led to the creation of a number of new organizational actors—most prominently Europol and Eurojust—that were charged with coordinating various aspects of the nascent European policy area including information sharing among domestic intelligence agencies and prosecutors.[51] The treaties also vastly increased the importance of council meetings among ministers for justice and home affairs, using the European Commission to provide administrative support for actions in this area, while until recently marginalizing the European Parliament. Justice and Home Affairs ministers meet regularly under the auspices of the Council of the European Union (the representative body of EU member states). For a number of years, ministers and the Council were able to proceed relatively unfettered by other institutions of the European Union.[52]

The two treaties described above provided the European Commission Directorate-General (DG) for Justice and Home Affairs with a substantial, albeit subordinate role given the "pillarization" of security policy. The passage of the Treaty of Lisbon in 2009 formally ended the distinction between the pillars of the single market and home and justice affairs.[53] At roughly the same time, the European Commission split its Justice and Home Affairs competences between two new DGs, creating the DG for Justice and Consumers and a separate DG for Migration and Home Affairs. This led to internal tension within the European Commission as the two DGs sparred over jurisdiction for homeland security and privacy issues. As later chapters discuss, such splits have had important consequences for policy: there is no simple "European Commission" position regarding many issues of domestic security and privacy.

In contrast, the European Parliament was largely excluded from the policy area for much of the period before and immediately after 2001. This caused much consternation in the early 2000s, when parliamentarians feared that justice and home affairs were becoming a new engine for integration within the European Union that systematically cut out the European Parliament. These fears eased after the Treaty of Lisbon came into force in 2009. This treaty provided the European Parliament with a much more substantial role in internal affairs.[54]

Just as the push toward the internal market spurred movement for regional internal security consolidation, it provided opportunities for actors more concerned with civil liberties and privacy. Dating back to the 1970s, many European countries had adopted comprehensive privacy legislation.

In addition to regulating the exchange and use of personal information in the public and private sectors, many of these laws established independent regulatory agencies—data privacy authorities—whose mandate was to oversee the implementation and development of national privacy regimes.[55] Much like a Federal Trade Commission (FTC) devoted solely to privacy (and increasingly to information access as well), data privacy authorities in France, Germany, and Sweden began to develop and implement national standards for data usage.[56]

Early on, these agencies recognized that their job had an important transnational dimension. Multinational corporations and pan-European public administration both relied heavily on cross-border transfers. Citizens could find their data passed on to foreign entities, which had to comply with different privacy regulations or no regulations at all. In 1979, a number of privacy authorities held their first transnational meeting in Bonn to discuss these issues. This meeting, the International Data Protection Commissioner Conference, started an organized network of privacy officials working to share best practices and develop a coherent set of privacy principles. Such principles were codified in the *OECD Guidelines on the Protection of Privacy and Transborder Flows of Personal Data.*[57] The guidelines reflected a set of fair information practice principles including giving individuals notice before data are collected, the ability to consent to data collection and usage, and the right to correct stored data. These basic concepts of data privacy inspired national legislation from Sweden's 1973 Data Act to the US Privacy Act of 1974.[58]

Over the course of the next decade, European privacy regulators developed a regional privacy agenda that would harmonize rules across the European Union at a relatively high level. After a series of confrontations where data privacy officials threatened to block information transfers within the European Union, the European Commission took up the issue.[59] It feared that without some compromise, it would be unable to deliver either on important aspects of the internal market (where national data privacy commissioners could block data flows from businesses or branches in one country to another) or on the Schengen Agreement (which data privacy commissioners threatened to impede flows of government administrative information). With the passage of the 1995 Data Privacy Directive, data privacy became embedded in the internal market project.[60]

The directive has had widespread implications for the transnationalization of domestic security within Europe. It consolidated regulatory authority over European privacy laws. Article 29 of the directive established a regulatory network that oversees the implementation of European rules. Composed of representatives from national privacy agencies, the Article 29 Working Party established itself as an influential voice for privacy within Europe and globally.[61] Its formal responsibilities include advising the European Union on privacy issues and legislation, evaluating the level of protection in other countries, and harmonizing enforcement within the member states.

Because the directive was passed as part of the single market initiative, it did not provide the Article 29 Working Party with formal authority over home and justice affairs. Privacy regulators created a shadow group known as the Working Party on Police and Justice, focused on the use of data by police and security-oriented actors. Informally, the Article 29 Working Party has become a powerful counterweight to firms and governments that skirt or bend European rules, and its opinions carry considerable weight with informed elite opinion. With the passage of the General Data Protection Regulation in 2016, which updated the 1995 directive, many privacy regulations have been harmonized across the member states and the enforcement powers of national data privacy authorities have been further expanded.[62]

Over the years, national privacy regulators and their network became flanked by additional privacy oversight bodies. The European Data Protection Supervisor position was established in 2004. It monitors and implements data privacy policy for the EU institutions and bodies. At the same time, it serves as an adviser to the European Commission on key data privacy issues. As a result, it often comments on and offers opinions concerning transnational and transatlantic data policy

The Privacy Directive included an important provision (Article 25) that regulates the transfer of personal information concerning European citizens to other countries. Article 25 states that data cannot be transferred to jurisdictions lacking adequate levels of privacy protection.[63] Most important, the United States has not been deemed adequate. Given the United States' limited privacy system, lacking an independent regulator and comprehensive coverage for the private sector, it is doubtful that it will obtain such status. These limits on cross-border transfers have provoked a series of conflicts between the United States and European Union. In 2000, for example, after concern that the Privacy Directive would hinder transatlantic electronic commerce, the two sides concluded lengthy and often-contentious negotiations over the Safe Harbor Agreement (see chapter 5).[64]

The Safe Harbor Agreement was ultimately struck down by the European Court of Justice in 2015 and was replaced in 2016 by a new arrangement known as the Privacy Shield, which is itself now under legal challenge (see chapter 5).[65] The arrangement allows US companies to commit to European standards for international data transfers, and be overseen either by the FTC or a European regulator. The fight over commercial privacy that led to the Safe Harbor Agreement was then followed by conflicts over air passenger data (see chapter 3 and the Passenger Name Record [PNR] agreements) and financial records (see chapter 4 and the SWIFT Agreement). In all three instances, early European initiatives to institutionalize regulatory authority within the European Union had substantial consequences for later disputes between the European Union and United States.[66]

Privacy also found its way into European electoral politics. While the European Parliament was once seen as marginal, it has steadily grown in significance since the early 1990s. Gradually it expanded its decision-making authority, first in the area of the internal market under the Treaty of Maastricht, and then in a broader set of areas including justice and home affairs with the passage of the Treaty of Lisbon. As its responsibilities grew, legislators began to develop policy profiles that serve them well in national elections. Green and Liberal parliamentarians, in particular, took on privacy issues as a means to distinguish themselves from their competitors. Taking on high-profile positions in the Committee on Civil Liberties, Justice, and Home Affairs, these members kept regional institutions focused on privacy.[67]

A number of other critical actors concerned with privacy issues have engaged in transnational homeland security debates. National constitutional courts in many member states have taken an activist position, promoting individual privacy.[68] The German constitutional court, for example, created an important line of precedent developing the concept of informational self-determination.[69] First elucidated in the 1980s in response to an overly detailed census questionnaire, the same logic was applied more recently by the court to European telecommunications surveillance rules. While the court's impact is ambiguous in some respects, it casts a shadow of authority over national and even European decisions that attempt to restrict personal privacy. The European Court of Justice, which issues authoritative rulings on the interpretation of EU law, has been substantially influenced by the German court's jurisprudence.[70] The European Court of Justice played an especially prominent role in the events described in chapter 5, where civil liberties actors employed the Court in their efforts to insulate European privacy rules from encroachments by the security community.

Complementing public sector initiatives, a number of NGOs positioned themselves as civil liberties and privacy advocates.[71] The European Digital Rights Initiative (EDRi), Statewatch, Privacy International, and the Working

Group against Data Retention are the most prominent such organizations in Europe. These groups disclose information about state surveillance activities, coordinate campaigns, file judicial cases, and update members on emerging privacy and civil liberties concerns. EDRi, for example, is a pan-European network of over thirty privacy and civil liberties organizations focusing on digital rights.[72] It has an office in Brussels, and employs six staff members. EDRi publishes a bimonthly newsletter with information about digital policy making in Europe called the *EDRi-GRAM*, lobbies European institutions on key legislation, and offers its members a platform to organize at the European level. Statewatch, which has existed since 1991, serves as an important information portal on home and justice affairs in Europe.[73] It maintains observatories on key European privacy and civil liberties issues, and frequently publishes leaked documents from the European institutions. While many of these groups are small and focused on a narrow spectrum of issues, they have forged a critical lobbying triangle with data privacy authorities and interested politicians in the European Parliament.[74] In recent years, they have increasingly turned to the European Court of Justice, where they have successfully defended European privacy and civil liberties protections (see chapter 5).[75]

This plethora of institutional arrangements and actors developed largely as a result of intra-European imperatives. The dynamics of European integration helped bring new actors into being providing both them and more long-standing organizations with the impetus and the means to struggle over institutional arrangements. These fights did not generate anything resembling a "unanimous" European position on domestic security and privacy. Instead, whatever institutional equilibriums developed were fragile and dependent on the shifting bargaining strengths of the different agents involved.

Hence, for example, security-focused actors were able to press for treaty changes that increased the ambit of the European Union, and to use these changes to bring through further changes in institutional rules and practices. Actors concerned with civil liberties, however, were similarly able to threaten the progress of the internal market and Schengen in order to try to get their way. The result was a compromise in which each side managed to shape the relevant institutions, even if each would have preferred a more encompassing victory.

Domestic Security in the United States before September 11

We now turn to internal developments within the United State prior to the attacks of September 11. The United States was an integrated economic and political entity long before the European Union. This created pressures and opportunities for internal actors such as the FBI to push for the ability to investigate crimes across different states of the United States from early in the twentieth century. That said, a truly comprehensive national security and intelligence apparatus did not appear until the World War II period. And even then, there was limited interest in transnational threats until after the end of the Cold War.

Policing in the United States is highly complex, involving interactions between local-, state-, and federal-level institutions. As Herman Goldstein (1977, 131) describes it, "The most distinctive characteristic of policing in the United States is the extent to which the police function is decentralized." This reflects both paths of institutional development over time and the US Constitution, which was specifically "designed so that the federal government may not directly control local law enforcement agencies."[76]

This meant that crime was dealt with at the state level until the early twentieth century. The FBI began as a modest bureau within the Department of Justice in 1908, and was originally charged with investigating crimes under the sparse existing federal criminal statutes.[77] Its ambit expanded to include domestic intelligence work and espionage as a result of World War I as well as the panic over the threat of Communist subversion. As new technologies (especially the spread of the automobile) made interstate crime easier to carry out, the FBI took on new authority, constructing a federal layer that worked over and between existing local- and state-level policing arrangements.

The role of this federal layer of police and domestic intelligence was transformed by World War II. The expansion of the FBI'S Special Intelligence Service into Latin America and the creation of the Office of Strategic Services during the war led to considerable bureaucratic infighting over who would be in charge of intelligence after the cessation of hostilities.[78] The FBI fought vigorously to maintain its international role and to stymie the creation of any peacetime intelligence agency.[79] Furthermore, President Harry S. Truman was nervous about creating what might become an "American Gestapo." Lawmakers nonetheless agreed to the Central Intelligence Agency (CIA), which would report to the newly instituted National Security Council and provide it with recommendations about the "intelligence activities of the various government agencies involved in national security." The NSA, established secretly in 1949 as the Armed Forces Security Agency, added to the mix, providing valuable communications intelligence on both US adversaries and allies.[80]

Over time, the CIA, whose mandate had been deliberately left vague, became more directly involved in covert action and espionage, taking advantage of the opportunities presented by the Cold War. This led to a distinction in practice between the FBI, which was focused on domestic issues, and the CIA, which was focused on international questions. The division of responsibilities caused some angst among lawmakers; the 1949 Jackson-Correa report argued that "fifth column activities and espionage do not begin or end at our geographical frontiers, and our intelligence to counter them cannot be sharply divided on any such geographical basis."[81]

Despite the notorious institutional rivalry between the FBI and the CIA, the distinction between domestic and international intelligence continued to get blurrier.[82] This eventually led to scandal when it became clear that not only the FBI but also the CIA and NSA had spied on US citizens, and engaged in various forms of covert action against them. Most notoriously, the FBI and NSA collaborated to tap the phones of Reverend Martin Luther King Jr. on the theory that he was part of a vast Communist conspiracy. The CIA maintained intelligence files on more than ten thousand US citizens, including members of Congress.[83] The NSA's Project SHAMROCK surveilled telegraph and telephone communication into and out of the United States, including communications by US citizens, without any warrants.

When these programs were uncovered, Senate hearings and hearings in the House of Representatives expressed serious concern about the activities of the FBI, NSA, and CIA. In 1978, Congress passed the Foreign Intelligence Surveillance Act (FISA) to prevent unsupervised programs from interfering with the privacy of US citizens, and made it far harder for US intelligence agencies to gather intelligence within the borders of the United States. It did not act on intelligence gathering outside the borders of the United States; instead, that was covered by an Executive Order.[84] FISA was later amended after Timothy McVeigh's bombing of Oklahoma City to allow for the collection of business records where there was reason to believe that a person was a foreign power or agent of a foreign power.

The new rules went together with a greater emphasis on curtailing organizational cooperation between domestically focused and internationally focused agencies. Extended and fractious turf wars meant that the US intelligence apparatus was extremely fragmented, with multiple agencies with redundant capacities and few linkages.[85] The CIA itself was effectively split into two agencies (operations and intelligence) with different roles and organizational cultures. Yet the split between externally focused intelligence agencies (most important, the CIA) and internally focused law enforcement agencies (most important, the FBI) was particularly crucial.[86] After September 11, Brent Scowcroft noted, "The borders, as far as the terrorists are concerned, have gone. There is no distinction for terrorists between inside and outside the United States and I think that makes much more serious the division that we have between the CIA and FBI."[87] The FBI systematically declined to provide information on investigations to intelligence communities or the White House, stating that it feared that information sharing might compromise prosecutions.[88] More broadly, organizational inertia led to extraordinary difficulties in transforming major US intelligence and law enforcement agencies so that they could deal with new issues and threats.[89] In the two decades before September 11, the pace of institutional change was notably lethargic in the United States in comparison to the European Union, which transformed its domestic security institutions over the same period, albeit from a much less organized base.

The dearth of specialized privacy regulators marked another important point of contrast between the European Union and United States. In 1974, the United States passed the Privacy Act, which provided US citizens with notable protections against government misuse of their data, but declined to offer blanket protections against commercial misuse. While the United States gradually built up a patchwork of rules covering many specific sectors (most notably health, but also including video rental records thanks to the efforts of journalists to uncover the rental habits of a Supreme Court nominee in the frustrated hope of finding evidence that he had depraved tastes), it never created any equivalent to the European Union's data privacy commissioners: independent officials charged with protecting the privacy rights of citizens.[90] Instead, the US government and its agencies treated privacy as another administrative obligation to be handled, along with a myriad other such obligations, by internal lawyers and other general-purpose officials.

This has changed in recent years as agencies have begun to create specialized internal bureaucracies to handle privacy issues. The FTC ended up assuming a privacy mandate by default for the various businesses under its ambit, using Section 5 of the FTC Act to selectively pursue sanctions against businesses that failed to live up to their stated commitments. It was, however, typically incapable of pursuing businesses that had not made such commitments.[91]

The United States, like the European Union, has a variety of NGOs with a direct interest in privacy. Typically, these organizations adopt a proprivacy stance. The Electronic Privacy Information Center is perhaps the most important specialized nonprofit covering privacy issues, with an interest in both commercial and governmental privacy issues.[92] The Electronic Frontier Foundation instead focuses on privacy primarily as a civil liberties issue and pays notably less attention to commercial aspects of privacy. The Center for Democracy and Technology is the product of a split between the Electronic Frontier Foundation's San Francisco head office and Washington, DC staffers in a previous incarnation, and tends to pursue a less activist approach than the Electronic Frontier Foundation. These organizations (especially the Electronic Privacy Information Center) have sought to use perceived pressure from the European Union in their efforts to push for legislative change in the United States.[93] Access Now!, a newer organization, looks to organize around digital rights issues and notably has a presence on both sides of the Atlantic.

In summary, the US approach to domestic security and intelligence is rooted both in post–World War II bureaucratic struggles, and in controversies over privacy and the state in the 1970s. These led to intense fragmentation, and after the revelations of the 1970s, a sharp split between agencies focused on domestic law enforcement such as the FBI and internationally focused intelligence agencies like the NSA. While the United States did institute privacy protections for its citizens (most notably FISA and the Privacy Act), these protections revolved around government rather than commercial activities, leaving the latter to be addressed by specific sectoral rules and by the logic of the market.

After September 11: International and Domestic Security Changes

The attacks of September 11 transformed transnational debates over privacy and security. At the global level, it demonstrated the relationship between economic interdependence and transnational threats with terrorists from a number of foreign countries deploying a symbol of globalization—airplanes—to destroy another symbol of globalization—the World Trade Center.[94] It also greatly intensified policy interdependence in the domestic security and privacy space as international organizations, the United States, and Europe began to respond. For the United States in particular, it made concerns about terrorism, which had been simmering in US policy circles since the end of the Cold War, immediately compelling and urgent. As a result, the United States and European Union underwent rapid reforms in their domestic security apparatus. A new sense of urgency regarding transnational threats as well as the changed institutional environment shaped the transatlantic disputes that we explore in the following chapters.

The United Nations was responsible for the most striking response internationally. It swiftly looked to take on a role, promoting cooperation on counterterrorism issues. In particular, Security Council Resolution 1373 adopted unanimously on September 28, 2001, by the United Nations marked an unprecedented level of action.[95] Unlike many UN resolutions, the resolution was adopted under Chapter VII of the UN Charter and is binding on all members.[96] Among other things, the resolution calls on members to criminalize acts of terrorism and punish it as a serious offense, promote intelligence sharing so as to combat terrorism, and adjust national laws so as to ratify all international terrorism conventions. Most important, the resolution calls on all members to become party to the 1999 International Convention for the Suppression of the Financing of Terrorism, which requires states to assist in freezing and seizing the assets of individuals or organizations engaged in funding terrorist activities. Additionally, the resolution created the Security Council's Counter Terrorism Committee, which monitors state compliance with the resolution. The Financial Action Task Force, which had initially had no competences over terrorism, has moved increasingly to cover antiterrorist financing measures.[97] As Nicholas Ryder (2015, 49) puts it, "The UN has become the fulcrum of the 'Financial War on Terrorism,' and its legislative agenda vehemently moved away from money laundering towards the financing of terrorism."

These changes have created some movement toward a common approach to terrorism across states, although this evolution has been hampered by the lack of a common definition of terrorism and continuing differences in national legal systems.[98] They have also led to legal challenges that focus on the apparent lack of due process associated with placing organizations on terrorist-financing watchlists that are sometimes based on secret information and difficult to appeal.

The attacks, unsurprisingly, had policy consequences within the United States too, even if they were less expansive than some might have liked.[99] Following the report of the September 11 Commission, there were important changes to practices within the intelligence community. The commission identified fragmentation and failure to share information as key reasons for the success of the terrorists.[100] Hence the intelligence community engaged in a wide-ranging effort to foster intelligence sharing through organizational changes and new technologies (such as Intellipedia) aimed at allowing the swift aggregation of dispersed information from across the scattered intelligence agencies. Many of the procedural roadblocks to cooperation between the CIA and FBI were dismantled.

The resistance of key actors such as the US Department of Defense (then led by Donald Rumsfeld) meant that the supervisory apparatus intended to ensure better cooperation between agencies was defanged while the obduracy of middle management made it hard to do away with traditional, more bureaucratic forms of information sharing. As with post–World War II efforts to make the CIA the key coordinator for all intelligence activities, proposals for a centralized national intelligence apparatus foundered on the rock of bureaucratic politics.[101]

Attempts to bring together various aspects of domestic security under one roof were somewhat more successful. The attacks of September 11 set in motion institutional reforms, which both elevated internal security efforts within existing agencies and centralized the oversight of many of these agencies under the rubric of the DHS.

The institutional transformation was not automatic. Soon after the attack, legislators attempted to transpose the Hart-Rudman recommendations by establishing a coordinating institution for homeland security issues within the federal government. The Bush administration initially blocked these efforts, resisting the creation of a federal bureaucracy. Over the course of winter 2001–2, the administration made a radical shift. Far from simply backing an independent coordination agency, the administration supported the biggest bureaucratic transformation in decades.[102] Over twenty agencies would be centralized and housed in the DHS, which would be given a mandate to protect domestic infrastructures and citizens. A motley bunch of organizations including US Customs (formerly part of the Treasury Department), the Immigration and Naturalization Service (formerly part of the Justice Department), and independent agencies such as the Federal Aviation Administration were brought together under one roof.[103]

At the same time, the Bush administration required that the transition be budget neutral. In other words, the agencies would be required to maintain their legacy mandates and take on the mantel of DHS tasks without new resources. The Bush administration ended up using the political opportunity created by the September 11 attacks to change the role of government in society.[104] As DHS opened its doors in March 2003, it not only created a focal point for national homeland security issues but also established an actor with a mandate to coordinate US security interests globally.

Despite these efforts, US policing remained remarkably fragmented and decentralized.[105] Particularly in contrast to countries such as the United Kingdom or Israel, US policing, intelligence, and internal security operations have long been distributed across a host of federal, state, and local agencies as well as across agencies at each level.[106] Various efforts to improve coordination across the federal, state, and local levels, including so-called fusion centers, swiftly evolved away from federal authorities' concern with tackling national threats, to provide more resources for state and local agencies' traditional concerns of local crime.[107]

At the federal level, individual departments and agencies created a multitude of initiatives aimed at reshaping domestic and international security. The FBI established a Terrorist Financing Operations Section, while the FBI, CIA, NSA, and Department of Defense participated in efforts to understand financing networks and use them as a lever against terrorism.[108] The Treasury Department proved especially aggressive in retooling itself to identify criminal financing arrangements, and disrupt and undermine them, using the preeminence of the dollar to open up financial relationships outside the United States.[109] Again, however, cooperation and coordination often turned out to be more difficult in practice than in theory.[110]

Legislative efforts sought to bolster organizational changes by giving law enforcement authorities new powers to demand information. Passed in October 2001, the USA PATRIOT Act broadened the authority of the federal government to obtain intelligence both domestically and abroad. A response to the September 11 attacks, the PATRIOT Act aimed to reduce technical barriers and legal standards that had been characterized as "walls" between different branches of investigation and intelligence gathering.[111] Of pivotal importance was the provision within Title II, Article 218, that amended FISA's requirements for judicial controls over intelligence surveillance. FISA created a specialized federal court, which oversees requests by federal agencies for surveillance warrants against foreign intelligence agents, and its proceedings are conducted in secret due to the national security issues involved. Whereas previously a FISA order could only be issued if the "primary purpose" of an investigation was for foreign intelligence, the PATRIOT Act reduced the threshold to a "significant purpose." A major consequence of this revision is that a warrant gained through in camera proceedings where there is less public access can now be used for criminal prosecution.[112]

Another controversial aspect of the PATRIOT Act concerns broad data collection powers contained in the so-called library records provision and the expansion of National Security Letters. Both allow for investigators to seize a wide range of business records. The library records provision covers both content and transmission information but requires a court order. National Security Letters, by contrast, have a narrower scope, focusing on transmission data, but do not require investigators to have a warrant. Both provisions come with gag orders so that businesses that provide information are not allowed to disclose the request.[113] The US government secretly interpreted these rules as allowing it to make blanket demands that telecommunications providers give it metadata in bulk rather than through specifically targeted requests as anticipated by the bill's drafters.[114]

The PATRIOT Act also authorized roving wiretaps, which are not constrained to tapping a single phone or provider, as well as wiretaps for noncitizens who are not associated with any foreign power. Although the PATRIOT Act was passed in Congress with an overwhelming majority in 2001, it has become increasingly controversial. Nevertheless, as the act was nearing expiration in 2011, President Barack Obama signed into law an extension of the aforementioned provisions.

In addition to these formal legislative changes, the US government has conducted a host of secret programs that expand transnational surveillance operations. In 2005, the *New York Times* reported that the NSA had been conducting a program of domestic warrantless wiretapping since 2002 without FISA approval. This was followed by the revelation in 2006 that the US government had been secretly requesting data from the Belgium-based Society for Worldwide Interbank Financial Telecommunication (SWIFT), which organized global financial messaging. In 2013, Snowden, an NSA contractor and former CIA employee, released a trove of data concerning US surveillance, demonstrating the extent of such surveillance as well as the limited ability and willingness of the FISA court to constrain such activities.[115]

Laura Donohue (2016) describes how the president authorized the NSA in 2001 to collect telephony and internet metadata en masse under the STARBURST program (later renamed STELLAR WIND), with no external oversight and under dubious legal authority. As Donohue notes, even the NSA was not allowed to read the legal justification for the program, which was eventually shifted to the pen register/trap and trace authorities in FISA after key Department of Justice officials threatened to resign. While STELLAR WIND appears to have been both illegal and unconstitutional,

Congress provided telecommunications companies with blanket immunity for their past participation.[116]

The Snowden revelations suggested even more sweeping information gathering on non-US persons, who were only scantily protected under US laws. Both Britain's GCHQ communications intelligence agency and the NSA engaged in warrantless interception of traffic between Google and Yahoo! data centers, providing them with 1.8 billion records over one single thirty-day period.[117] One of the key problems of US data gathering from the internet and other advanced communications networks has been the difficulty of distinguishing between domestic and non-US traffic, which are supposed to be covered by different legal standards and principles. Moreover, efforts by US officials such as President Obama to reassure the US public that it was not the subject of surveillance since it enjoyed protections that were not granted to non-US persons have not been treated with extraordinary enthusiasm outside the United States.[118]

While security and intelligence agencies have seen their budgets expand and coordination increase, US civil liberties advocates face obstacles in the transnational homeland security environment. The failure of the 1974 Privacy Act to create an independent privacy commissioner has had stark long-term consequences.[119] Broadly speaking, US NGOs lack a consistent advocate within the executive branch. The Clinton administration did create a chief privacy office within the Office of Management and Budget, but it was quickly disbanded under the Bush administration. Not only is there a domestic gap in public-private advocacy but the lack of a US privacy office excludes the United States from full participation in international efforts. National civil liberties organizations such as the American Civil Liberties Union (ACLU) have only recently formally acknowledged the transnational dimension of the issue. In 2008, the ACLU spurred the formation of a transnational network of similar organizations, which meets biannually to discuss common concerns, share best practices, and build mutual institutional capacity.

In an important development, several federal agencies have created internal privacy offices. Both the DHS and the Justice Department have chief privacy officers. The DHS has a relatively large office, with a budget of nearly $8 million and a staff of forty-six as of 2017.[120] It has an international division, and actively comments on and participates in transnational developments. Despite the rise of internal privacy expertise within the DHS, Justice Department, and other agencies, these officials have a precarious role within international debates.[121] While tasked with managing information processing and collection within the administration, they are also required to represent the administration position. As they lack institutional independence and are political appointees, they do not have the clout of data privacy authorities in Europe.

The EU response to September 11 and subsequent terrorist attacks was far less sweeping. As Jörg Monar (2015, 335), rector of the College of Europe, notes,

> The EU has clearly not replaced Member States in this domain, and limitations of its legal competences, institutional framework and internal counterterrorism measures—which have invited comparisons with a "paper tiger" in counter-terrorism matters—have a continuing restrictive impact on its international role in counter-terrorism.

Member states continue to exercise their competences on antiterrorism and other domestic security matters as well as reserve the right to negotiate national agreements on judicial cooperation with third countries.[122] Consequently, key aspects of domestic security remain at the nation-state level, and EU-level competences are dominated by the Council's Justice and Home Affairs incarnation. The Council has established internal institutions to improve coordination and information gathering, including the European Union Intelligence Analysis Centre, which coordinates with national external intelligence services. The Council's counterterrorism coordinator has no direct powers or authority, but plays an important agenda-setting role as well as managing external relations on security-sensitive topics.[123]

Elsewhere, the European Union has had greater difficulty in dealing with domestic security issues that emerged after September 11.[124] The EU Framework Decision aimed at restricting terrorist financing was passed in December 2001—but was already in progress before the attacks. Efforts by the European Union to implement actions against specific groups and individuals identified on UN watchlists have been hampered by the European Court of Justice, which ruled in its 2008 *Kadi* decision that these watchlists did not provide sufficient means of redress to be considered legitimate.[125] The Treaty of Prüm, which was ratified in 2005, and signed by Austria, Belgium, France, Germany, Luxembourg, the Netherlands, and Spain, gives participating states access rights to a variety of information sources (such as DNA analysis and vehicle registration data).[126] Some of the convention's rules have been adopted into EU legislation.[127]

The European Council's 2004 Declaration on Combating Terrorism called on member states to cooperate more fully on police and judicial matters, and to coordinate with Europol and Eurojust. Its associated Action Plan consisted in large part of previously existing initiatives that were repackaged as playing a counterterrorism role.[128] A Belgian-Austrian proposal for a European intelligence agency was "summarily rejected" by the big states. The subsequent European Union Counter-Terrorism Strategies appear to in large part be a branding exercise rather than significant policy measures.[129]

In the wake of the declaration, Eurojust has acquired an internal team of antiterrorism specialists, while Europol has increased in importance with its staff growing from roughly three hundred in the early 2000s to over twelve hundred by 2017, and has been incorporated more directly into the EU institutional framework after the Treaty of Lisbon.[130] It has come to play a vital role in facilitating information transfer between EU member states through the Secure Information Exchange Network Application, and in January 2016, established a Counter Terrorism Center, which is intended to be "an enhanced central information hub by which the member states can increase information sharing and operational coordination." In the wake of the Paris bombings in 2015, it facilitated Taskforce Fraternité, which has been cited by the European Union's counterterrorism coordinator as a model for cooperative ventures between Europol and member states.[131] Even if the aegis of Europol has increased, it is still modest; like Eurojust, the institution plays a coordinating role among the member states instead of being a major actor in its own right.[132] The EU's Framework Decision on the Arrest Warrant and Surrender Procedures, adopted in 2002 and amended in 2009, provides a common European Arrest Warrant, making it easier for member states to surrender wanted individuals to other member states.

Terrorist attacks, including the Madrid attack in 2004, helped pave the way for the 2006 EU Directive on data retention, which obliged member states to adopt common rules under which telecommunications providers maintain records on traffic data.[133] The European Court of Justice found in 2014 that the EU Directive was invalid because it breached the Charter of Fundamental Rights of the European Union. The Court noted in particular that the traffic data that was gathered could be transported outside the European Union,

> with the result that it cannot be held that the control, explicitly required by Article 8(3) of the Charter, by an independent authority of compliance with the requirements of protection and security . . . is fully ensured. Such a control, carried out on the basis of EU law, is an essential

component of the protection of individuals with regard to the processing of personal data.[134]

The Court hence suggested its willingness to take an activist stance on information exchange with non-EU authorities, creating an important precedent for the later cases discussed in chapter 5.[135]

In general, the European Union has been slower than the United States to adopt major institutional changes in the wake of September 11. Its relative lethargy is the consequence of three factors. First, many of the challenges combine national intelligence questions, which are not an EU competence, and police and home affairs issues, which are a shared competence between the European Union and its member states. Member states (especially large ones with their own independent intelligence capacities) have been highly reluctant to countenance measures that might impede their own freedom of action and external relationships, which in some cases (e.g., the United Kingdom until it leaves the European Union) are arguably better developed than their relations with other member states. The result is semidisconnected institutions and competences under which some matters are kept out of the European Union's ambit altogether, others are shared only at the member state level, and others still are fully part of the European Union but are limited in scope.

Second, policing arrangements, even absent the thorny questions of intelligence sharing, are complex and vary dramatically from state to state. Some states have highly devolved policing systems (e.g., Belgium). Others have nationalized police forces, or some blend of nationalized and local structures. All this, combined with deep-rooted national patterns of cooperation, and differences of language, culture, and legal system, make it difficult to achieve deep cooperation on domestic security matters. Third and finally, the European Union is itself a complex law- and rule-making system, with many different veto points, making it hard to carry through large-scale institutional reforms.

Figure 2.2 summarizes the major developments in privacy and security discussed in the chapter. Emphasizing the period since the 1970s, the events described above the time line focus on privacy, while the events noted below the time line center on security. We hope that the visual depiction of the chapter helps readers understand the chronology of the various transformations happening both within the European Union and United States as well as those occurring between them and globally.

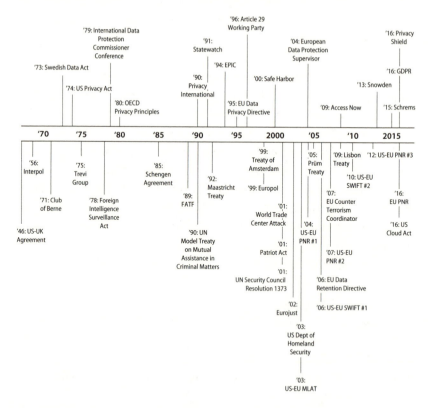

FIGURE 2.2. Development of Transatlantic Privacy and Domestic Security

Conclusion: Changing Relations between the European Union and United States

The existing patterns of privacy and security governance in both the European Union and United States that we describe individually in the main part of the chapter are already quite complex. They have been further complicated by interaction effects between the two systems, which we seek to identify more specifically in the remaining chapters of this book. US and European officials signed a number of bilateral deals in the wake of the attacks of September 11. In addition to the PNR agreements (2004, 2007, 2012), the SWIFT Agreement (2006, 2010) and the Umbrella Agreement (2016), which are subject to detailed discussions (see chapters 3, 4, and 5), the two jurisdictions signed a mutual legal assistance treaty in 2003, a cooperation agreement between Europol and the United States in 2001, and one between Eurojust and the United States in 2006. These agreements created nascent cooperative relationships among major law enforcement agencies on the two sides of the Atlantic.

Equally, actors in each system engaged in unilateral actions that have implications for actors in the other. For example, the United States adopted a host of unilateral counterterrorism activities with transnational implications. Many of these policies included overt legislative change such as the PATRIOT Act, but also include a range of secret initiatives conducted covertly by intelligence agencies. In 2018, the United States extended its reach with the passage of the Cloud Act, which grants the US government access to data held by US firms in offshore data centers. The overall effect of these policies has been to widen the net of US government surveillance to include both domestic and international targets. At the same time, these changes have weakened the due process mechanisms that typically constrain government overreach.

This has had political consequences in the European Union. The 2013 revelations that the NSA tapped political leadership in major European countries as well as potentially engaging in large-scale forms of intelligence gathering stoked existing concerns in Germany and elsewhere about US intentions. It led senior decision makers in Germany to revisit their concerns about the Five Eyes arrangement, unsuccessfully demanding Five Eyes status in Germany's information-sharing arrangements with the United States.[136] At the level of parliamentarians and ordinary citizens, it provoked widespread fear and consternation, especially in countries like Germany where privacy was already an important issue.

Yet actors within the European Union have also engaged in unilateral actions. The increasing willingness of European privacy regulators and the European Court of Justice to block international data transfers to protect domestic arrangements is causing nervousness among US firms and officials, since it both threatens commercial relations and seeks to constrain what US officials and former officials see as legitimate exercises in protecting the US homeland.[137]

The sensitivity on both sides highlights changes in the relationship. Economic integration proceeded through globalization and regional integration, generating policing and internal security issues. Organized crime, drug trade, and human trafficking all raised the salience of key homeland security domains, such as border control, customs, and immigrations. Governments—especially in Europe—developed institutions to manage transnational homeland security. In the wake of the Schengen Agreement, the European Union created the third pillar for justice and home affairs, which then received an explicit international mandate under the Treaty of Amsterdam. By the end of the 1990s, the European Union experienced a governance revolution with the institutionalization of Europol and the Treaty of Lisbon.

After September 11, the locus of far-reaching institutional change moved from Europe to the United States. The attacks shifted the debate on two levels. They created a common set of threats—transnational terrorism— around which transatlantic cooperation seemed necessary. Moreover, they centralized US agency activity under the auspices of DHS and increased its attention to homeland security concerns.

This interaction brought the two jurisdictions into much closer contact on homeland security issue than they had been for much of the postwar period. With distinct institutional legacies concerning homeland security, civil liberties, and privacy, these interactions sparked a series of conflicts that were as much about the renegotiation of domestic bargains as they were about international stalemate. The remainder of the book examines how different political groups responded to these pressures, and how these strategies altered domestic and global institutions. In the next chapter, we explore the specific case of passenger data in the aviation sector. In so doing, we connect the kinds of descriptive transformation detailed above to the causal processes that we discussed in chapter 1, showing how the politics of interdependence is associated with particular actor change strategies.

3

Competing Atlantic Alliances and the Fight over Airline Passenger Data Sharing

In late 2002, European airlines had to confront a seemingly unsolvable problem. After the attacks of September 11, the United States passed legislation requiring foreign air carriers to transfer detailed personal information on their passengers to US Customs. Any failure to comply with these rules would risk extensive fines and potentially the loss of landing rights. If they met US security demands, however, European air carriers risked violating European privacy laws, exposing themselves to different regulatory sanctions. Rule overlap created an impossible catch-22 for firms, stranding them between the directly conflicting demands of transatlantic counterterrorism cooperation and privacy protection. This dilemma generated a roughly decadelong dispute over the sharing of PNR data between the United States and European Union. Ultimately the two sides reached an accord, and in its wake, the European Union changed its internal rules so as to require similar information of flights entering Europe.

Existing accounts of this dispute tend to depict it as a battle between a security-focused United States and a privacy-focused European Union, in which the United States succeeded in imposing its own approach on a reluctant European Union.[1] Javier Argomaniz (2009b, 128) concludes that "US dominance has been apparent in the negotiations as well as in the final contents of the 2007 PNR agreement." Alternative accounts describe the controversy as the result of a common shock (the advent of terrorism) working out in different ways in different systems, or as a process of normative convergence across the European Union and United States.[2]

These standard explanations start from the assumptions about interactions between unitary states that Helen Callaghan (2010) has dubbed "methodological nationalism." They disagree on what drives interstate dynamics, respectively emphasizing interstate bullying, domestic institutions, and normative agreement. They agree that the key interactions are between discrete and monolithic states. Each, consequently, underemphasizes the importance of interdependence between different national systems and the ways in which politics in the transatlantic space often spans geographic boundaries.

Our alternative approach, developed in chapter 1, highlights how interdependence not only generates common problems but also differentially creates transnational opportunities for actors hoping to contest or protect their existing domestic institutional bargains. In particular, the chapter underscores the competing factions within each jurisdiction, and how they took advantage of or resisted these political opportunities. The PNR dispute was shaped, on the one hand, by security-oriented actors within both the European Union and United States who forged a transnational alliance to transform European rules, and by the efforts of their opponents (who were primarily located within Europe, and who were concerned more with civil liberties and privacy) to insulate the European Union from external influence, hence potentially undercutting their internal adversaries.

In the remainder of this chapter, we examine how actors in the United States and European Union used these strategies of cross-national layering and insulation to shape the consequences of the transatlantic dispute. We show that neither the European Union nor the United States had unified preferences. The US DHS pushed the European Union to introduce measures that it had been unable to shepherd through the US political system because of strong political opposition from the domestic civil liberties community. At the same time, its proposals were not simply forced on an unwilling European Union; while these policies were strongly opposed by some actors within the European Union, they were welcomed by others.

This produced a situation where one alliance, which was not happy with the European status quo on privacy, used cross-national negotiations to change it. US negotiators (in coalition with European security officials) sought to build an alternative to European privacy rules in which PNR data could be shared with the United States and in turn with European security officials. This alliance developed principles that were intended to resolve business uncertainty among the airline industry, soften the opposition of the privacy coalition, and expand data transfers.

On the other side of the argument, the defenders of the privacy status quo used various domestic policy levers to try to insulate existing EU institutions from the transatlantic security community. These ranged from threatening European market access to seeking to undermine the nascent transnational agreement by taking it to the European Court of Justice. As in the case of financial data (which we examine in the next chapter), key European actors favoring greater attention to security concerns saw US pressure as an opportunity to reshape EU institutions in ways that favored them, while those who favored privacy sought to protect existing institutions against these pressures.

Importantly, security actors in the United States and Europe built transatlantic agreements, which over time gained the support of the aviation industry (which sought legal certainty) and leached away support for pure resistance strategies. Ultimately, the interactions between transatlantic security officials not only arrived at a transnational solution to the problem but also helped build the necessary political foundations for the adoption of an internal PNR system within the European Union modeled on the EU-US agreement. Intra-EU battles, coupled with the cross-national layering strategies of security officials from both jurisdictions, explain why and how US demands had consequences both globally and for Europe. The chapter, then, focuses on the strategies of the competing alliances as they alternatively attempted to resist and bring through this institutional change.

Domestic US Politics: Defense through Data Collection

Border control has historically been a critical site of surveillance where governments attempt to prevent people whom they consider undesirable from entering their sovereign territory. Globalized commercial air transport and the rise of transnational terrorist networks confronted governments with new security challenges, but they also provided opportunities for surveillance as governments could tap into the information that airlines and other agencies used to identify their customers.[3] After September 11, the US government tried to increase its access to commercial data to surveil domestic air passengers, but ran into strong resistance from a vigorous civil liberties lobby. DHS proposals to construct a national information-gathering system were resisted by US privacy advocates such as the ACLU, which successfully constructed an unlikely coalition of progressive liberals and libertarian conservatives to stymie the creation of purely domestic databases.[4] After being blocked at home, the US government explored alternative international sources of data.

Gathering data on airline passengers had some precedent. Starting in the late 1990s, the FBI and Federal Aviation Administration developed a screening system to prevent explosives from entering the checked luggage system. Under the Computer-Assisted Passenger Prescreening System (CAPPS) system, airlines used a limited amount of PNR data to identify luggage that should receive additional attention prior to flight. After September 11, DHS proposed to take the system over and expand it, and to link PNR data to other databases kept by the government and private sector to identify individuals who would receive additional personal screening at security checkpoints. This shifted policy from screening luggage to screening people, using a range of personal data such as reservation histories to construct individual risk scores. Known as CAPPS II, the proposed policy greatly expanded both the data to be analyzed and the extent of privacy intrusion that might result. Eventually, proponents hoped, CAPPS II could be used to assist law enforcement agencies and prevent risky individuals from flying.[5]

In one of the most successful post–September 11 civil liberties advocacy campaigns, the ACLU targeted CAPPS II as an excessive invasion of privacy. The ACLU (2003) warned that "this system threatens to create a permanent blacklisted underclass of Americans who cannot travel freely." Working both with its membership and ties to elected officials, the ACLU orchestrated a campaign that depicted CAPPS II as an Orwellian program that excessively expanded government authority and was rife for abuse. The campaign successfully highlighted a number of high-profile mistakes in which prominent people found themselves labeled as "high risk" by the database.

The ACLU found allies in industry, which worried both about the financial cost of the program and reputational damage for airlines. As Garth Jopling, president of the Association of Corporate Travel Executives, explained, "It [CAPPS II] went against the grain of the average U.S. traveler to stand for investigation over the purchase of a plane ticket. The program also failed to satisfy corporate America's concerns over projected costs relating to delays, missed flights and false-positive readings."[6]

Congress finally intervened, requiring that the Government Accountability Office conduct an audit to assess the intrusiveness of the program and delaying the program until the office could demonstrate that CAPPS II would pass a series of privacy protection standards. Bowing to both public outcry and political pressure, the Transportation Security Administration, an agency within the DHS, canceled the program in 2004.

Facing stiff opposition, the Transportation Security Administration sought to create a successor program, known as Secure Flight, in 2005. After years of development, Secure Flight was finally made operational in 2010. In contrast to CAPPS II, Secure Flight is focused on improving no-fly lists by identifying passengers correctly. Prior to departure, passengers enter their legal name, date of birth, and gender so as to better match this information to government-held no-fly lists. While some have criticized possible mission creep in the Secure Flight program, it is far more constrained than the original CAPPS II program and in many respects more limited than the EU-US PNR agreement that we discuss later. The data provided is circumscribed and is held for only seven days before being deleted. While internal resistance strategies did not completely stymie domestic air passenger surveillance, they greatly weakened it.[7]

Rule Overlap: Reaching out for Data across Borders

DHS found it far easier to demand data on international travelers. In large part, this was because of preexisting institutions for managing the movement of individuals across borders. US border control agencies already had a high degree of autonomy in controlling who and what entered the country—having the power, for example, to conduct extensive searches without a warrant and to deny entry to non-US citizens with little effective judicial recourse. Providing US customs officials the power to require new information was presented as an extension of existing practices given the security concerns rather than a fundamental invasion of civil liberties along the lines of CAPPS II.[8]

Prior to the September 11 attacks, border control agencies typically collected passport information at the border. Known as Advanced Passenger Information, these data provided basic information on the identity of the person traveling such as name, gender, age, citizenship, and travel documentation.[9] It is routinely captured by the machine-readable data kept in a passport and swiped as an individual proceeds through customs. While such data are useful in establishing identity and visa status, they offer limited additional opportunity for building up detailed risk profiles.

PNR data are kept by the airlines in their reservation systems and contain much broader data ranging from credit card numbers to meal selection. After September 11, this provided the opportunity for the more wide-ranging screening of international travelers. The Aviation and Transportation Security Act of 2001, passed swiftly after the terrorist attacks, required that foreign air carriers report PNR data to US Customs before permitting entry.[10]

US authorities intended to scrutinize these data using profiling and network analysis software to identify suspicious behavior patterns and connections to potential criminal targets. The US DHS, for example, operates an Automatic Targeting System that analyzes a host of data including PNR to develop a risk score for travelers. As Stewart Baker (2010, 81), former head of policy at the DHS, later explained,

> Data was once costly to retain, store, and analyze, but now it was becoming cheaper and easier every day. What's more, the airlines whose passengers were overloading the old border system were using new technologies to identify and manage the travel of those same passengers. If we could use their data to identify the handful of risky passengers who needed an interview, we could do our screening while the plane was in the air.

The US government furthermore demanded that US Customs have direct access to European airline databases for security reasons as the need arose. Most airlines do not maintain their PNR data themselves but instead outsource storage to a Computerized Reservation System (CRS). Of the four major CRS providers, three are headquartered in the United States (Sabre, Galileo, and Worldspan) while one is based in Spain (Amadeus) and stores data in Germany but also has a datacenter in the United States. This constellation of data storage facilities allowed US officials to obtain data from these CRS companies' US data centers rather than from foreign air carriers and to share data with other US agencies than only US Customs.[11]

The US government began demanding that foreign governments comply with these demands in late 2002. By pressing the European Union to accede to these demands, security-oriented groups in the United States sought to defend US rules, which enjoyed a high degree of legitimacy within the United States in the wake of the recent attacks. They also tried to reopen European privacy rules, which they perceived as hampering the international fight against terrorism.[12]

US demands for airline passenger data were obviously in tension with the European privacy rules described in chapter 2. The augmented surveillance effort posed at least three challenges: the expansion of the data obtained (including sensitive information such as meal choice and financial data), the broad sharing of data with third parties (other government agencies and private contractors), and the extended retention period (DHS maintains PNR data for up to fifteen years). Actors such as the European data privacy authorities (who were the key privacy regulators in the member states) and the European Parliament sought to protect the existing European privacy regime against the threat of foreign encroachment.[13] Both had some commitment to civil liberties, but both also stood to lose if the European Union reached an administrative compromise with the United States. Data privacy commissioners would find their effective power to interpret and enforce rules trampled and weakened, while the European Parliament would lose hard-won clout over both intra-European policy setting and international agreement making.

Internal Dissent in the European Union

Under Article 25 of the Data Privacy Directive, the European Commission takes the lead in assessing whether foreign jurisdictions have or do not have "adequate" data privacy rules, which would allow data to be exported to them. When the controversy over airline data began, the Commission's Internal Market Directorate, which promotes internal market harmonization, was in charge of data privacy issues. It quickly found itself sidelined, however. In the description of one prominent Internal Market Directorate official, "We were under instructions in this particular DG to keep out of it as much as possible. We were not encouraged to be very forward."[14]

The Commission did not take a forceful stance on European privacy rules, worrying that it would be seen as hampering the fight against terrorism.[15] Instead, it sought to protect European airlines from clashing EU and US rules as best as it could by trying to obtain an adequacy ruling for US Customs, thereby allowing it effectively to accept the US approach. Given the quintessentially global nature of the aviation industry, the Commission hoped that it could find a quick compromise that would mitigate any economic impact for European airlines.[16] The importance of the transatlantic air transport market led to Commission fears that failure to resolve the dispute could threaten a major component of European competitiveness.

Furthermore, some security officials were actually quietly in favor of the US demands. EU interior ministries tended to back a prosecurity perspective, and to be impatient with privacy and civil liberties arguments. Highly influential officials like Germany's Wolfgang Schäuble supported PNR and wanted to share information with the United States even if this was legally dubious.[17] This created a tacit alliance between US officials and

EU interior ministries, who had an interest in pushing forward an agenda based around security cooperation and pushing back against what they saw as obtrusive privacy regulations.[18] Within the European Commission too there were strong disagreements internally over how issues such as PNR ought to be handled.[19]

After several rounds of negotiations between the Commission and the newly created DHS, the two sides developed a Joint Statement in February 2003.[20] In the agreement, the Commission pledged to delay the implementation of European privacy laws and permit data transfers. The United States agreed to a series of privacy concessions including limiting the sharing of information with other US agencies, restricting access to the data within US Customs, removing sensitive data from analysis, deleting data after three and half years, and committing to a periodic joint review of DHS management of data. The Internal Market Directorate indicated that data privacy authorities might accept the Joint Statement as sufficient to permit data transfers. Many officials within the US government believed that they had made important concessions during the process.[21] Officials on both sides of the negotiation process saw the Joint Statement as reflecting a genuine spirit of compromise by the two parties that recognized and attempted to balance privacy interests and those of information sharing.

The European privacy regime provides opportunities for other actors to veto policy proposals. Even though the Commission took the lead in negotiating, it was subject both to member state supervision and to pressure from the European Parliament and national data privacy authorities (who play an important advisory role through the Article 29 Working Party). While member states were split, both the Parliament and data privacy authorities had a stronger interest in maintaining the existing European privacy regime than did the relevant European Commission officials. Both of these groups were deliberately and systematically excluded from the EU-US forums where PNR was being discussed. Because they had no direct access to negotiations, they used the institutional tools at their disposal to try to insulate the existing regime from the proposed international compromise.

The European Parliament worried that the agreement was propelling privacy issues from the realm of market governance into the burgeoning area of justice and home affairs. As discussed in chapter 2, the role of Parliament in the so-called third pillar of the European Union (covering justice and home affairs) was extremely limited. Some figures in Parliament feared that justice and home affairs was replacing the EU internal market process as the main motor of European integration, effectively cutting the Parliament out of increasingly important areas of decision making.[22] In this context, the Parliament believed that the agreement set a dangerous precedent.[23]

Data privacy authorities, for their part, saw the agreement as threatening European privacy law. They had played a critical role in pushing comprehensive European legislation to replace the preexisting patchwork of national approaches. The agreement seemed to heavily water down Europe's privacy regime for the sake of EU-US relations and domestic security concerns. Again, they believed that this plausibly set a dangerous precedent for the future.[24]

National data privacy authorities began deliberately to oppose the agreement from within, trying to insulate the existing European privacy regime against external pressures. They repeatedly and publicly rejected the Commission's interpretation of the legislation, and used their delegated authority and expertise to undermine internal support for the Joint Statement. This began in October 2002 when the Article 29 Working Party preemptively released an opinion arguing that such transfers were in direct violation of the 1995 Privacy Directive.[25] The regulators did not seek to ban PNR transfers as such, but indicated their hostility to US direct access to European airline databases, the sharing of sensitive data such as meal choices that might indicate religious affiliation, the extended retention period, the vague standard for collecting and transferring the information to other agencies, and the lack of a formal control mechanism to monitor use by US Customs.[26] The Commission faced the difficult task of publicly justifying its compromise with the United States in the face of continual opposition from the Article 29 Working Party and potentially conducting a "comitology" review (i.e., a review under the Commission's delegated powers) in which it would have to contradict the opinion of the relevant technical experts.

In addition, data privacy authorities started to use their nationally delegated authority over the transfer of personal data across borders to try to force the Commission to renegotiate the agreement so as to better preserve the existing regime. In March 2003, the chair of the Article 29 Working Party and the head of the Italian data privacy authority, Stefano Rodotà, warned the European Parliament that continued transfers might result in regulatory or judicial intervention. Given the requirements of the European Privacy Directive, data privacy authorities might be forced to sanction carriers that transferred data under the Joint Statement.[27]

This began to happen. The Italian data privacy commissioner required Alitalia to provide US authorities only with the information contained in a passport.[28] Similarly, the Belgian authority ruled in late 2003 that US-EU transfers violated data privacy laws.[29] In short, national data privacy authorities used their nationally delegated power to try to reinforce the European Union's existing approach to data regulation and to undermine the nascent transatlantic PNR regime from below.

Leveraging ties to policy makers at different levels, the arguments of the Article 29 Working Party quickly found their way to the European Parliament, which had authority to review and amend first-pillar policy under the codecision process. European parliamentarian Sarah Ludford (UK-Liberal) summarized the assertions of Article 29 Working Party chair Rodotà as a major challenge to the Commission's authority:

> This is a stunning rebuff to the Commission. He [Rodotà] said in essence that National Data Protection Commissioners and courts were not free to suspend application of relevant laws just on the say-so of the Commission. That must be right. It is a reminder to the Commission that if it will not be the guardian of Community law, then others have to be.[30]

The alliance between the data privacy authorities and pro-civil-liberties European parliamentarians pushed the Commission to return to the negotiating table as Frits Bolkestein (2003), of the Internal Market Commission, explained in a letter to Tom Ridge, head of DHS:

> Data protection authorities here take the view that PNR data is flowing to the US in breach of our Data Privacy Directive. It is thus urgent to establish a framework which is more legally secure. . . . The centerpiece would be a decision by the Commission finding that the protection provided for PNR data in the US meets our "adequacy" requirements.

To be clear, data privacy officials were not opposed to international cooperation per se. They had determined that such transfers could be permitted to Canada and Australia. They were only willing to permit these transfers since they did not undermine the existing EU regime because of the amount of data involved as well as the restrictions placed on the storage and use of the data.[31] Similarly, the European Parliament was not opposed to cooperation with the United States in principle as long as it took place under an agreement that respected both the European Union's existing approach and the prerogatives of the Parliament.

> It would be in the European Union's interest to have a much greater exchange of information with the United States; providing it was governed by a proper international bilateral agreement. . . . Unfortunately, when

the US started to put pressure on the European Union to deal with PNR questions, the commission chose to approach it—I think under pressure from the member-states—in a way that was not going to involve the European Parliament at all. They initially told us, in September of 2002, that they would give us . . . rights to sign off on the agreement. That was then withdrawn; then they decided on a different approach. And we felt in the end . . . that we were talking about too many categories of data without adequate safeguards as to what this data would be used for; who it could be passed on to; and so on.[32]

As Rodotà (2003) argued in an address to the European Parliament, the concessions made by the United States were not sufficient to satisfy the Article 29 Working Party. The Commission risked further delay and institutional conflict with the Parliament in the form of a drawn-out codecision process if it failed to move the agreement closer to the demand of the Parliament and the data privacy authorities.

Thus, the first stage of the dispute over PNR saw a conflict between two major coalitions. One, consisting of EU and US domestic security officials, agreed on the primacy of security, while facing different institutional constraints in their different systems, and sought to bring through an agreement that could work above those institutions so as to allow the ready exchange of passenger information.

The other coalition mostly consisted of actors within the European Union—importantly the European Parliament and national-level data privacy authorities. Their goal was to insulate existing privacy institutions as best as they could either by reshaping the proposed agreement so that it did not challenge these institutions or by blocking it altogether. Their insulation strategies consisted of a mixture of veto threats and informal authority based on officially recognized expertise.

The Ironic Outcome of Domestic Insulation Strategies

After continued negotiations with the United States, the Commission agreed in December 2003 to the transfer of data from European airlines to US Customs. This would not include direct access to carrier databases, and the information transferred would filter out sensitive information. The compromise solution included the reduction of the categories of data collected from thirty-nine to thirty-four, the deletion of sensitive data, limiting the purpose of collection to terrorism and transnational crime, a retention period of three and half years, a sunset clause that forced renegotiation after three and half years, and annual joint audits of the program.[33] This reflected some concessions to the Parliament and data privacy officials. While the latter were unable to get their preferred outcome—the adoption of data privacy legislation for the private sector in the United States—they forced both the Commission and the United States to reach a compromise that bolstered the privacy protections in the agreement.[34]

The Parliament and data privacy officials were still dissatisfied with the compromise, and continued to use insulation strategies to resist the implementation of the agreement. The Parliament filed a suit with the European Court of Justice (2004) in summer 2004, despite uncertainty as to whether it had an actionable case.

> The Parliament sought the advice of its own lawyers on this, and the advice was not clear one way or another. But this didn't surprise us terribly. Our own in-house lawyers don't like Parliament to go to court so they tend to advise against it. This has been our experience on previous matters. On the other hand, on previous occasions when we have had to use the court, the court has often found in our favour. So we thought it was worth a shot.[35]

Following the logic presented by the Article 29 Working Party, the Parliament argued that the agreement was in violation of Article 8 of the European Convention on Human Rights, which protects the private life of European citizens.[36] Specifically, data in the United States were not monitored by an independent regulatory agency and the limitation of purpose was weak, allowing security agencies to use the information for unspecified "transnational crimes."

The European Court of Justice ruled against the agreement but on purely procedural grounds.[37] The Court concluded that the Commission did not have the authority under the first pillar to negotiate the agreement because it involved issues directly tied to justice and home affairs. The Court sidestepped the more fundamental debate about privacy, requiring that the agreement be renegotiated under the third pillar.[38] In short, it found no basis for supranational action. The court decision basically sent the negotiating parties back to the table with the European Union negotiating under new institutional parameters, under which the Parliament had little say.

As per the third-pillar rules, the Council now took on the lead role, supported by the commission directorate responsible for home and justice affairs. Within the Council, the interior ministries took responsibility for the negotiations.

This shift in institutional procedures was to the advantage both of EU officials in domestic security as well as justice and home affairs who typically cared more about security than economic relations or civil rights, and US officials impatient with European privacy law.[39] It also gravely weakened the formal authority of both the Parliament and the Article 29 Working Party of data privacy authorities. The Parliament had only limited rights under the third pillar, and because the EU Data Privacy Directive was passed under the first pillar, the Article 29 Working Party had no formal role in third-pillar affairs. As MEP Sophie in't Veld concluded, "Unfortunately, the outcome of the court hearing was such that we basically sidelined ourselves."[40]

Ironically, in using an important domestic lever of resistance—judicial review—defenders of the European Union's existing privacy regime precipitated themselves into a situation where they were far less easily able to use insulation strategies than hitherto. The means that they had used to try to insulate the regime from external pressure, by asserting the supremacy of privacy law over security concerns, allowed the Court to invalidate the agreement on the grounds that it was more directly connected to domestic security than it was to economic markets. This undermined the existing agreement and ensured that any renegotiation would happen under conditions where members of the civil liberties coalition had little direct influence.

The efforts of some European officials to insulate European institutions against other European officials and US officials who wanted to change those institutions backfired. It created the conditions for a new—and much more sweeping—effort to reshape European rules around the privacy of airplane passengers.

Mounting Regulatory Uncertainty and Industry Calls for Compromise

The efforts of Parliament and others to insulate EU institutions created additional uncertainty for industry. After nearly five years of negotiations, the issue of PNR transfers had still not been resolved. Moreover, the court decision did not offer a clear path for resolving the problem, which revived industry worries about rule overlap. Most carriers transferred data to US officials but were still vulnerable to sanctions from European data privacy officials.

US officials, who were impatient with the lack of a permanent agreement, frequently raised the specter of fines or flight disruptions so as to assert their bargaining strength.[41] This was accentuated by organizational changes in the DHS. Between the finalization of the Joint Statement in February 2003 and the European Court of Justice decision in May 2006, US bureaucracies underwent a remarkable transformation. Although President Bush appointed the first DHS director in September 2001, this was primarily an advisory position, providing support to the president on issues of counterterrorism. It was not until November 2002 that Congress authorized the creation of a cabinet-level department, and the department did not officially open its doors until March 2003. In early 2005, Secretary Michael Chertoff replaced Tom Ridge and began a major organizational consolidation, including the creation of a director of policy who could oversee DHS strategic planning and coordination across the sprawling department.

Secretary Chertoff, together with his first director of policy, Stewart Baker, prioritized the removal of barriers to information sharing. The new leadership viewed stovepiping and the failure to share data between law enforcement agencies as key causes of the intelligence failure of September 11. From this perspective, the commitment to data limitation in the EU-US PNR agreement, which prevented US Customs from sharing data with other agencies, represented just another dangerous constraint on law enforcement. Baker (2010, 104) concluded that "this was a bad deal. We needed to get out." In a *Washington Post* op-ed, Chertoff (2006) went as far as to publicly decry the agreement that his own administration had previously negotiated. In the wake of the European court decision, DHS representatives did not merely seek to reenact the status quo ante but also to renegotiate the terms of the agreement to limit constraints on data sharing, remove restrictions of sensitive information, and extend storage periods. As Baker (2010, 117) explained it, "We [DHS] were determined not to reinstate the old agreement. Secretary Chertoff and I simply would not accept a made-in-Europe version." Graham Watson, a British MEP, summarized the dilemma facing the airlines: "Either they violate EU law and give the US what they want, or they risk the States turning around and saying your airplanes can't come here."[42]

The stakes of the PNR debate for industry were considerable. European airlines depended on transatlantic flights for revenue. Moreover, investments made by the industry to meet US demands for data raised overhead costs. Industry wanted both a commitment that flights would continue and confidence that the financial burden of facilitating PNR would be contained.[43]

Both before and after the court decision, industry repeatedly called for a return to legal certainty surrounding transatlantic flights.[44] Association of European Airlines secretary-general Ulrich Schulte-Strathaus summarized the predicament by saying, "Our airlines are subject to conflicting regulatory requirements from opposite sides of the Atlantic—an untenable situation for airlines and passengers alike."[45]

Airline associations lobbied extensively to try to push both sides toward a solution. As described by one parliamentary official heavily involved in the debates, "Basically, IATA [the International Air Transport Association] [did the lobbying] because obviously airlines are in a terrible situation if they go with either U.S. law or European law, and obviously they had a great interest in resolving the issue."[46]

The Security Community Strikes Back: The Construction of a Cross-National Layer

Even as privacy advocates pursued domestic insulation strategies within the European Union, security officials developed a transnational platform through which to press a cross-national agenda. Security officials on both sides of the Atlantic acknowledged the frictions that arose from the extraterritorial implication of the US response to the attacks of September 2001. Two of the issues—port screening and airline data—involved the transportation sector, a domain that security officials saw as critical to a comprehensive homeland security strategy.

To address these concerns and prevent frictions from upsetting expanded surveillance efforts, US and European officials created the High Level Political Dialogue on Border and Transportation Security in April 2004. This informal network of officials concerned with homeland security issues on the two sides of the Atlantic sought to develop policies on information sharing and promote successful cooperation. Importantly, membership centered on those bureaucracies that represented security interests such as DHS and Customs on the US side, and the Justice and Home Affairs Directorate in the European Union. As Patryk Pawlak (2009b, 571), a scholar of homeland security cooperation, concluded, representation in these forums "was designed in a way to exclude any direct involvement of DPAs [Data Privacy Authorities]." Eventually, the High Level Political Dialogue on Border and Transportation Security was integrated into the High Level Contact Group on Data Protection, where discussions between security-oriented officials continued.

These transnational interactions proved decisive in allowing agencies both to clear up points of disagreement and to build a common transatlantic homeland security agenda. In addition to information sharing and agenda setting, the results of the dialogue were frequently used in domestic jurisdictions to overcome bureaucratic opposition.[47] More generally, these informal links forged trust between officials who previously had little experience with each other or, more generally, in working with foreign officials in international negotiations.

The European Court of Justice decision allowed the transnational security community to reassert itself. In the months following the European Court of Justice decision, a new round of negotiations began. This time it was led by the Council on the European side and the DHS on the US side. As these negotiations started, a critical shift had begun on each side of the Atlantic: the elevation of security interests. On the US side, the DHS began to transform itself from an inchoate amalgamation of disparate agencies to a more concentrated and focused organization.[48] DHS started to take a much more aggressive position than traditional foreign policy agencies had envisioned in the PNR negotiations. At the same time, control over negotiations shifted on the European side, thanks to the European Court decision, to the Council. Although the Council is in theory a single legal entity, in practice it is represented in particular issue areas by the ministers of EU member states concerned with overseeing that area. In this instance, the Council is comprised of interior ministers, who were far more concerned with security questions than are their internal market counterparts.[49] The transatlantic security alliance, then, was able to steer the negotiations away from the previous and more privacy friendly Joint Statement.

It was clear from public remarks made by interior ministers that they wanted a speedy agreement with the United States that would clarify relations and maintain counterterrorism cooperation. Wolfgang Schäuble (2006), who served both as German interior minister and European Council president during the negotiations, argued that "they [passenger data] are the most important clues to recognizing potential terrorists." In a review of leaked cables between US officials, *Der Spiegel* observed that "the Bush administration saw Schäuble as a sort of Trojan horse in Europe, a man who could help Washington achieve its goals."[50] In the view of US officials, Schäuble was willing to oppose the legal opinion of data privacy officials and the privacy-oriented coalition in order to overcome logjams and to expand transatlantic information sharing.[51] Going even further, Schäuble built on the agreement with the United States to propose that Europe too ought to adopt a PNR, concluding that "we need this [PNR] in Europe."[52] The Commission quickly followed suit, proposing a European PNR arrangement in 2007 that was closely modeled on the EU-US agreement.[53] As Baker (2010, 84, 141) described it, "Other countries weren't firmly opposed to sharing information. After all, that would make their border officials more effective, too. But sharing information with the United States was bound to meet some political resistance at home. Our allies needed help in overcoming that resistance." Baker also emphasized the importance of the shift to interior ministers as the lead negotiators: "With Schäuble and Frattini leading Europe's team, we hammered out a deal with far less drama than in the first talks."

By July 2007, a final agreement had been reached.[54] From the perspective of data privacy advocates, it contained few improvements over the Commission-brokered deal and in many areas was weaker. It specified the transfer of similar types of data to those detailed in the earlier agreement. The agreement also called for the use of a "push" system whereby airlines would send data to US Customs as opposed to the original "pull" system whereby US Customs would have had direct access to European air carrier databases. In a blow to data privacy protection, it included an extended data retention period of seven years. In addition to this, a "dormant" period of eight years was created. This classification of data allowed information to be kept but not used in active searches. The agreement did not prohibit the further transfer of data from US Customs to other agencies or to third countries—previously a major issue for the European Parliament. "The problem is not with the US itself. It is the fact that data are shared with other US allies; with other agencies, and so on."[55]

In theory, data could be shared with a large number of US agencies and foreign security services. Finally, many of the privacy protections were not contained in the agreement itself but rather in an accompanying exchange of letters, all of which could be unilaterally withdrawn at a later date. Most advocates of strong data privacy rules have concluded that despite a number of protections, the agreement offered fewer safeguards than the compromise struck down by the European Court of Justice and provides the United States with significant amounts of unmonitored data.

Thus after the European Court of Justice decision, policy on PNR was dominated by a cross-national alliance of security-minded officials who wanted to roll back previous privacy protections. Even officials like Baker, who was notorious for his impatience with perceived EU squeamishness, did not see themselves as imposing a solution on Europe. Instead, they worked together with European allies in key interior ministries who were independently eager to emphasize security questions over privacy concerns. This in turn helped lay the groundwork for new institutional changes within Europe: the creation of a European PNR system that would take the approach of the EU-US agreement and apply it to internal EU affairs.

The Limited Consequences of Lisbon

Just as all sides had hoped to be rid of the PNR debate, a further institutional twist reopened the long and hard negotiations. As the 2007 PNR agreement had been negotiated under the third pillar of the European Union, its implementation depended on approval by a sufficient number of national parliaments. Before this approval process had finished, the European Union introduced a major constitutional reform through the Treaty of Lisbon. This treaty greatly increased the European Parliament's authority in home and justice affairs. When the treaty was adopted in December 2007, the 2007 PNR agreement became preliminary since it had not been fully implemented, pending adoption by the European Parliament. In May 2010, the Parliament adopted a resolution requiring the renegotiation of the agreement so as to better protect the privacy concerns of European citizens. In particular, the privacy advocates in the Parliament focused on the period of data retention, redress mechanisms, and the justifications for data searches.

Once again, civil liberties advocates in the Parliament along with data privacy authorities looked to use domestic insulation strategies to shape the contours of the regulation.[56] As MEP in't Veld warned, "Now we have the power, and they have to listen to us."[57] In interviews and public comments, parliamentarians warned of a veto if their demands were not met. This threat initially seemed credible given that six of the parliamentary groups in the Parliament had signed on to the resolution pushing for greater concessions. Additionally, the Parliament had recently flexed its muscles by rejecting the initial proposal of a cross-border financial-data-tracking program between the United States and SWIFT in 2007 (discussed in greater detail in chapter 4).

While defenders of the existing regime regained some of the institutional levers that they had lost in the 2006 court decision, they faced both a consolidated transnational security alliance and internal dissent within the Parliament regarding how best to move forward. One important consequence of the Treaty of Lisbon was to split Justice and Home Affairs into two DGs at the Commission and to make the Home Affairs DG the main negotiator of the PNR agreement. DG Home Affairs parallels the interests of interior ministers at the national level and had long been interested in concluding the international PNR agreement as well as setting up a similar PNR system within Europe. The Council was similarly positioned in support of a reinstatement of the 2007 agreement as interior ministers had worked hard to conclude that deal and had no enthusiasm to start from scratch. Parliament, in contrast, was divided between Christian Democrats (many of whom now favored a stronger law-and-order approach) and liberals and left-wingers (who were more suspicious of the PNR deal).

The Parliament and its allies were unable to work across borders to create coalitions with privacy-focused actors in the United States. The key problem that they faced was that there were no US equivalents of European data privacy authorities that could be interlocutors to work together with European officials to reshape US policy. Even though the ACLU had succeeded in resisting a PNR-like system domestically, they were not appropriately organized to engage in transnational political campaigns.

Neither parliamentary relations with US lawmakers nor informal links to some US civil liberties groups provided a viable substitute. While parliamentary exchanges between the European Union and United States had been going on for some time, these had resulted in few policy-oriented or actionable proposals. In 2008, a delegation of civil-liberties-minded MEPs visited Washington, DC, to develop such contacts but found themselves late to the game and unable to exert much influence. Structural inequalities between the power and political role of EU parliamentarians and US members of Congress meant that the latter did not really recognize the former as peers. To combat this perception, the European Parliament opened a Washington bureau in April 2010.[58] At this point, it was in any event likely too late for the European Parliament to construct an alternative transnational blocking coalition.

Nor could the Parliament easily forge an effective alliance with nonstate actors in the United States. While some parliamentarians had informal relations with privacy advocacy groups, these organizations were best capable of action when they could work together with industry to push back against government regulation. Yet the key actors in industry, the airlines, had no interest in trying to undermine a deal that resolved continued and worrying legal uncertainties.

Furthermore, facts on the ground were beginning to change in the member states in ways that undermined the Parliament and data privacy commissioners. The United Kingdom and a few other states adopted PNR systems similar to the EU-US system, putting pressure on the Commission to both level the playing field within Europe and hence shift the regulatory status quo. The United Kingdom not only began lobbying for a speedy conclusion of the EU-US PNR deal but also for the European Union to adopt a PNR system.

Finally, industry pressed politicians to avoid a return to the uncertainty that had previously surrounded PNR. The 2007 agreement was seen by many in the aviation sector as an acceptable compromise that ended a long period of instability. Not only did industry want to end the back and forth but businesses too were frustrated by the shifting terms of agreement as each proposal led to new requirements and associated implementation costs.

EU and US negotiators reached a deal in late 2011 that reflected the content of the 2007 agreement. The major difference between the two agreements was a refinement of the data retention clause. Data would be maintained in an active database for five years, and after the initial six months, data would be depersonalized. After the six-month window, data could still be personalized but this would require a higher level of authorization. Following this active phase, data would be held in a dormant database for up to ten years, at which point it would be anonymized. In a last-ditch effort to scuttle the deal, MEP in't Veld, who served as rapporteur for the agreement, recommended rejection, concluding that "the new agreement represents a deterioration on many points."[59] Commissioner Cecilia Malmstrom, head of DG Home Affairs, believed, in contrast, that the agreement contained "robust safeguards."[60] In the end, the Parliament approved the agreement in April 2012 on a vote of 409 to 226 against and 33 abstentions.

The vote was carried in large part by representatives of the European People's Party, which is the conservative party in the Parliament, and was persuaded both by industry's and the security community's arguments. As Timothy Kirkhope, a British MEP, contended, "The importance of PNR data for our security cannot be underestimated. This agreement secures passengers' rights and safety, and it cements the crucial EU-USA security partnership."[61] By contrast, in't Veld underscored the political repercussions of the common sense of purpose that had been created among security officials on both sides of the Atlantic, remarking, "I sometimes feel people negotiating on behalf of the EU are negotiating on behalf of the US."[62] The 2007 deal created an important cross-national layer, which leached away opposition both from industry and in the Parliament.

The Transformation of Europe's Policy Trajectory

Even as negotiations continued with the United States over a transatlantic PNR agreement, the security community within Europe was laying the groundwork for a transformation of European policy. In particular, the Justice and Home Affairs DG of the Commission along with national interior ministers began to promote a European PNR regime based on the same proposals that they had crafted together with US security officials. Initial drafts sought to collect PNR data for foreigners entering the European Union, but interior ministers, especially the United Kingdom's home minister, hoped to expand the system to collect data on domestic as well as international flights. Despite repeated efforts by the European civil liberties community to use domestic levers to insulate European policy from transnational spillovers, the European Union adopted an EU PNR system in 2016. The precedent of the EU-US agreement was key to the development of proposals for a European PNR system, the proponents of which "stressed the fact that if the EU has allowed the exchange of PNR with third countries, like the USA and has started negotiations with Canada, it is nonsense to refuse it within the EU."[63]

Drawing on the interactions with the United States, the Commission was an early supporter of a European PNR system as part of a larger package of antiterrorism efforts.[64] Then Commissioner for Justice Franco Frattini argued on multiple occasions that a European PNR was a vital tool for the successful protection of European citizens against potential terrorist attacks. Commission interest in a European PNR system dated back at least to 2004, shortly after the completion of the Joint Statement with the United States, when it sent a communication to the Council and Parliament on the issue.[65] The Commission looked to internal security to demonstrate its relevance to European citizens—a strategy that became more attractive after the failed referendum on the European Constitution.[66] In addition to promoting pan-European legislation, the Commission simultaneously funded fourteen national PNR systems, which many in the civil liberties community viewed as a Trojan horse for future pan-European rules. As in't Veld warned, "Giving money to the member states to create national systems, so that all of a sudden there is a need for harmonization, 'hey look we have a reason for a directive,' it's called bribing and I find this a despicable way of making policies and law."[67] Their worries were prescient: European Council president Donald Tusk used concerns about fragmentation between different member states' approaches in his final push to get the legislation passed.[68]

Similarly, national interior ministers were consistently strong advocates for a European PNR system and used their interactions with the United States to justify their policies. The German internal minister, Schäuble, argued that given the EU-US PNR system, a failure to adopt a PNR system for Europe would be "inexcusable."[69] Even Germany's justice minister from the Social Democratic Party supported the proposal.[70] The British government went so far as to call for the data to be used for more general public policy purposes than just fighting terrorism.[71] A Commission-sponsored questionnaire sent to the member states found that a majority of members supported the initiative, and a meeting of national internal ministers called for the speedy adoption of a European PNR. Slovenian interior minister Dragutin Mate, reporting for the EU presidency in January 2008, claimed that "there was general support from all ministers on a European Passenger Name Record."[72] At the meeting of the home and justice ministers in November 2008, the French presidency released a report supporting a European PNR system.

In summer 2009, the Council submitted a revised draft of an EU PNR proposal for consideration, and the agreement was then written up by the Commission. While differing slightly from the EU-US PNR agreement, its genetic imprint was clear. In particular, the EU PNR agreement called on member states to create Passenger Information Units (PIU), which would serve as repositories for PNR data. Like in the EU-US PNR agreement, airlines would be required to transfer PNR data to PIUs prior to landing or departure from EU territory. PIUs could then retain anonymized data for up to five years. While the directive requires PNR data to be reported for all external flights entering or leaving the European Union, it also allowed member states to set up PNR requirements for internal flights within the European Union. Noting the connection between the EU-US PNR agreement and the EU PNR proposal, Jan Albrecht (2012), a Green MEP, concluded, "The Commission wants to introduce a system along the lines of that in the United States."

Privacy advocates in Europe used a series of procedural tools to delay passage and undermine support for the internal reform. Most notably, Green and Liberal Party members of the civil liberties committee of the EU Parliament blocked the EU PNR proposal in April 2013.[73] Their position was supported by the Article 29 Working Party as well as the European Data Protection Supervisor, who argued that the legislation was overly broad.[74] At the same time, the EU Parliament took an agreement to share PNR data with Canada to the European Court of Justice, hoping to find a sympathetic ruling that would boost the legitimacy of its claims.

Although the Court eventually ruled against the PNR agreement with Canada, its ruling came too late. Efforts to block the EU PNR failed as internal political support for an EU system grew, particularly in the wake of the Paris and Brussels attacks of 2015 and 2016, respectively.[75] Furthermore, border control became newly salient as the European Union began to deal with the political fallout of the migration crisis, in which hundreds of thousands of refugees from war and economic turmoil sought a better life in Europe.[76] While migration and the terrorist threat boosted the salience of the issue, interior ministers and Commission officials once again relied on the EU-US PNR agreement to justify the EU PNR plan. In making the case for an EU PNR, French minister of the interior Bernard Cazeneuve is reported to have pressed parliamentarians using the argument that "the United States security services know more about who takes European flights than do the EU member states themselves."[77] Similarly, MEP Timothy Kirkhope, who served as the legislation's rapporteur, contended, "It is [a step that] all EU governments and indeed the United States government have requested as a very important tool to tackling terrorism."[78] Moreover, European security officials repeatedly called on their US counterparts to justify the usefulness of the program for counterterrorism purposes.[79] These arguments slowly peeled away opposition within the Parliament, leaving the Greens as the only group to vote cohesively against the deal.[80]

The EU PNR directive was ultimately adopted by the European Parliament in April 2016 by a vote of 461 in favor, 179 opposed, and 9 abstentions.[81] The privacy community in Europe has not totally given up. In July 2017, the European Court of Justice ruled on a case brought by the European Parliament regarding a PNR agreement between the European Union and Canada, finding that the agreement needed to include additional privacy safeguards. The ruling does not apply directly to the US agreement or the internal EU PNR system, but it will provide privacy advocates further tools to continue the struggle to protect privacy from security encroachments.[82] While these insulation strategies produced some concessions, which led to important privacy safeguards in both the EU-US agreement and the EU system, they were insufficient to prevent another coalition of actors from using cross-national layering to transform both transatlantic and intra-European rules.

Conclusion

For over a decade, US and European officials, firms, and privacy activists have engaged in a bitter struggle over how to balance security demands for access to information over airline passenger data while protecting privacy. All sides believed that the stakes were high. One argued that government access to the data was necessary to stop the next mass casualty attack, while the other warned that they would facilitate massive state surveillance. Although it is easy to claim that the conflict was a simple product of US bullying or alternatively the emergence of a new terrorist threat, neither captures the complex dynamics of the interaction, or the important changes to privacy and security policies globally and within Europe.

Specifically, the chapter demonstrates that the demands of the DHS led to new institutions being created, both in the transatlantic relationship and in the European Union itself. This was possible because there was a group of actors within the European Union that was unhappy with existing EU privacy institutions and willing to make common cause with security-oriented actors within the United States in pursuit of institutional change. When the opponents of change—those who wanted to insulate the European Union from transatlantic negotiations—made a crucial misstep, security-minded officials in the United States and European Union were able to join forces to layer an extensive and far-reaching agreement over existing EU arrangements. These transnational agreements over time leached away European opposition to transatlantic information sharing over passenger data and created a platform for further policy change within the European Union. In a counterfactual world where the United States had to rely on external pressure and coercion alone, the results would surely have been different. While the European Union might have had to accede to some US demands, given the intensity of US preferences and US bargaining power, Europe would have made the minimum necessary concessions and not introduced institutions that were likely to lead to substantial changes in its own internal handling of PNR.

Of course, the migration crisis and terrorist events in the European Union plausibly played a key role in softening opposition to transatlantic and EU-level changes in the rules governing PNR at crucial instances. These demand-side arguments, however, do little to explain the critical political interactions that determined the extent and scope of policy changes. Most obviously, the US administration, even though it demanded PNR from the European Union, was not able to introduce similar domestic rules on its own territory. Furthermore, when the European Union introduced its own PNR arrangements, it did not resemble the United States' domestically focused Secure Flight Initiative. Instead, it was a direct genetic descendant of the EU-US PNR agreement, which advocates of EU PNR employed in order to prepare the way for European policy changes. EU and US responses were not the product of common shocks experienced by disconnected systems; they were the result of iterated interactions within and between the two polities. As a European Parliament official who was deeply involved in EU-US privacy debates remarked, "It is obvious that the US PNR system was an inspiration for the [European system]."[83]

While it is true that there was some exchange of policy ideas between EU and US officials as a result of their interactions, this most certainly did not translate into a general convergence of norms across the two polities.[84] Rather, both polities continued to be riven by discord along with disputes between actors who often retained different understandings of the appropriate relationship between security and privacy. The determining event in the PNR saga was not a shift toward consensus but instead a court decision that undermined the opponents of PNR and empowered those who wanted to emphasize security over privacy.

Thus as this chapter shows, the key actors in the PNR saga were not the two systems of the European Union and United States, nor even the United States and the individual states that composed the European Union. Instead, they were political actors beneath the level of the state, such as the European Parliament and European data privacy officials, interior ministers, and the DHS. These actors often had quite-different interests than the perceived interests of the states in which they were located. Their interests furthermore shifted as their organizational form changed (e.g., as DHS became an actual organization). As globalization progresses, actors' ability to pursue their interests will vary depending on their access to the relevant transnational forums. Those with access to these forums will be able to use them either to defend or to change domestic institutions. Those without will have to rely on purely domestic tools, which they will use, as best as they can, to try to insulate domestic regimes from international pressures.

Ultimately the PNR saga underscores how transatlantic interactions themselves redistribute power. The alliances that respectively opposed and supported greater information sharing have engaged in a decades-long fight to shape the terms of privacy and security. Apparent victories have been challenged, and agreements or laws have been overturned. The parties involved rarely give up in the face of defeat, instead seeking alternative pathways to their objectives. Rather than reaching a final equilibrium, in which one group "wins" and another "loses," the case of PNR shows how power and influence ebb and flow according to the changing ability of actors to access domestic and international opportunity structures. At the same time, it demonstrates the force of incremental processes of institutional change that complement and even sometimes supplant sudden shocks.

This explains how actors in the European Union sought to fend off a new international regime mandating information exchange, which threatened existing EU rules on privacy. Data privacy officials and concerned European parliamentarians did not have much access to the transnational forums in which EU and US officials sought to resolve their differences. Indeed, these forums were in part designed specifically to exclude privacy-friendly officials. This led them to try to insulate domestic politics from the international regime, even as other actors within the European Union tried to use this regime to further their own preferences for change.

The actors who favored the domestic status quo failed at least for the time being, thanks both to unanticipated consequences of their choices (an unhelpful decision by the European Court of Justice) and the ability of their opponents to use international negotiations to push for changes in ways that eventually divided the defenders of the existing regime. The result had some ironies: US negotiators were better able to get the European Union to accept concessions than to influence their own colleagues in the US government. Yet the ironies were limited: US officials were better able to extract concessions because key EU counterparts shared their desire for change so that both could push together for a reorganization of information-sharing rules in the European Union. In the next chapter, we show how the strategy of cross-national layering led to an equally fundamental transformation of rules in the case of financial data.

4

Cross-National Layering and the Regulation of Terrorist Financial Tracking

On June 23, 2006, the *New York Times* published an article that led to a transatlantic crisis. The article detailed a secret data-sharing program between the US Department of the Treasury and a little-known Belgian organization called SWIFT.[1] SWIFT is the primary digital backbone of the global financial services industry, handling millions of secure payment messages per day. The US government subpoenaed SWIFT after September 11, 2001, looking to leverage these financial transaction data in its fight against transnational terrorism. After the *New York Times* story, SWIFT was caught between the conflicting imperatives of US security rules and EU privacy regulations. Even as the European Union and United States sought to resolve their separate dispute over the sharing of airline passenger data, they found themselves embroiled in a second controversy centered on banking and finance.

In chapter 3, we demonstrated the importance of cross-national alliances for transatlantic politics over privacy and security. Now we turn to a parallel case—disputes over financial data—to explore more explicitly the specific mechanisms through which these substate dynamics generate institutional change. Traditional accounts of regulatory disputes between jurisdictions such as the European Union and United States see them as problems of system clash. They look to explain regulatory disputes over issues such as consumer protection, the environment, health standards, or production processes.[2] These regulations determine how national and international markets work, and often distribute their economic benefits across market actors.[3] Some accounts emphasize how different switching costs make it unattractive for one jurisdiction to change its rules to better conform with another's, leading states to exercise their market power in order to try to shape outcomes.[4] Others focus on how the domestic institutions of aggregation shape actors' preferences and bargaining power by providing them or denying them veto points in the policy-making process.[5] Both of these accounts assume that preferences result from processes of domestic interest formation external to the theory and that bargaining takes place between discrete jurisdictions.[6] Furthermore, they look to predict one-off outcomes of either stalemate (where states cannot agree, leading to a lasting standoff) or convergence (where jurisdictions' rules converge as a result of efficiency or power dynamics).

As the previous chapter makes clear, we start from different microfoundations, arguing that both the formation of preferences and bargaining take place across different jurisdictions, rather than within or between them. Moreover, the product of these interactions often do not fit neatly into the boxes of either stalemate or policy convergence. Specifically, we show how cross-national layering changes global dynamics by circumventing or even transforming domestic rules. The "SWIFT dispute," which involved access to global financial transaction data, provides an apt case to investigate our causal account, and to assess the respective merits of various approaches to understanding the struggle over freedom and security.

As we show, the initial dispute between the European Union and United States over access to financial data led to an unsurprising compromise in which the United States continued to access data located in the United States. This bargain, however, was the beginning rather than the end of the process of institutional change. It created transnational forums, which were dominated by security officials on both sides of the Atlantic. These officials had a strong interest in tilting the internal balance between privacy and security within the European Union away from privacy and toward security. They had previously been unable to push these changes through conventional EU legislative processes, where key veto players (most especially privacy-oriented MEPs, but also some privacy-friendly ministries and institutions within member states) prevented legislative change. These security officials hoped to use transatlantic negotiations over electronic data and other privacy issues to craft an agreement, layered over the existing

European privacy infrastructure, that would create a new status quo for later institutional changes at the domestic and international levels.

The key to this cross-national layer was the inclusion of a *reciprocity requirement* that allowed European security officials to policy launder arrangements for greater information sharing through transatlantic cooperation. The SWIFT agreement included a clause, known as Article 10, which allows European officials to make requests of US counterparts for data originally transferred to the United States from Europe. The transnational layer, then, routed around internal EU privacy law as European security officials could obtain European data from US counterparts that they would have great difficulty in accessing under domestic rules.

For a long time, the European security coalition did not need changes to domestic rules because the transnational agreement provided it with the necessary data, allowing it to sidestep difficult domestic political battles. At the same time, the gradual institutionalization of reciprocal arrangements for information sharing undermined opposition to the transnational agreement within the Parliament, and gave rise to exchanges in which EU and US security officials could cooperate with little effective oversight. Now security officials are raising the possibility of domestic reforms for information collation and analysis. They can do so because they have effectively used cross-national layering to finesse domestic opposition, transforming the political context so as to undermine resistance.

Moving beyond Systems Clash

Standard accounts of regulatory disputes such as the SWIFT controversy frequently turn to one of two approaches to understand their dynamics: preference aggregation and veto points, or market power. Both inform the simplistic depictions of the United States as Mars and the European Union as Venus (although they may surely be deployed in more sophisticated ways), and have been used to understand transatlantic tensions over information sharing. We briefly summarize each before turning to our argument focusing on cross-national layering.

Preference aggregation approaches emphasize how domestic and international institutions of interest aggregation influence interest group preferences, which are filtered through veto points so as to constrain international negotiators.[7] In such accounts, interdependence shapes the preferences of domestic interest groups (e.g., importers versus exporters), but it neither affects their bargaining power (which is a product of the veto points inscribed in domestic institutions) nor leads directly to institutional change. These accounts suggest that countries will agree when the constraints of domestic veto points on both sides provide some minimal space of mutually acceptable positions. Which position is chosen, then, depends on the particular configurations of veto power and the ability of states to credibly threaten to withdraw if they do not get an outcome that satisfies the relevant domestic constituencies.

In contrast, market power arguments emphasize how jurisdictions with large markets leverage market access to influence others' regulation.[8] Both the United States and European Union, for example, employ equivalency clauses to condition market access on the adoption of compatible rules in other jurisdictions. This can be reinforced indirectly by processes like "trading up."[9] These approaches see interdependence between different national systems as causing regulatory clashes, but maintain that these clashes are resolved through bargaining between discrete national units based on market size.

Such explanations provide indeterminate predictions in situations where two powers with similarly large markets need to reconcile their approaches. Under these circumstances, scholars turn from differences in market size to preference compatibility as the key variable. In these accounts, the degree of preference compatibility depends on whether it is cheap or expensive for states to switch to the other's standards (or some mutually agreeable compromise) given their existing approaches.

Approaches emphasizing preference aggregation and market power have similar empirical expectations across many dimensions. Both stress how powerful markets set global rules, and emphasize the importance of traditional jurisdictional and sovereign borders. They assume that states have relatively predictable preferences, which reflect economic fundamentals as refracted through legislative institutions. Preference aggregation accounts suggest that convergence will happen where there is a win-set of outcomes acceptable to all actors with domestic veto power. Market power arguments expect global convergence to happen in the (likely rare) cases when great powers have similar domestic regulatory structures. We summarize these approaches' causal logic for regulatory disputes in figure 4.1.

Although both approaches are intuitively plausible, they are partly belied by the empirics of transatlantic data-sharing disputes. Cooperation has increased over time, even in cases where great powers have different regulatory systems, switching costs have been high, and the number of veto players has increased.[10] That said, such cooperation has not been straightforward.

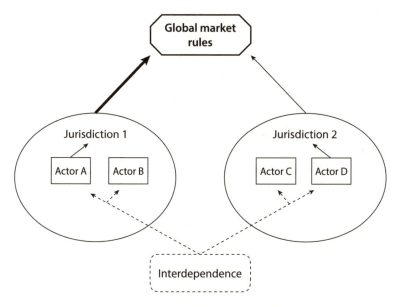

FIGURE 4.1. Preference Aggregation / Market Power Model of Global Politics

Often it takes unconventional forms, routing around traditional bilateral treaties, and instead relying on transnational executive agreements and domestic legal changes.

Our alternative approach is described in detail in chapter 1. For the sake of convenience, we briefly summarize again the key differences between our argument and the preference aggregation and market power approaches. First, we start from the assumption that when rule overlap has destabilizing consequences across different jurisdictions, actors look not only to domestic resources but also to transnational alliances as a means of pressing to protect domestic institutions that they value or undermine institutions they abhor. This implies that jurisdictions like the United States or the European Union should not be treated as a monolithic bloc since they contain within them diverse interest groups seeking to use international interactions for their advantage.

Second, their ability to work across borders will depend on whether they have access to relevant opportunity structures such as transnational forums. For example, actors who do not like existing domestic institutions, but have access to the international opportunity structures that would allow them to build cross-national alliances, will look to build cross-national institutional layers that over time destabilize existing domestic institutions, providing them with a backdoor route to change. The opportunity structures created by interdependence crucially are not equally distributed among actors.[11]

In our account, then, the key variable in disagreements between big jurisdictions is neither switching costs nor the specific configurations of domestic veto points within each jurisdiction. Instead, it is the availability or nonavailability of opportunity structures, which allow some actors (but not others) to craft cross-national institutional layers that have long-term domestic consequences, altering international regulatory dynamics. For a visual depiction of this process, see figure 4.2.

In the succeeding sections, we examine how well these different approaches explain the dispute over financial data and also assess the merits of more specific accounts of the SWIFT dispute. Some existing accounts focus on the power of the civil-liberties-oriented European Parliament, which had only exiguous competences over homeland security issues before the Treaty of Lisbon and an effective veto thereafter when it gained the ability to reject international treaties.[12] This version of the preference aggregation argument would see the 2009 treaty as the decisive factor shaping the bargaining process.

Other accounts see the SWIFT dispute as a learning process, and emphasize instead compatibility between the values and interests of the European Union and United States. For example, Marieke De Goede (2012b) highlights how similarities between US security concerns and the European approach to risk management made it easier for the two sides to come together once a formal process was in place. Here, compatible risk assessments concerning

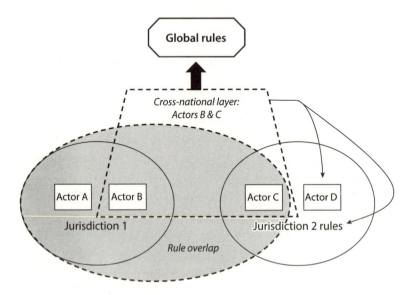

FIGURE 4.2. Cross-National Layering Model of Global Politics

terrorism produce cooperation between two jurisdictions with roughly equal market power.

Our cross-national layering argument instead examines whether or not a transnational forum existed, and which actors had access to it. In EU-US disputes over information sharing, the relevant forums of high-level officials were open to security-focused officials and closed to privacy-focused ones. This leads us to predict that security-oriented actors in the United States and European Union could coordinate to build cross-national arrangements intended to weaken domestic privacy arrangements within the European Union. These arrangements enhance predictability for affected businesses such as SWIFT and the banking communities with interests in both jurisdictions. This, in turn, destabilizes institutional bargaining within the European Union, as actors who had previously sought to defend existing institutional structures defected so as to continue to influence rule making in a modified institutional setting. Here, the key causal factor is the varying access of subnational actors to the relevant cross-national forums.

Financial Surveillance and Rule Overlap

International financial markets provide a cornerstone of globalization; banks, investors, and corporations rely on access to foreign financial markets to trade, hedge against risk, and build global supply chains. This creates a dense network of financial flows.[13] At the same time, criminal and terrorist organizations take advantage of these very same structures to promote and conduct illicit activity.[14]

Just as with air transportation, the attacks of September 11 highlighted how international economic exchange provides great economic benefits and increases interdependent risks. The United States moved quickly to press for antiterrorist measures, while the European Union moved more slowly. This led to clashes between US and EU rules on information sharing as the United States pushed through antiterrorism laws that had international consequences for Europe.[15] EU institutions initially resisted external pressure, only to later start emphasizing security concerns.

The US Department of the Treasury, in particular, investigated how it might respond to cross-national terrorism through leveraging the institutions created to manage globalization. In addition to beefing up anti-money-laundering operations, the Treasury created the Terrorist Financial Tracking Program (TFTP), which attempted to identify and cut off the international funding of terrorist networks.[16]

The US government had a number of coercive tools to pressure banks or individuals engaged in such activity, but it first needed to locate the perpetrators. It sought to do this by conscripting SWIFT.[17] Founded in 1973, SWIFT is a cooperative venture, run as a limited liability company incorporated in Belgium, that plays a key role in facilitating interbank financial transactions.[18] It operates a secure messaging network, which banks use to communicate with each other and to organize up to $6 trillion in interbank transactions daily (the actual financial transfers occur separately). SWIFT messages include data on the amount in a transaction, the currency, the date, the customer's name and financial institution, and the beneficiary's name and financial institution.[19] They thus provide crucial information on cross-border financial transfers, with one former government official calling SWIFT "the Rosetta stone" for financial data.[20] The importance of SWIFT to the global financial system is illustrated by the sheer number of messages that it facilitates on a day-to-day basis and how it has grown (see figure 4.3).

US officials had previously tried to persuade SWIFT in the 1990s to provide them with access to data, but with no great success.[21] As Lenny Schrank, former chief executive of SWIFT, later reflected, "This was when we first began to think the unthinkable: that maybe we have some data that authorities would want, that SWIFT data would be revealed . . . and what to do about it. . . . [N]o one thought about terrorism at that time."[22] Following September 11, US law enforcement and intelligence officials were in

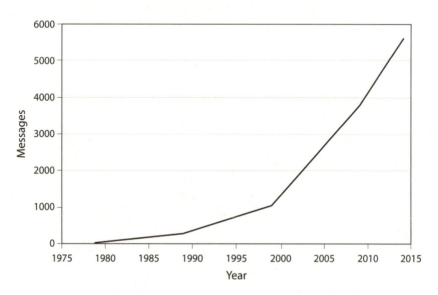

FIGURE 4.3. Annual SWIFT Messages in Millions

a far stronger bargaining position. After informal discussions between the Treasury and SWIFT, the United States started to serve SWIFT with broad subpoenas known as National Security Letters demanding the handover of data on financial transactions.[23] SWIFT, on investigating its legal options, concluded that the subpoenas were valid and compulsory, and hence complied.[24] The US Treasury and SWIFT reached a secret agreement under which the Treasury would carry out specific searches related to targeted investigations. Generalized data mining and searches not related to terrorism were precluded by this agreement. SWIFT data were then held by the Treasury in encrypted form in a "black box." CIA officials (the CIA managed the program) could then perform searches by name, thus automatically decrypting relevant information in order to provide useful search results.[25] Roughly one subpoena a month was served on SWIFT during the 2001–9 period.[26]

The problem for SWIFT was that by complying with US authorities, it was breaking European privacy law. SWIFT was domiciled in Belgium, which like other European countries, had adopted privacy legislation based on the EU Data Privacy Directive.[27] The directive prevents the transfer of data concerning EU citizens to jurisdictions that fail to maintain an adequate domestic privacy regime and the limited US privacy regime is not considered adequate.

SWIFT was clearly nervous about its legal position. In 2003, it told US officials that it was thinking of pulling out of the arrangement (which had been put together as an emergency response in the immediate wake of September 11), and was only dissuaded from doing so by the direct intervention of senior US officials (including Alan Greenspan) and the introduction of an external auditing firm, Booz Allen Hamilton, to oversee the process.[28] The United States further undertook not to publicly reveal that SWIFT was the source of the data. From 2004 on, "scrutineers" with appropriate clearances and who were employed by SWIFT were able to monitor searches.[29]

SWIFT furthermore advised the National Bank of Belgium along with other members of the G10 group of central banks that it was subject to a US subpoena.[30] The National Bank of Belgium did not feel competent to issue any opinion on SWIFT's compliance with the subpoena. The bank also appears to have declined to inform other authorities, including most prominently the Belgian Privacy Commission, which is responsible for administering Belgian privacy law.

Rule Overlap and the *New York Times* Exposé

This delicate equilibrium—in which SWIFT broke Belgian privacy law by complying with US law—persisted until June 2006, when the *New York Times* published details of the arrangement despite strong pressure from the US administration as well as from both Republican and Democratic elected officials to remain silent.[31] In an extensive front-page article, Eric Lichtblau and James Risen (2006) detailed the program along with the secret controversies surrounding it.

The revelation further exposed fissures within Europe as politicians and regulators tried to take advantage of rule overlap to press their case for either privacy or security. Belgium's privacy regulator conducted an investigation, which expressed some sympathy for SWIFT's position, but found that SWIFT was indeed breaking national privacy law, that US subpoenas were not a sufficient excuse, and that any bank that used SWIFT's services might possibly be in breach of European data law too. It called for "a solution at European level for the communication of personal data to the UST [US Treasury], with respect for the . . . principles which apply under European law."[32]

The Article 29 Working Party similarly found the program to be illegal and highlighted the failure of the G10 group to inform other European authorities of the problem. It furthermore suggested that G10 member banks (as users themselves of SWIFT's messaging services) might be liable under European privacy law:

> The hidden, systematic, massive and long-term transfer of personal data by SWIFT to the UST in a confidential, non-transparent and systematic manner for years without effective legal grounds and without the possibility of independent control by public data protection supervisory authorities constitutes a violation of the fundamental European principles as regards data protection and is not in accordance with Belgian and European law.[33]

Even though the SWIFT arrangement broke the law, key security-oriented officials in important EU member states were privately sanguine about it. One German official opined in private to US Treasury officials that she thought Germany would have "done the same thing."[34] A UK Treasury official went even further, telling the United States that Britain's "primary objective [was] to maintain the flow of data and [US government] access to it."[35] Nicolas Sarkozy, then minister for the interior in France, expressed his encouragement for the continuation of SWIFT, after an appropriate agreement had been reached, in a private letter to the US ambassador.[36]

Reasserting the Status Quo: The 2007 Exchange of Letters

Many of these officials also warned that it would be necessary to find a compromise to placate the public and dissatisfied MEPs. European authorities hence needed to discover some face-saving compromise to modify the US fait accompli, which the United States had little desire to change except at the margins. European officials did have the implicit ability, had they wanted it, to threaten action against not only SWIFT but also banks that used SWIFT's services if they did not seek alternative arrangements. There would have been political complications: European data privacy authorities did not want to be seen as obstructing measures that the United States could argue were genuinely helpful in fighting terrorism.

The United States enjoyed the additional advantage that SWIFT "mirrored" its data across two locations—storing replicated data on two servers, one in Europe and one in Virginia. As such, the data accessed by the United States was technically on US soil and required no request for international data transfers (in contrast to some of the PNR data discussed in chapter 3). Until SWIFT altered its data architecture or Europe banned data transfers to the United States, the default mirroring system allowed US authorities to claim access to data located within its own jurisdiction.[37] Again, the United States had fallback options stemming from its market power—but like the European Union's options, these might have substantially disrupted international financial flows.

While both the European Union and United States had the capacity to make credible threats, neither wanted to deliver on them because key national officials in the European Union were privately unconcerned by the SWIFT arrangements, and because both sides feared that open hostilities would be economically and politically costly. Key officials on both sides favored some continuation of the arrangement.

This created incentives to reach a compromise. The result was an agreement, negotiated over the next several months and concluded in June 2007, that made some concessions to privacy advocates in Europe at the cost of preserving a version of the new status quo in which data transfers continued. Initially, the European Commission asked for a formal agreement with the United States governing these transfers. Not only did the United States prove intransigent, but some European officials too preferred a less formal and binding arrangement. The final result was an exchange of letters (which were nominally independent of each other to avoid the appearance of a binding formal agreement that might require domestic ratification) in which the United States agreed explicitly that the program should be confined to antiterrorist uses and undertook to provide protections to Europeans that resembled those offered to US citizens under the 1974 Privacy Act. The United States also agreed to have a senior EU representative vet its system to assess whether its claims about the program's probity and usefulness were true.[38]

On this basis—as well as a commitment from SWIFT to sign on to the Safe Harbor arrangement and end data mirroring in the United States—the Council (which represents European member states) and Commission expressed their confidence that SWIFT and its clients would be in compliance with EU law. All financial institutions would have to inform their customers about the possibility of their information being transferred to US authorities. The European Parliament (as well as the Article 29 Working Party), which had also expressed serious concerns about SWIFT and would almost certainly have taken a stronger oppositional stance, had no decision-making competence. International negotiations dealing with issues concerning justice and home affairs as defined by the European Union's (now largely defunct) pillar system provided few formal competences to the Parliament and the data privacy community, and thus offered a permissive environment for the creation of transnational institutions.

Transnational Alliance Seeks to Recast the Privacy/Security Balance

The first stage of contact between the EU and US systems potentially fits the predictions of *both* market power and preference aggregation accounts. A market power account would highlight the willingness of key players in the Europe Union to accept the SWIFT arrangement as plausible evidence that the preferences of pivotal European states and the United States were largely compatible. Such accounts would predict correctly that a deal could be achieved that would likely be closer to the United States' stated position than the European Union's position, given differences in bargaining strength and the intensity of preferences between the European Union and United States. A preference aggregation account would emphasize the limited competences of the European Parliament (which would almost certainly have sought to veto the arrangement) as a critical factor in explaining how the deal was achieved. The form of the deal—an exchange of nonbinding letters—minimized the influence of the European Parliament, as German minister for the interior Wolfgang Schäuble was swift to underscore in a private conversation with US officials.[39]

What happened next is more difficult to explain. Instead of a static compromise between the European Union and United States, which simply continued US access to SWIFT data held on US territory, the EU-US accommodation became the starting point for dense relationships between officials on both sides of the Atlantic. These officials' actions took place within the broad contours of the SWIFT deal (and the PNR deal discussed in chapter 3). They did not, however, leave these deals unchanged. Rather, the officials sought to use them as a starting point to advance their policy goals across both jurisdictions, and ultimately, to reshape privacy and security practices within the European Union.

Officials on both sides of the Atlantic who were influential in the SWIFT discussions were strongly dissatisfied with an institutional status quo within the European Union that often privileged privacy concerns.[40] This caused considerable frustration among European security officials, especially after September 11 and a series of attacks on European soil. They were unhappy with what they saw as the inability of the European Union to coordinate seriously on antiterrorism policies because of restrictions on data sharing and data analysis.

While the privacy rules provided exceptions for security-related information, they still made data sharing more cumbersome and conflictual. High-ranking officials such as Schäuble, who had himself been permanently disabled by a terrorist attack, wanted a better "balance" between antiterrorism and privacy rights, complaining of a "lack of understanding" in Germany and the European Union of how data privacy rights constrained access to and use of security-relevant information.[41] After the SWIFT scandal broke, a Dutch interagency group privately told US officials that "there is a general consensus within the [Dutch government] and the Dutch Central Bank on the need to shift the current debate on SWIFT procedures away from only data privacy issues to broader national security interests."[42]

These frustrations were shared by many US officials, who saw Europe's attachment to data privacy rules as hampering international cooperation in the fight against terrorism. Only a few weeks after the September 11 attacks, President George W. Bush wrote a letter to the European Commission's president proposing a massive increase in the European Union's willingness to share data with the United States, and telling the European Union that it should "consider data protection issues in the context of law enforcement and counterterrorism imperatives."[43] After the SWIFT controversy broke, US officials quietly urged sympathetic officials to do all they could to shift the emphasis in the broader EU debate away from privacy and toward security.[44]

No Quick Internal Fix

It was clearly difficult to reform these rules inside the European Union. Under codecision rules, the European Parliament was willing and able to block legislative changes that might undermine privacy.[45] While it had passed some changes to existing privacy laws (most notably mandating the retention of data by communications providers), this was in response to direct and immediate security threats. Within the Parliament, there was a core group of privacy advocates from the Green and Liberal parties that often found allies within the larger Socialist bloc.[46] The Parliament's obduracy was reinforced by the member states' data privacy commissioners, both in their national role and as members of the EU-level Article 29 Working Party. Although the Article 29 Working Party had no formal veto power, it did have the right to be consulted, and was able to mobilize opposition in Parliament and among its national members against potentially privacy-invasive changes.

This presented security officials in member states' ministries of the interior as well as in the European Council and the European Commission with considerable difficulties. Given the multiplicity of veto points in the EU legislative process and the blocking power of the Parliament, there was no realistic prospect of substantially reshaping EU internal privacy laws. It was often possible for security officials to work around the Parliament; most cooperation on justice and home affairs took place under so-called third-pillar articles, where the Parliament had no veto. It was also clear that the European Parliament was going to gain additional influence over justice and home affairs legislation under the Treaty of Lisbon, which was to come into effect in late 2009.[47] Furthermore, many areas of information sharing involved justice and home affairs along with areas of privacy regulation where the Parliament plausibly had competences. This raised the possibility of lengthy and difficult "legal basis" disputes in which Parliament could take the Council or Commission to court over specific pieces of legislation or forms of cooperation, arguing that they needed to base the legislation on treaty articles that would provide the Parliament with a greater say.[48]

Building a Cross-National Layer

Institutional change concerning privacy regulation within the European Union was nearly impossible. The incipient transatlantic relationship on security and privacy, however, provided European security officials with attractive-seeming opportunities to create a layer of institutions at a level that their opponents had great difficulty influencing. Privacy-oriented MEPs and EU data privacy officials—two of the most important actors opposing EU-level legislative change—could be excluded from transatlantic discussions on security where they did not have direct competences. Instead, these discussions were dominated by the Council and Commission, which had negotiated the SWIFT agreement. These actors wished to build the EU-US relationship so that it moved closer to their shared interest in maintaining security. US and European security officials established a series of transatlantic networks in which they hashed out principles and guidelines to achieve their policy goals.

The Council was strongly responsive to the expressed desires of interior and home affairs ministries in the member states. These were typically impatient with European privacy law, which they saw as a constraint hampering meaningful security cooperation. EU foreign relations experts—who played a role in early negotiations—soon gave way to home affairs officials, who tended to take a more security-oriented approach to negotiation with their US counterparts.[49]

The European Commission's data privacy unit had been transferred from Internal Market DG in March 2005 to the Justice, Freedom, and Security DG, where it played the lead role in early negotiations over SWIFT.[50] It was soon sidelined in favor of the policing unit, which took over negotiation and implementation, nearly completely freezing out the more data-privacy-friendly elements within the Commission, to their considerable frustration and unhappiness.[51]

Again, EU-US working relations excluded the European Parliament and the Article 29 Working Party. Officials on the Council and Commission hence had a strong incentive to manage their relations with the United States under the third pillar, avoiding the need to consult with a Parliament that was clearly unhappy about data transfers to the United States. Again, the concerned officials deliberately constructed their dialogue with the United States so as to avoid any need to consult with or inform the Article 29 Working Party.[52] The European Data Protection Supervisor provided informal advice at some points in the negotiation process, but was typically obliged to follow discussions from a distance.

This resulted in the creation of interlinked transatlantic forums, which aimed not only to facilitate the transfer of financial information but also to shape other aspects of the EU-US privacy relationship in particular and the homeland security relationship more generally. The PNR data dispute had previously led the European Union and United States to establish a High Level Political Dialogue on Border and Transportation Security, as mentioned in chapter 3. This provided EU and US officials with a space where they could discuss emerging issues and try to prevent controversies before they arose. It also created a model for a wider-reaching dialogue on EU-US privacy relations. In November 2006, a High Level Contact Group of senior EU and US officials was initiated to begin talks over more far-reaching proposals (the group's work culminated in a proposal for an "Umbrella Agreement" on privacy and domestic security, which we explore in detail in the next chapter). The High Level Contact Group developed guidelines and practices that would facilitate data sharing across the Atlantic.[53] It was within this discussion that the notion of reciprocity, which would later play a crucial role in the cross-national layering process, was raised. In particular, the group flagged reciprocity in data sharing and data-sharing practices as a key feature for future binding agreements.

European security officials did not plan to build a European system to monitor financial flows using SWIFT's data in the short term since they believed that this would prove politically controversial and difficult to push through. They did, however, anticipate reaping considerable benefits from a streamlined system of information exchange both across the Atlantic and among European member states. Such a system could be layered on top of existing privacy institutions—and over time, come to modify and even perhaps replace them. The rules that were agreed on between the European Union and United States would help reshape relations among member states too, tilting the balance away from what they saw as an excessive concentration on privacy and bureaucracy, and toward what they anticipated would be a more efficient focus on national security.

This strategy amounted to a tacit agreement between EU and US security officials to create an international regulatory solution that they hoped would both cement relations and ease problems of security cooperation (especially on the European side) by supplementing, modifying, and perhaps over time even supplanting the existing EU privacy framework with one more amenable to security concerns. By creating common principles and procedures, applying them to existing and emerging controversies, and then seeking to have them become the formal basis for EU-US relations, these officials hoped to transform both transatlantic relations and EU politics in ways that would have been conducive to their institutional interests.

Neither market power nor preference aggregation arguments encompass the kinds of causal mechanisms through which this transnational forum of security officials came to have power and purpose. Market power accounts treat the preferences of great powers as a product of domestic institutions, which in turn are exogenous. They provide little scope for understanding why domestic officials who are frustrated with their own jurisdiction's institutions might look to create common cause with like-minded officials from elsewhere. Preference aggregation accounts, for their part, are perfectly well suited to explaining why EU security officials were unhappy with domestic institutions that gave veto power to officials and actors who cared more about privacy. Neither addresses the ways in which cross-national alliances, when they have access to the relevant opportunity structures, gradually reshape vexing domestic practices. Hence, both would treat transatlantic forums as talking shops better suited for ventilating gripes than achieving actual change.

The account that we lay out in this book, in contrast, emphasizes how opportunity structures enable some coalitions of actors to achieve change in their home jurisdictions through cross-national layering, while frustrating others who do not have access to these forums. We now turn to examine whether this happened.

Sands Moving under the Feet of the Compromise

As the High Level Contact Group sought to create a broad framework for the EU-US privacy relationship, the issue of SWIFT data transfers started to reemerge in a new form. The initial EU-US deal had been based on the United States' direct access to SWIFT data (SWIFT had an operations center in the United States). When SWIFT relocated its US operation center to Switzerland, the original deal proved moot. The United States had a strong interest in maintaining access to SWIFT data, and wished to export it in bulk from the European Union to its existing system for analysis and storage. The European security officials who had come to dominate decision making similarly had a strong interest in keeping the arrangement intact as the US Treasury selectively fed information obtained through searches to its European counterparts.

At the same time, the European Union anticipated ratifying the Treaty of Lisbon in 2008–9. This treaty, among other changes, granted the European

Parliament much greater decision-making powers in the area of justice and home affairs. If any new SWIFT deal was reached after the treaty had come into effect, the Parliament would have an opportunity to veto it through its power of assent.[54]

A new SWIFT arrangement had implications that went far beyond the exchange of financial information. It would serve as a test case for the broader EU-US homeland security relationship. A successful deal on SWIFT would pave the way for further agreements on specific issues (the PNR deal needed to be renegotiated too) and general ones (the legally binding EU-US treaty proposed in the Council's Stockholm Programme). A failure to reach agreement on SWIFT would, in contrast, be a "nuclear option" that could plausibly stymie the future development of a transatlantic institutional framework.

EU and US officials coordinated on a quite-different approach than they had adopted for the initial SWIFT agreement. First, they sought to create an interim agreement as a stopgap to prevent any loss of coverage, but also to set the agenda for a longer-lasting agreement. Second, they went some distance toward including actors who had been more or less excluded from previous dialogues: the European Parliament and the European Data Protection Supervisor's office. Third and most important, they leveraged the international precedent on reciprocity that had been set in the High Level Contact Group to shift political alliances in the Parliament.

By early 2008, security officials hoped that the European Parliament's previous hostility to EU-US cooperation had diminished over time. Increased exchange between the European Union and United States had changed the facts on the ground, and led to greater mutual understanding, perhaps isolating the die-hard opponents of cooperation in the minority. They also believed that the Parliament was likely to be more cooperative after it acquired its new powers under Lisbon. They wished to delay proposing any ambitious proposal until after Lisbon to avoid a perceived "provocation" to Parliament. The Parliament pressed for some time for a unified EU data privacy regime, which would rationalize the relationship between the different directives covering data privacy issues. Senior officials in the Commission hoped that this could be turned into a new dispensation that would have a stronger security element than the existing regime. The reality of active exchange of information with the United States could supply a plausible precedent for further activity within the European Union. Senior officials recognized that the data privacy authorities were less likely to be cooperative, but hoped that off-the-record discussion of the importance of security cooperation might soften their opposition.

A Brash Move by the Council Backfires

This gradual process of changing minds suddenly became a lot trickier when the SWIFT deal had to be renegotiated on an expedited basis. Council and Commission officials sought initially to win the Parliament over by providing it with a much greater degree of involvement. In contrast to previous negotiations, they consulted with the Parliament throughout the negotiation process, as if it already had the rights it would acquire when the Treaty of Lisbon came into force. They furthermore pressed the United States to agree to a short time horizon for any agreement so that it could be renegotiated again after Lisbon came into effect. While officials expected that the interim agreement would offer a template for any long-term agreement, Parliament would at least have some opportunity to have its say. Finally, the negotiators sought input from the European Data Protection Supervisor and persuaded the United States to agree to incorporate several of his suggestions in the final text.

This effort at agreement involved some concessions on the US side, recognizing that it needed to secure the acquiescence of EU actors such as the Parliament that had not previously been involved.[55] The European Union agreed to ensure that "designated providers" identified by both sides would provide the United States with the information it needed to fight terrorism. Searches would be targeted as narrowly as possible, and automated data mining would be specifically precluded. Unused data would be deleted after five years. EU member states, Europol, and Eurojust could use the Treasury facility and staff to conduct their own searches. The parties would review the arrangements after six months and whenever one of the parties so requested. EU-based individuals could request their data privacy authorities to verify that their rights had been respected. In contrast to the original arrangement, these conditions took the form of an actual agreement rather than a mere exchange of letters. This agreement was the end result of difficult negotiations; at the beginning, at least one EU negotiator had doubted that the discussions would succeed.

As it became clear that there was opposition within Parliament to the proposed deal, the Council investigated backup options, with greater alacrity than adroitness.[56] At the last moment, through two successive maneuvers, it sought to ensure that the Parliament would not have the opportunity to turn the agreement down. First, it tried to sign the agreement on the day before the Lisbon requirements came into play. The Council fumbled, failing properly to conclude the agreement and hence not completing the process in time to avoid the Lisbon requirements.[57] Then the Council delayed its request for parliamentary consent until just before the agreement was due to go into effect so that the agreement would already be operative (with accompanying legal obligations and protections) before the Parliament had a chance to vote on it.[58] These maneuvers led to vociferous complaints from MEPs and failed to produce the desired result. Despite an appeal from US secretary of state Hillary Clinton and US secretary of the treasury Timothy Geithner, the agreement was voted down by the European Parliament, by 378 to 196, on February 11, 2010.[59]

Underneath the rhetoric about privacy lay an institutional fight between the various bodies of the European Union about how the Treaty of Lisbon would be interpreted and to whose institutional advantage. US observers believed that the "no" vote was in large part the result of interinstitutional politics within the European Union. As described in one diplomatic communication, "MEPs of all stripes saw this as an early opportunity to exert their new post-Lisbon powers and send a message to the Commission and Council."[60]

Turning Transnational Gains into Political Influence

The Parliament's position, though, had changed in ways that were not recognized by its critics across the Atlantic. The new treaty, together with the layer of transatlantic institutions, provided the Parliament with different incentives than had existed some years previously. It was willing in principle to reach a deal—as long as it got direct recognition of an enhanced role for Parliament in the transatlantic relationship.

Although the failure to pass the agreement sent shock waves through the EU and US relationship, the rough outlines of a modified deal that would be acceptable to a majority in Parliament were not difficult to discern. While a core group of parliamentarians in the Green and Liberal party alliances had up to now played a key role in blocking security proposals, it had relied on allies in the Social Democratic group to supply the necessary votes. The Social Democratic bloc, however, was split on the privacy issue. As it became clear that the agreement provided benefits to national police and intelligence agencies as well as Parliament's institutional position by giving it with new forms of oversight, the security alliance slowly peeled away MEPs from the center.

The norm of reciprocity, formalized in Articles 9 and 10 of the agreement, played a vital role in persuading MEPs. Article 9 authorized the US Treasury to pass relevant leads on to its European counterparts. Under Article 10, European security officials could now make requests of the US Treasury to conduct financial tracking searches that would be legally and technically difficult for the same European agencies to conduct themselves. European privacy regulations limited the types of searches and the extent of data mining. Moreover, many European intelligence agencies did not have the capacity to conduct analysis at the same level as their US counterparts. One European official argued, "The truth is that we in Europe don't have the technical ability to interpret this stuff. We rely on the Americans to process it and pass it on as intelligence."[61] Similarly, the European Peoples Party concluded in its press release on the agreement that "the EU also needs to be able to obtain information from the US database."[62]

Just as the transatlantic security alliance had hoped, the institutionalization of EU-US information exchange changed the Parliament's underlying understanding of its goals. As European police services began to make systematic use of the US Terrorist Financing Tracking Program to pursue their own security needs, it became more and more difficult for MEPs to oppose EU-US cooperation outright.[63] Moreover, key MEPs gradually became persuaded that the European Union should have its own similar program, which would naturally be accountable in some form to Parliament.

This would have the twin benefits of providing the Parliament with a direct bargaining role in transatlantic relations along with increased oversight of the ever-proliferating web of informal relations among police and security services within the European Union. If the Parliament was prepared to accept an institutional deal on SWIFT, it could try to turn these institutions to its own purposes.

Hence the Parliament's negotiating position not only called for greater privacy protection but also for changes to the transatlantic security relationship and internal EU institutions. Many of its demands on privacy were negotiable. Its institutional demands proved less so. The Parliament deplored the way in which it had been excluded from previous negotiations. The rapporteur's report recommending a rejection of the SWIFT deal noted that

furthermore, what might have kicked off as an urgent temporary measure (in reply to 9/11) became *de facto* permanent without specific approval or authorisation by EU authorities or a real transatlantic evaluation of its impact and forward looking transatlantic negotiations covering at the same time security, judicial cooperation and data protection impact. Clearly, such proceedings did not help in building up mutual trust for transatlantic cooperation on counter-terrorism purposes.[64]

The implication was clear, and was clearly understood by its intended audience. On March 24, 2010, the European Commission proposed a revised negotiating mandate, which was accepted by the Council in April.[65] Under this proposal, the European Parliament would be kept "immediately and fully informed" at all stages of the negotiation.[66] This not only helped greatly to smooth the specific negotiations but created an important precedent for the Parliament's role in future negotiations too. When a deal was finally concluded in July, the Parliament's rapporteur specifically noted that "the agreement also marks a new step in Parliament's powers, ensuring European democratic oversight over international agreements."[67]

Many of the more specific changes to the agreement that the Parliament demanded were also to its institutional advantage. The Parliament had initially requested

the European Commission to submit recommendations for the immediate opening of (new) negotiations with the United States on both, financial messaging data for counter-terrorism investigations and privacy/personal data protection in the context of the exchange of information for law enforcement purposes. . . . [T]he concerns of—and recommendations made by the European Parliament as well as the EDPS and Working Group Article 29—are expected be reflected. . . . [A]ttention should be given to a "European" solution for the supervision of data exchange, i.e., to determine an EU independent (judicial) authority which would be empowered to verify the TFTP operations (and even to block the TFTP system). The prerequisite for this European solution is a binding international agreement on privacy and personal data protection in the context of the exchange of information for law enforcement purposes.[68]

The Parliament clearly wanted a deal with stronger protections for the data of European citizens. It also envisaged that this deal would be institutionalized in ways that benefited the Parliament. While Parliament pressed for an European official to oversee data extraction in Washington, DC, it insisted that this official be appointed on the same basis as the European Data Protection Supervisor, with significant input from the Parliament. It abandoned its demand for an independent judicial authority in favor of an arrangement under which Europol would consider requests for data, even though Europol was not a judicial authority, and furthermore, as the European Data Protection Supervisor pointed out, was only dubiously independent.[69] Europol had recently been incorporated as an official institution of the European Union, providing the European Parliament with some influence over its role and budget. Europol's new responsibilities might plausibly bring it further within the framework of the Treaty of Lisbon and hence into the Parliament's sphere of influence.

Most ambitiously, the Parliament signaled its willingness to see the European Union introduce its own TFTP program, which would most likely be administered by Europol. The Parliament indicated that one of its main sticking points was the transfer of bulk data to the United States. While Europol could mitigate this problem through checking that US data requests were appropriate before they were fulfilled, the problem of external transfer still remained. From Parliament's perspective, this problem would be obviated if there were a European equivalent to the TFTP, which could carry out its own independent analysis of European data, both for the benefit of European law enforcement officials and intelligence agencies, and on request, for US authorities. Under such an arrangement, only the reports would travel across the Atlantic, not the raw data.

Earlier, Council officials had declined to raise the possibility of an European TFTP for fear that it would alienate the Parliament. In the wake of Lisbon, however, Parliament negotiators were quick to see the possible benefits of such an arrangement. If it were to come into operation, it would need Parliament's support. And this support could be exchanged for influence and oversight authority over its actions. Accordingly, the Parliament resolved on May 5, 2010, on a "twin-track approach which differentiates between, on the one hand, the strict safeguards to be included in the envisaged EU-US agreement, and, on the other, the fundamental longer-term policy decisions that the EU must address." This "twin track" clearly linked developments in the EU-US relationship back to institutional change within the European Union. Parliament further noted that

> the option offering the highest level of guarantees would be to allow for the extraction of data to take place on EU soil, in EU or Joint EU-US facilities, and ask[ed] the Commission and the Council to explore . . . ways to

phase into a medium-term solution empowering an EU judicial authority to oversee the extraction in the EU, on behalf of Member States, after a mid-term parliamentary review of the agreement.[70]

These suggestions were taken as an invitation to create a European TFTP program along US lines. The final EU-US agreement seemed to foresee this outcome, while a Council / European Commission declaration following from the agreement "acknowledges in the longer-term, the ambition for the European Union to establish a system equivalent to the TFTP, which could allow for the extraction of data to take place on EU soil," and observed that the United States "has committed in the Agreement to cooperate and provide assistance and advice to contribute to the effective establishment of such a system."[71]

Institutional Change after SWIFT

The Parliament's hopes were systematically disappointed. After member states and the Commission secured an agreement on the TFTP, they sidelined the proposals that would have provided the Parliament with greater oversight while enhancing cross-Atlantic cooperation at the expense of EU-level transparency and accountability. The result is a set of institutionalized forms of information exchange among security officials that are inscrutable to the public since not only the information but also aspects of the rules under which the information is provided are considered to be classified information.[72]

In 2011, the European Commission presented an initial report on the options for a European TFTP equivalent or European Union Terrorist Finance Tracking System (EU TFTS), noting that there were "solid grounds for believing that an EU TFTS will also provide significant added value to the efforts of the EU and the Member States," listing several possible options for how the EU TFTS could be organized. It also noted that despite the safeguards for the existing TFTP system, "arguments have been made that the provision to a third State of such large amounts of personal data constitutes an unwarranted infringement of the fundamental rights of these citizens."[73] In a later document in 2013, the Commission reversed its favorable initial assessment of the case for an EU TFTS. It found that an EU-based system for analyzing TFTP data "would not generate additional intelligence benefits for the EU or the Member States," might slow down analysis, and would not guarantee better protection of personal data.[74] Other options were presented as unworkable because member states would never allow the European Union to develop a fully centralized system, while a decentralized system would run the risk of communications failures between the member states. This led the Commission to recommend that there was no clear case for an EU TFTS system.

A 2014 report commissioned by the Parliament's Committee on Civil Liberties, Justice, and Home Affairs dissented, noting that the TFTP system did not provide a solution under the Commission's own criteria since it did not limit the transfer of personal data to third countries. This was a breach of faith with the European Parliament since "for many MEPs the promise of data analysis capacities on European soil through an EU TFTS was one of the preconditions for approving the EU-US TFTP Agreement in 2010."[75] The Parliament, however, had little that it could do except to complain.

Regular reports by the European Commission on the implementation of the TFTP agreement took a more sanguine view, mentioning occasional difficulties but finding in general that the procedures were working well. In particular, the reports argued that the reciprocity procedure worked well in allowing European intelligence officials to obtain information from their US counterparts that they would have otherwise had difficulty obtaining. In a series of joint reviews of the agreement, the two sides noted that European requests under Article 10 grew from 15 in 2011 to 192 in 2017 (see figure 4.4)

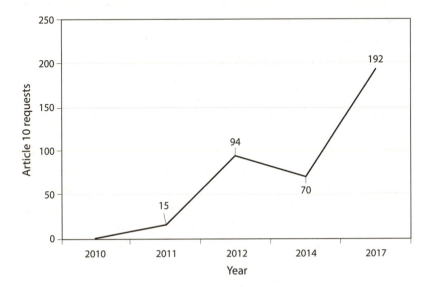

FIGURE 4.4. Article 10 Requests, 2011–17

with requests from 2017 generating nearly 9,000 leads. This does not include a sizable number of US-initiated data sharing that occurred under Article 9.[76] An independent analysis of the TFTP program by the Royal United Services Institute in the United Kingdom concluded that "the programme must thus be considered an integral part of the EU framework for combating the financing of terrorism."[77]

Privacy Advocates Continue the Struggle

These reports did not satisfy the TFTP's critics in the Parliament and elsewhere, especially since they declined to provide specific information on large swathes of TFTP activities and indeed classified all of the documents relating to important aspects of the agreement. This led MEPs, including in particular the libertarian Dutch MEP Sophie in't Veld, to try to expose the TFTP to greater public oversight in legally innovative ways. In an initial lawsuit before the European Court of Justice, in't Veld sought access to legal documents relating to the European Union's negotiation position. When this was only partially successful, in't Veld turned to a different strategy, complaining (as an ordinary EU citizen rather than an MEP) to the European Ombudsperson about her lack of access to the technical modalities document in which the technical aspects of the TFTP agreement were addressed.[78] The Ombudsperson agreed with her complaint, but was unable to supply her with the document since the United States refused to allow European authorities to provide it.[79] There was a clash between the apparent obligations under the agreement concluded by the Commission and the oversight powers of the European Union's domestic institutions, which Europol's supervisory body resolved in favor of the international agreement.

> The technical modalities were agreed without the legislature's involvement and Europol basically said that they had to consult the third party [the United States]. The document is actually an EU document, which was drawn up by the Joint Supervisory Body, which supervises Europol. But they said that information in the document came from the US, so they would have to consult the US. . . . So basically, Europol went to the US, and asked the US authorities—they refused and then our inspection was refused.

The European Parliament's Committee on Civil Liberties, Justice, and Home Affairs expressed its displeasure with this outcome in a subsequent meeting.

Basically [there was] a lot of unhappiness that there is no democratic oversight of this agreement—that the Parliament doesn't have any oversight, the ombudsman doesn't have any oversight, so that was . . . a major problem. There is no special reading room for the Parliament so they cannot ensure the agreement is being implemented the way the legislators intended, and the Ombudsman also doesn't have access to the documents.[80]

Despite the apparent limits of insulation strategies, as discussed in the next chapter, this conflict may give rise to future litigation in the European Court of Justice.[81]

Internal TFTP Emerges as Complement rather than Supplement

In the wake of terrorist attacks in Brussels and Paris, security officials in the European Union have started to argue again in favor of an EU TFTS but on a different basis.[82] In February 2016, the European Commission suggested that the European Union should consider a system to monitor payments made through the Single Euro Payments Area system that are not covered under the existing agreement, and hence not systematically available either to the European Union or United States.[83] The European Union's anti-terrorism coordinator in turn noted that "an EU system complementary to the TFTP should be considered in due course."[84] In December 2016, the relevant commissioner stated that

when the Commission presented its action plan to counter terrorism financing back in February, we agreed to look further at the EU-US TFTP and whether a complementary EU system might be necessary. In 2013, we looked at this issue and concluded no complementary EU system was necessary. Since then quite a few things have changed: the terrorist threat has increased and changed in nature, the way that terrorists finance themselves is different, there have been enormous technological advances in the areas of payments so lots of new ways of transferring money which are not covered by the TFTP. On that basis, we're committing in today's Security Union report to consider the options further, do the appropriate studies, and we'll report back by the summer.[85]

Instead of rolling back the existing TFTP system in favor of an EU-based approach along the lines that the Parliament asked for, this proposal preserves the existing system and supplements it. In Mara Wesseling's (2016, x) summary, there has been a "shift in conceptualization, from a system that would *replace* part of the EU-US TFTP Agreement to a *complementary* system that would focus on intra-European SEPA data, which is not currently covered by the agreement." Such a system would replace existing, ad hoc, and ramshackle procedures for information exchange between member states with a more streamlined and centrally organized approach. It is likely to spur further political arguments, both about its relationship to the existing TFTP system and the appropriate procedures for information sharing. Nonetheless, if this system is introduced, it will mark the culmination of a new stage of institutional change.

Conclusion

This chapter examines an important case of how cross-national layering led to critical policy change concerning information sharing and surveillance. Dominant approaches have enormous difficulty in explaining this outcome. There has been no significant shift in market power between the European Union and United States; both retain enormous influence over international markets, yet the European Union has altered its position and internalized arrangements that build on a US initiative that at first was illegal under European law. While market power approaches perhaps treat this as a case of preference change, they cannot explain why the preferences of the European Union changed using their own frameworks. Preference aggregation accounts too have enormous difficulty in explaining observed outcomes. When the Parliament got effective veto power, the space of possible agreeable outcomes seemed to expand rather than to diminish, including for the first time a domestic institutionalization of the TFTP that had previously seemed unthinkable. Moreover, the actual form that this institutionalization took was not what Parliament anticipated, or wanted.

Instead, the mechanism of change appears to have involved cross-national layering. EU security and justice and home affairs officials were frustrated, as were their US counterparts, by their inability to overcome a coalition within the European Union that sought to block security measures that might infringe on personal privacy. This coalition primarily consisted of privacy-oriented MEPs and data privacy authorities as well as some sympathizers within the European Commission and national justice ministries. While it was not powerful enough to block all change, it surely was able to slow or sometimes completely stymie forms of information exchange that would arguably be privacy invasive.

This led security officials in the member states, on the Council, and in certain parts of the Commission to adopt a policy of cross-national layering. By creating international arrangements, they could over time undermine the domestic coalition that was blocking change by transforming the interests of key coalition members. The SWIFT agreement built on the track that had already been partly laid down by the PNR negotiations to provide these security officials with a transnational forum where they could develop alternative, more security-focused arrangements. Thus, an apparently straightforward deal between the European Union and United States became the seedbed for a proliferating relationship between security officials on both sides of the Atlantic. Over a period of several years, these officials sought to create an EU-US institutional dispensation under the banner of reciprocity, which would reconcile the different regulatory systems, and allow for much more far-reaching forms of information exchange and security cooperation.

These efforts enjoyed considerable success. As one skeptical MEP described it, the proposal for a European TFTP

> fits the trend whereby whatever instruments the US has for counter-terrorism and other law enforcement purposes is copied by the European Union. I have with great hesitation voted for the final agreement. One of my problems was indeed that via the back door, a European TFTP will be created. It is the umpteenth example of what we call policy laundering. There have been many examples where either the US or the member state governments who usually work in tandem want something; the European member states know that if they present such a proposal to their national parliaments there is no way in hell they are going to get it, so what they do is they hide behind some international agreement in order to get it.[86]

By creating transnational relationships and associated agreements, these officials provided the European Parliament, a key member of the blocking coalition, with good reason to moderate and eventually partly abandon its commitment to the privacy of European citizens. The existence of these relationships posed a threat to a Parliament that wished to accrue as much power as possible. Accordingly, the Parliament was prepared to fundamentally change its approach so that it no longer opposed security-oriented measures, provided that it was given a substantial stake in the emerging relationship. The European Parliament, which had previously been vigorously opposed to the TFTP, not only accepted its logic but also agreed to incorporate it into the European Union's institutional framework in the belief that this would give it greater oversight and control. These hopes were frustrated, giving rise to the effective institutionalization of the TFTP as a core element of the European Union's antiterrorist strategy. Now security officials are looking to build on these foundations by creating the formal institutions for a new and complementary EU-level arrangement, which will not replace the EU-US TFTP but instead extend its logic to a separate European payments system, establishing the already-existing arrangements of reciprocity on a new institutional basis.

To be clear, this stage of institutional change is less a final culmination than a new battleground, on which we expect the various antagonists to continue to conduct skirmishes and forays in the hope of turning the next stage of combat to their advantage. Still less does it reflect the domination of the United States over the European Union. In the next chapter, we turn to different and unexpected developments that show how the coalition of actors who lost out over both PNR and SWIFT have been able to use the opportunity structures created by interdependence to the partial dismay of security officials on both sides of the Atlantic.

5

Insulation and the Transformation of Commercial Privacy Disputes

In June 2013, the *Guardian* broke a series of stories based on leaked information about US and European surveillance activities. Drawn from a cache of documents smuggled out of the NSA by Edward Snowden, the stories revealed massive data collection efforts, which ranged from tapping the data pipes of the internet and global telecommunications to monitoring the cell phones of world leaders, most notably German chancellor Angela Merkel.[1]

While the Snowden revelations generated a series of specific political crises over summer 2013, it also set in motion powerful dynamics, which continue to remake transatlantic data and security policy as this book goes to print. The leaks revealed important connections between commercial data transfers and government surveillance. While many had suspected such connections, most notably the late civil liberties writer Caspar Bowden, this irrefutable evidence was used by privacy advocates to gain access to domestic opportunity structures that had previously been closed off so that they could try to insulate European privacy rules from transnational pressures.

This chapter, then, tells a story that contrasts sharply with the accounts in chapters 3 and 4. Those chapters described how security actors created a cross-national layer that transformed the environment for institutional change and explored how difficult it was for actors oriented toward civil liberties to insulate domestic institutions against these pressures. Civil liberties groups could not fight back effectively because they had limited access to the relevant platforms for transnational cooperation and only had limited domestic levers to protect against transnational arrangements.

In this chapter, we demonstrate how potent insulation strategies are when domestic institutions are more favorable. The Snowden documents created a situation of rule overlap between security and commercial data regulations. Social media and internet service providers found themselves trapped between the legal requirements of commercial data sharing, which limited the onward transfer of data to outside organizations, and the intelligence community, which increasingly demanded access to massive amounts of data. Civil-liberties-oriented actors used this rule overlap to exploit judicial and regulatory channels, including the European Court of Justice and national data privacy commissioners. By linking the issues of commercial data and security-based information sharing, civil-liberties-oriented actors targeted transnational change strategies and insulated European privacy rules.

Substantively, we examine a different set of privacy relations, which at least initially did not appear to have any implications for domestic security: those concerning commercial privacy. Before September 11, the European Union and United States had already fought a major battle over the circumstances under which commercial actors could or could not use the personal information of European citizens. This battle led to the creation of the Safe Harbor Agreement, in which both sides settled on a hybrid arrangement where companies agreed to respect a watered-down version of European rules, with the potential of enforcement actions by the FTC. While many privacy advocates considered this arrangement unsatisfactory, it appeared likely to endure. The European Commission officials who negotiated the agreement saw it as a satisfactory means of defending a preexisting political bargain within the European Union, which they did not wish to reopen, while perhaps disseminating EU privacy practices to the United States.

The Safe Harbor Agreement, however, had more or less the opposite effect. As US negotiators hoped, it provided US e-commerce companies with the institutional means to superficially satisfy EU regulators while developing business models that were at odds with the values of Europe's privacy regime. Snowden's revelation of how the US intelligence community had access to information held by major US e-commerce firms transformed debates over commercial privacy and opened up a means for EU privacy advocates to start insulating the EU regime against US encroachments. Specifically, it demonstrated that the apparent accord between the European Union and United States over commercial privacy was in fact a situation of overlapping and clashing rules, in which European rules to protect citizens' data were directly at odds with the US willingness to use this data in privacy-invasive ways.

This allowed Max Schrems, a privacy activist based in Austria, to identify a path through which he could use the Snowden revelations to undermine Safe Harbor and commercial data sharing more generally. When Ireland's data privacy authority declined to investigate Facebook's recourse to Safe Harbor, Schrems began a legal process that culminated in a European Court of Justice ruling that overturned Safe Harbor, leaving businesses and politicians scrambling to come up with a replacement. Intense negotiations led to legislative change in the United States and the creation of the so-called Privacy Shield arrangement, which offered stronger protections to European citizens than Safe Harbor, but is likely to come under sustained legal challenge.

These two phases—the phase in which Safe Harbor was negotiated, and the phase in which it was overturned—illustrate the strategies that different kinds of actors are likely to deploy in an age of interdependence. The first stage illustrates how actors with access to cross-national negotiations will deploy defend and extend. When the European Union and United States initially faced off over commercial privacy on the internet, the agenda was set by formally appointed negotiators who had, by definition, extensive access to the relevant transnational forums, and a mandate and desire to protect existing institutional arrangements. Thus, both the US Department of Commerce and the European Commission sought to defend their specific domestic institutional arrangements, and if possible to extend them, by creating circumstances under which their adversary's system would be gradually subverted over time. The problem that negotiations had to solve was that neither EU or US negotiators were willing to make concessions on changing preexisting institutions.

The second phase was different, with new tensions that stemmed from the fact that the Safe Harbor Agreement had slowly eroded European privacy protections for citizens against large multinational corporations. Now the agenda was set by EU-focused activists and data privacy authorities who wished to insulate their institutions against US-style business models. These actors were invested in existing privacy law and the institutional bargains that made it enforceable. They did not themselves have direct access to international negotiations. Hence they wanted, as their predecessors had, to insulate European privacy rules from the encroachment of US firms and privacy approaches. The difference with the previous struggle over airline passenger data was that new and publicly salient information made it impossible to elide the clash between European privacy standards and the information-gathering actions of US-based actors. Rather than simply focusing on domestic legislative reforms, privacy activists in Europe leveraged political opportunity structures to target transnational agreements. This meant that negotiators played a reactive as opposed to active role, trying to preserve cross-Atlantic information exchange against the highly credible threat that European data privacy agencies and the European Court of Justice might hamper or block future data exchange. The chapter therefore both shows how defend-and-extend strategies of bargaining may lead to domestic institutional change, and how disgruntled actors may respond to this in a subsequent phase, deploying insulation strategies in order to undermine transatlantic efforts to emphasize security at the expense of privacy.

The Commercialization of the Internet and Digital Disputes

When data exchange first became a transatlantic policy problem, it was interpreted in commercial terms, with a specific focus on privacy issues. In the mid-1990s, the European Union introduced comprehensive privacy legislation to prevent privacy concerns from hampering European integration. The Privacy Directive had important external consequences, leading to fears within the United States that the directive might cripple the burgeoning e-commerce sector.[2]

The conflict over commercial data flows stemmed in large part from the beginnings of economic interdependence in e-commerce. While it is hard to imagine today, the internet did not exist as a commercial space until the mid-1990s, having been limited during its early existence to research and noncommercial purposes. The relaxation of US rules on the commercial use of the internet and the release in 1994 of Netscape Navigator, one of the first commercial web browsers to allow secure and encrypted communication, helped a much broader base of individuals and firms to use the internet for business purposes.[3]

The Privacy Directive included a clause with clear extraterritorial consequences for countries such as the United States, preventing data transfers to jurisdictions that had weak protections. Specifically, Article 25 stipulated that transfers could only go to countries outside the European Union if those countries had an "adequate" level of privacy protection. Where the Commission found that a country did not have adequate protection, member states were obliged to take the necessary measures to block data flows to that country. The Commission could find that a country provided adequate protection, and could also negotiate with outside countries to bring them to improve their protections and make them adequate from the European Union's perspective.

This was intended to block an obvious loophole in EU law; without such a rule it would be easy for multinational corporations to transfer personal information on EU citizens to a third jurisdiction with weak privacy rules and process it there, doing an end run around EU privacy protections. The rule, however, was not only intended to defend the EU approach to privacy but to extend it worldwide too. Officials in the European Commission wanted to remedy the risks of international flows by encouraging other jurisdictions to engage in negotiations with the Commission to improve their privacy rules and standards so as to achieve adequacy. Hence the European Union quite explicitly sought not only to protect its own system but also to bring the rest of the world into closer conformity with its understanding of privacy through building institutions that resembled the EU model.[4]

This was not motivated by a deep commitment to the values of privacy; the officials responsible for negotiation were at the European Commission's Internal Market DG, which had previously opposed strong privacy regulation within the European Union. Instead, it stemmed from more prosaic considerations. Internal fights over privacy had endangered the European Union's market integration project until national privacy officials and the Commission had struck a difficult political bargain. Under no circumstances did the Commission want this internal bargain to unravel, prompting it to try to defend the rules in multilateral discussions and export the EU approach to other countries.[5]

Many of the European Union's trading partners did indeed accede to the EU approach.[6] The United States presented the most obvious risk of holdout given its clout and adherence to a different approach to privacy. While the European Union created comprehensive privacy rules that covered most market activity and included oversight by independent regulatory agencies, US privacy law followed a sectoral approach with privacy rules for some sensitive sectors but not others, where industry self-regulation prevailed.[7] The United States did not and does not have a dedicated privacy agency that provides independent oversight for privacy concerns. Ultimately, Europe did not view US rules as adequate as per the clause in the 1995 Privacy Directive.

The US approach to privacy was just one aspect of its larger understanding of the appropriate regulatory approach to the digital economy. As firms and policy makers sought to manage the pressures of increased global competition in traditional industrial sectors, e-commerce offered the potential for innovation and job creation. Market players on both sides of the Atlantic saw the transatlantic marketplace as a key source of potential growth. As described by Ira Magaziner, the US e-commerce "czar,"

> In 1994 . . . President Clinton asked me to have a Cabinet level group to look at one or two things that we might do were he to be re-elected. . . . [W]e . . . determined that something which was not on the original list we were looking at, which was the commercialization of the Internet would offer the potential to drive the world economy for the next couple of decades if we could set up the right policy environment for it. . . . [W]hat we believed was that if the government could resist over-regulating, over-censoring, over-taxing the Internet, that it had the potential to really drive economic growth.[8]

The US government too wanted to protect its own regulatory approach from international incursions and decided that the best way to do this would be to spread it internationally. In Magaziner's words,

> The U.S. government believes that it's best for our economy and best for the development of this new digital age to try to set a predictable legal environment globally for the conduct of commerce. . . . [I]n general, we think that governments should stay away from regulating, over-taxing, or censoring the Internet. . . . [I]f they create this as a regulated industry in some way—that will strangle the growth potential that we see. . . . [D]evelopments should be led by the private sector, and privately established codes of conduct should govern, not government regulations.[9]

Magaziner and other officials worked on creating a "Framework for Global Electronic Commerce," which was published by the White House on July 1, 1997. This framework sought to embed and protect the US self-regulatory approach as the global standard, hence both shielding US e-commerce from foreign regulators and encouraging the latter over time to take a more laissez-faire approach.

This antiregulatory emphasis meant that the United States was greatly alarmed at the European Union's directive. Magaziner noted that

> a lot of our companies were reacting with great concern, and coming to us in government and saying this is a nightmare, and it's going to affect

our investments in Europe. . . . [T]hey were facing a huge investment plus that there was a risk that the normal data that they needed to operate their business with subsidiary companies and so on, would be put in danger. . . . They thought it was a potential disaster.[10]

Negotiating the Safe Harbor

This threatened to ignite the first major trade war of the digital era. Key actors in both the European Union and United States saw themselves as protecting important domestic institutions. The risk of a breakdown in relations over the issue led both sides to begin negotiations aimed at finding a solution. The European side of the negotiations was conducted by officials from the Commission's Internal Market DG, in consultation with Enterprise DG and other interested parties.[11] These officials' major goal, as already discussed, was to protect the directive and the complex political bargain that it represented.[12] The US negotiations were led by the US Department of Commerce, occasionally consulting with the Department of the Treasury, the FTC, the US Trade Representative, and the Office of Management and Budget via an interagency process.[13] Commerce officials wanted to protect the interests of US business, which they saw as best served by a continuation of the US system, under which e-commerce businesses and others had only to obey lax or nonexistent privacy rules.

Each set of negotiators refused to countenance substantial changes to its own domestic institutions, while demanding that the other conceded on theirs. As Ambassador David Aaron, the undersecretary for international trade, put it, the Europeans "want us to invent a regime that looks like theirs. . . . [W]ell, we aren't going to do that." Yet as Spiros Simitis, a commission adviser and highly influential voice in European privacy debates, laid out the European perspective: "Americans still have the illusion that they can change the directive, but they can't. . . . This is not bananas we are talking about. . . . This is about what we consider a fundamental claim to privacy, and therefore there is a limit to compromise."[14]

EU and US negotiators were initially skeptical that a deal could be reached; European negotiators at first saw themselves as engaged in a process of damage control.[15] As an EU official described it, "There was a lot of angst around that this could spin out of control. There weren't any obvious solutions here; it was very black and white in the beginning, the comprehensive legislative approach and the piecemeal self-regulatory approach in the US."[16]

An idea floated by Ambassador Aaron provided an unexpected possible solution.[17] Aaron, who had previously worked in the financial sector, was familiar with the concept of safe harbor, under which if businesses behaved in a certain kind of way, they were presumed to have safe harbor from enforcement. This prompted him to suggest that the Commission consider whether the Commission could provide an adequacy finding for US companies rather than the United States as a whole. European officials, who very much wanted a deal that would provide them with a colorable solution, but that would preserve the existing EU institutional framework, were intrigued. The crucial question was of enforceability: the European Union still wanted some assurance that businesses' promises would be underpinned by some regulatory framework. Here, the FTC played a crucial role. Under Section 5 of the FTC Act, the FTC is empowered to fine businesses that fail to live up to their promises to consumers. Thus businesses could commit to abide by privacy principles that reflected EU preferences to some considerable degree, while the FTC could punish businesses that failed to abide by their promises.

This basic framework became the foundation for the Safe Harbor Agreement—the final deal struck between the European Union and United States in 2000. The Safe Harbor Agreement took the form of an exchange of letters between the European Union and United States, and an adequacy decision by the Commission agreeing that businesses that signed up to Safe Harbor would be in compliance with the directive if they exported personal data to the United States. In practice, the arrangement had three pillars. First were the Safe Harbor Principles, a set of basic privacy principles that reflected those contained in the EU Privacy Directive (and that the United States had previously indicated in other forums were best practice that firms ought to look to). All firms that registered as Safe Harbor participants had to agree to abide by these principles and a set of frequently asked questions about their interpretation that had similar standing to the principles themselves.[18] They furthermore had to sign up either to self-regulatory organizations or the FTC, which would address complaints and resolve disputes over privacy. Second, the FTC agreed that it would entertain complaints from Europeans who felt that their privacy had been invaded by US firms that had signed on to Safe Harbor. Third and finally, European data privacy authorities could block data flows if they were advised by the US government or the relevant self-regulatory organization that a firm was in breach of the Safe Harbor Principles. European data privacy authorities could also suspend flows unilaterally, but under highly restrictive conditions, while the

European Commission could withdraw its adequacy finding if it thought that the arrangement was not working.

This arrangement did not please some privacy advocates in the European Union. Although the Article 29 Working Party of data privacy authorities voted unanimously in favor of the Safe Harbor, certain regulators were privately highly skeptical. Moreover, the European Parliament, which did not have veto power over the terms of the arrangement as such, voted against Safe Harbor, albeit in a sufficiently ambiguous way that the Commission could interpret its disagreement as tacit acquiescence.[19] Within the United States, privacy advocates were largely skeptical about Safe Harbor, but had few tools to make their protest register with the US government.[20]

From the perspective of the actual negotiators, Safe Harbor was a success, protecting the existing institutional arrangements of each of the negotiating parties while avoiding a potentially serious dispute between them. Each set of negotiators could credibly argue that it had done its job. While the United States could continue to claim publicly that its basic policy stance of protecting privacy through self-regulation was unchanged, the European Union could say that it had succeeded in dictating the terms of self-regulation.

Each side hoped that the Safe Harbor would not only defend its existing institutional approach to privacy but perhaps gradually extend it over time as well, subverting the institutions of the other jurisdiction. Magaziner worried that the European Union's role in setting the terms of regulation would have negative long-term consequences.[21] Nonetheless, he anticipated that "if the privacy protections by the private sector can be spread internationally, that will become the de facto way privacy is protected, and that will diffuse this disagreement."[22]

The Europeans, for their part, hoped that the spread of European privacy principles would change the approach of major US corporations and perhaps help generate pressure to transform the US privacy regime along European lines. As described by a negotiator, the alternative mechanism of "contracts only deal with the transfers that they are concluded to deal with. They are much less likely to have any secondary or spin-off effects. Whereas the Safe Harbor was much more likely to have a general upward pulling or pushing effect on privacy in the US in general. Including through the alternative dispute resolution mechanisms."[23]

Thus the process leading up to the Safe Harbor Agreement and the arrangement itself fit well with the expectations of this book's arguments. The key actors driving the process on both sides were negotiators, who obviously had access to the relevant international discussions where the European

Union and United States sought to resolve their differences. The lead negotiators came from entities that had a major interest in preserving existing domestic institutions in their home jurisdictions. The European Union's Internal Market DG had just shepherded through a vastly complex piece of legislation that was intended to resolve, once and for all, the threat that data privacy issues posed to the completion of the European Union's internal market. It had a strong interest in protecting domestic rules that it itself had conceived. The US Department of Commerce, for its part, was highly sensitive to the wants of US firms (its first request for public comment on Safe Harbor was tellingly addressed to "Industry Representatives"), which were in general allergic to regulation and wished the existing US emphasis on self-regulation to continue unchallenged.

This confluence of access and interest meant that both sides were strongly committed to preserving their existing domestic bargains. What is remarkable is that it initially seemed that they had discovered a way to have their cake and eat it too by creating an interface between the institutional approaches of both sides.[24] Each side, however, not only wanted to defend its own institutions but, if possible, to extend them. Both the European Union and United States viewed the Safe Harbor as a potential Trojan horse through which their preferred mode of regulation could be smuggled into the system of the other actor, with possible long-term subversive consequences.

In contrast to standard rationalist depictions of international bargains, this agreement was premised on disagreement: the two parties, rather than converging on a common estimate of the respective risks and probabilities, as the game theoretic assumption of common knowledge requires, in fact placed different bets on the future. The Commission bet that US businesses, as they adhered to Safe Harbor, would internalize European privacy rules and build pressure for stronger privacy in the United States. The Department of Commerce, in contrast, bet that the Safe Harbor would allow US companies to avoid European sanctions while adhering to a largely self-regulatory regime, hence creating a widening space for company self-rule. It was hard to see how both could be right.

The Implementation of Safe Harbor

Over the next several years, the US view of Safe Harbor proved more accurate. There was little evidence of an overall push toward increased privacy regulation in the United States. Occasional mutterings from the FTC never translated into serious legislation. In contrast, Safe Harbor quickly became a key means through which companies with large operations in the United States could move data back and forth between the European Union and United States. By 2004, thousands of companies had signed on to the Safe Harbor. At the same time, the transatlantic digital marketplace grew exponentially.[25] US firms benefited tremendously, with information technology companies like Google and Facebook winning larger market shares in many European countries than they had in the United States, even though their business models seemed directly at odds with the intentions of European privacy law.

It did not take long for critics to emerge. As social media services exploded and ever more amounts of data were collected, privacy advocates argued that US firms were not meeting Safe Harbor standards.[26] Equally troublingly, they argued that the process for redress was not transparent, as it was difficult for European citizens to bring complaints to the FTC. The French data privacy authority, for example, claimed that many more complaints were brought to the FTC than the FTC acknowledged having received.[27]

A series of public and private sector reviews of Safe Harbor demonstrated that there were weaknesses in the agreement. A 2004 implementation study commissioned by the European Commission, for example, concluded that "key concepts such as 'US organization,' 'personal data,' and 'deceptive practices' lacked clarity. Moreover, the jurisdiction of the FTC over certain types of data transfers was dubious."[28] The Safe Harbor Agreement faced increasing hostility within Europe as scandals erupted over US-based information technology firms. For instance, Google's monitoring of residential Wi-Fi traffic, as its cars were imaging neighborhoods for its Street View service, caused considerable unhappiness in Europe.[29] In 2008, disgruntled MEPs commissioned a report from the consultancy group Galexia.[30] This report argued that firms listed as members of Safe Harbor had failed to renew their registration, that a large number failed to comply with basic privacy standards, and that alternative dispute resolution providers identified by firms were unaffordable to consumers. These complaints led some German data privacy authorities in 2010 to require that companies exporting data not simply rely on the Safe Harbor list but also verify that the recipient of any data was fulfilling its obligations and report their compliance efforts.[31]

Despite these doubts, the European Commission continued to support the agreement during the 2000s, leading to a general assumption that Safe Harbor would continue to operate.[32] In 2012, Viviane Reding, European Commission vice president, and justice commissioner and US commerce secretary John Bryson made a public declaration that "the United States and the European Union reaffirm their respective commitments to the U.S.-EU Safe Harbor Framework."[33] Reding furthermore made a forceful defense of the agreement in October 2012, concluding that "Safe Harbor will stay."[34] Both the European Union and United States accepted that Safe Harbor had to be reformed and updated. In the description of one former senior Department of Commerce official, "Certainly we were aware of the complaints. The first study came up with evidence that there were companies that were not adhering [to Safe Harbor rules]. . . . 2009 was when the FTC began enforcement actions on Safe Harbor."[35]

Despite the claim by some US observers that European privacy policy was a form of tacit protectionism, European policy makers had much to lose from an end to Safe Harbor.[36] Companies like Google, eBay, and Apple employed thousands of workers across Europe. Moreover, important European firms conducting business with the United States used Safe Harbor too to handle, for example, transfers of employee data. Even when it began to face concern about the rupture of Safe Harbor (described in more detail below), the European Commission (2013, 6–7) continued to make the economic case for maintaining the agreement:

> The Safe Harbour scheme is an important component of the EU-US commercial relationship, relied upon by companies on both sides of the Atlantic. . . . [I]ts revocation would adversely affect the interests of member companies in the EU and in the US. The Commission considers that Safe Harbour should rather be strengthened.

The Umbrella Agreement, and Delinking of Security and Commerce

Debates over commercial privacy had been quite successfully isolated from the more fractious arguments over domestic security described in the previous two chapters. Assessing the impact of US security legislation passed in the wake of the September 11 for the Safe Harbor Agreement, a European Commission implementation study concluded, "Since the new US legislation only rarely contradicts the SH principles for data covered by SH, these conflicts do not appear to undermine the level of protection for any significant flows of personal data to the United States. The controversial provisions of the USA PATRIOT ACT are essentially irrelevant for SH data flows."[37]

As negotiations advanced on security issues, security and commerce began occasionally to interact with each other. Thus when the SWIFT organization entered into the Safe Harbor after it had restructured its data flows, EU and US policy clearly distinguished between the commercial flows enabled by Safe Harbor, and the purportedly distinct question of government use of information from those flows for security and policing cooperation.

As relations between the European Union and United States became more systematized, moving from the High Level Dialogue to a more expansive High Level Contact Group, the ambitions of negotiators grew. As described by one negotiator, the European Union and United States initially wanted to create building blocks for a future agreement, creating a kind of catalog of parts that could be incorporated into agreements on particular matters.[38] They increasingly sought not only to confer, identify, and resolve potential problems in the policy process before they broke out into overt conflict but also to spur more general cooperation on security questions. The group started its work in February 2007, aiming to create a general framework within which EU and US privacy controversies could be resolved, allowing for much greater and more structured engagement on internal security issues.

EU officials sought to create a two-step process through the High Level Contact Group. First, they hoped that its discussions would clear the ground for a political agreement. This agreement would clarify, minimize, and ideally eliminate the areas of dispute between the European Union and United States. Second, they anticipated that this political agreement would in turn pave the way for a more formal legal agreement a few years down the line. Such an agreement would create binding rules governing transatlantic data exchange on security issues.

US officials—who always worried that the European Union would cease cooperating because some actors in the European Union viewed US privacy protections as inadequate—were less concerned with grand visions and more with concrete deliverables.[39] In particular, they wished to ensure both that the EU framework for data privacy in the transfer of security-sensitive information would not create any roadblocks to cooperation, and that continuing issues of contention such as PNR and SWIFT would be permanently resolved. These worries came to a head in a diplomatic demarche issued by the United States on November 7, 2008, seeking to head off "premature" discussions by the European Council of Permanent Representatives, which the US feared might foreclose debate of the points it felt to be most important to a proper deal. The EU interlocutor retorted that a presentation of the work in progress would "give the Presidency firm support against the constant challenges from the European Parliament and 27 Member State parliaments," noting that "some EU members had criticized a lack of transparency about the HLCG's work."[40]

The High Level Contact Group took longer to reach a conclusion than EU and US officials had initially hoped. The group issued its first report in May 2008, which was followed up by an addendum in October 2009.[41] The group sought to reach an agreement on basic principles of personal data privacy, which officials saw as having prevented cooperation in the past or as having the potential to prevent cooperation in the future. This goal was recognized by the European Council in December 2009 in its Stockholm Programme, which defined EU priorities in the area of justice and home affairs between 2010 and 2014, when it invited the European Commission to "propose a Recommendation for the negotiation of a data protection and, where necessary, data sharing agreements for law enforcement purposes with the United States of America, building on the work carried out by the EU-US High Level Contact Group on data protection."[42] While the group succeeded in creating some degree of accord, it did not reach agreement on a few key principles. The group agreed that the principles should be applied for "law enforcement" purposes—but could not agree on what "law enforcement" meant. The European Union wished to confine law enforcement purposes to criminal offenses, while the United States wanted to also extend it to violations of law relating to border enforcement, public security, and national security as well as to noncriminal judicial and administrative proceedings linked to such offenses or violations.

Additionally, the sides remained at odds on the issue of redress. The European Union argued that redress ought to involve impartial and independent tribunals, while the United States sought to claim that some laws treat nationals differently. The issue at stake here was that the US Privacy Act of 1974 and other protective legislation apply only to US nationals. The United States sought to have administrative procedures rather than legal rights accepted as a form of redress.

Indeed, the DHS had already agreed to provide limited administrative redress to non-US persons who had data in "mixed systems of records" in a 2007 Internal Guidance Memorandum.[43] The United States, however, was reluctant to provide judicial redress, all the more so because this would require US law to establish new rights for foreign citizens—a cause that rarely generated great enthusiasm among US legislators. While negotiators were able to make substantial progress on other issues, the debates on judicial redress stalled on US unwillingness to accommodate demands that the European Union felt were politically necessary given increased pressure from a newly empowered Parliament.

The United States and European Union also disagreed on the sidelines about the definition of an individual, and on what constituted independent supervision (the United States wanted to have internal controls, such as data privacy officers attached to individual agencies, while the European Union wanted regulators with some degree of autonomy). Apart from these ambiguities, the principles encountered skepticism from outside officials, who had not been consulted.[44]

Despite these disagreements, the two sides pushed for the negotiation of a more formal EU-US deal on privacy for security information that could take the form either of a binding international agreement or soft law. The first was their recommended option:

> Both sides agree that an international agreement binding both the EU and the US to apply the agreed common principles in transatlantic data transfers is the preferred option. In negotiating a binding international agreement the EU and US should strive to obtain the recognition of the effectiveness of each other's privacy and data protection systems for the areas covered by these principles. In addition to the agreed common principles, further work could be undertaken to identify detailed key issues to be addressed in such an agreement. Whilst it is difficult/impossible to envisage an international agreement covering all types of law enforcement data, a binding international agreement would offer the advantage of establishing the fundamentals of effective privacy and personal data protection for use in any future agreements relating to the exchange of specific law enforcement information that might arise between the EU and the U.S. As a binding instrument, it would provide the greatest level of legal security and certainty.[45]

They recognized that this would require further consultation with the European Parliament, which now had the power to provide or deny consent for any agreement that was reached. If it required additional implementing legislation, it would furthermore require congressional ratification. The report hinted that a soft law solution might offer some benefits should these hurdles be insurmountable. Yet as time went on, both sides continued to negotiate in the hope that they could create a comprehensive agreement on law enforcement and privacy that would supply a general template for public sector data exchanges.[46] Accordingly, negotiations on a so-called Umbrella Agreement to cover all data transfers for police and judicial purposes began in March 2011. This effort, led by security-oriented actors in the European Union and United States, attempted to create a firewall between information sharing for law enforcement and intelligence and commercial information sharing as addressed by the Safe Harbor Agreement.

The Snowden Affair and the Blurring of Commercial and Security Data Exchanges

In 2013, the transatlantic privacy debate was dramatically reshaped by Edward Snowden's revelations. A former national security employee and contractor with access to top-secret documents, Snowden released information to the world about a number of surveillance programs, including surveillance by the NSA. These revelations documented how the US national intelligence community monitored electronic communication domestically and globally.

The most important consequence of these revelations for EU-US relations was that they highlighted the extent to which US rules clashed with European ones. This had not gone entirely unnoticed before Snowden. Caspar Bowden, who had cofounded the Foundation for Information Policy Research and had later been appointed chief privacy adviser for Microsoft, called out the ways in which FISA requests made by the US national intelligence community endangered the privacy of European and non-US citizens. In a series of speeches between 2011 and 2013, Bowden sought to highlight the contradiction between EU laws protecting citizens' privacy and US laws allowing mass surveillance of non-US citizens, but to little avail. An increasingly embittered Bowden (2014) concluded afterward that only the Greens in the European Parliament were "helpful"; other audiences (including NGOs, privacy officials, technical experts, and politicians) were uninterested or nonresponsive, and in one case actually laughed at his arguments.

After the Snowden revelations, no one was laughing. The documents demonstrated in compelling detail how commercial flows of information to the United States might have unexpected consequences for privacy and security.[47] European civil liberty groups were especially troubled by accounts of the NSA's PRISM program. Under this program, the NSA was able to monitor the internet traffic of many of the largest information technology companies and had access to a significant amount of data maintained by the companies. While the US administration argued that use of the data was limited to targeted searches, many feared that the program included indiscriminate collection, leading to much controversy, especially given the noninituitive ways in which terms like *bulk collection* and *targeting* were used by the US intelligence community. Equally troubling, information technology companies claimed that they had no knowledge of the data collection, leading to allegations that the NSA had direct access to the physical networks underlying the internet. Regardless, major internet platform companies found themselves trapped between rules governing surveillance data sharing such as the US FISA law, and rules governing commercial data sharing such as the Safe Harbor Agreement and European privacy laws.

The United States' initial response did little to assuage Europeans. President Obama, looking to reassure Americans that their privacy was not being invaded, stressed that PRISM surveillance "does not apply to U.S. citizens and it does not apply to people living in the United States."[48] This statement provided scant comfort to those who failed to enjoy either of these specific privileges, and spurred considerable alarm among US allies as well as global e-commerce companies that were exposed to the unhappiness of customers and regulators in other countries.[49]

The evidence suggested that US intelligence was undermining the privacy of EU citizens by accessing data flows both within and outside the United States. It was the former that was more politically relevant. It was nearly impossible for EU authorities to prevent US surveillance of data outside US borders, even if it had wanted to, since this fell into the legal gray zone of spying and surveillance. Furthermore, EU spying agencies often tacitly or actively supported the efforts of the United States to engage in large-scale surveillance both because they hoped to benefit from it too and because they feared being cut off from other actionable intelligence if they did not accommodate US efforts.

Of course, EU intelligence and policing agencies also engaged in surveillance, both of their own citizens and of the citizens of other EU member states. Data flows to the United States were a different matter, however, even if they were possibly less invasive. Paradoxically, it was more difficult for EU actors who were dissatisfied with the post–September 11 security arrangements to address surveillance activities within the European Union than outside it. Surveillance by European states was difficult to address in the context of the European Union's treaties, while US surveillance was conventional espionage by a third party and hence not protected by EU law.[50]

If surveillance used data that had left the European Union and entered the United States through commercial channels, there was a possible opening to be exploited by privacy activists and privacy officials. Two European

Commission studies tasked with evaluating the Snowden documents found that US government agencies had widespread access to the personal information of European citizens stored on the databases of US companies.[51] Additionally, they found that European citizens had no clear mechanism to seek redress for any possible abuse of the use of such data.

This had obvious implications for Safe Harbor. As Reding pungently put it, reversing her previous support for the agreement, Safe Harbor "might not be so safe after all," and instead might be a "loophole" that allowed companies to move data to the United States, where "data protection standards are lower than our European ones."[52] Previously, there had been no effective basis for challenging information exchange between the European Union and United States. Now the Snowden revelations highlighted how this commercial exchange facilitated wide-scale surveillance.

Together, these led the European Commission to press for revisions to Safe Harbor. In July 2013, the European Commission announced that it was reviewing Safe Harbor. German Data Protection Commissioners (2013) soon piled on further pressure, arguing that "intelligence services constitute a massive threat to data traffic between Germany and countries outside Europe." The commissioners specifically noted that the European Commission had always said that it would suspend the transfer of data under Safe Harbor and standard contractual clauses (another data transfer mechanism) if there was a "substantial likelihood" that the Safe Harbor Principles or standard contractual clauses were being violated, and then stated that "this was now the case," calling on the Commission to "suspend" the Safe Harbor until further notice. They further suggested that companies sending personal data to the United States "bear the responsibility" for ensuring that the data were not subject to large-scale surveillance, intimating that they might take direct action against recalcitrant businesses themselves should the Commission fail to act.

In its report, issued in November of the same year, the European Commission (2013b) was obliged to conclude that "Safe Harbour also acts as a conduit for the transfer of the personal data of EU citizens from the EU to the US by companies required to surrender data to US intelligence agencies under the US intelligence collection programmes." It argued that "revocation [of Safe Harbor] would adversely affect the interests of member companies in the EU and in the US," recommending instead that the Safe Harbor Agreement be strengthened and stating that the Commission would engage with the United States "as a matter of urgency" to conclude negotiations by June 2014. Improvements to Safe Harbor should then address the structural shortcomings related to transparency and enforcement, the substantive Safe Harbor principles, and the operation of the national security exception. The European Commission (2013b) also noted,

> US President Obama has announced a review of US national security authorities' activities, including of the applicable legal framework. This on-going process provides an important opportunity to address EU concerns raised by recent revelations about US intelligence collection programmes. The most important changes would be extending the safe-guards available to US citizens and residents to EU citizens not resident in the US, increased transparency of intelligence activities, and further strengthening oversight. Such changes would restore trust in EU-US data exchanges, and promote the use of Internet services by Europeans.

This led to a series of initial negotiations between the European Union and United States focused on reforming Safe Harbor, albeit with less alacrity than the Commission had at first hoped. Commission negotiators saw this as an opportunity to update an instrument that had not kept pace with rapid developments in technology and their use.[53] They also hoped to raise the question of national security agencies' access to data collected under Safe Harbor. The original Safe Harbor text had said that the principles could be derogated "to the extent necessary to meet national security, public interest, or law enforcement requirements."[54] The EU side interpreted this as requiring that national security agencies had access to EU citizens' data exported under Safe Harbor only when strictly necessary and proportionate. In the words of one negotiator,

> On top of it . . . came the Snowden revelation which raised the issue of interpretation of the famous provision that said "yes, public authorities can access data transferred under the old Safe Harbor including for national security purposes when strictly necessary." The Snowden revelation, to say the least, raised questions on compliance with this necessity test.[55]

As described by a former US official,

> Before Snowden, the conversation was improving with DG Justice. There was a sense that their institutions and ours were working in similar directions. . . . [A]t least among key decision makers in the Parliament and other people who were paying attention, we were making some

headway, and getting them to understand US protections. . . . That was really undone by the Snowden revelations.[56]

It proved extremely difficult, however, to get national security agencies in the United States—the responsible parties—to take negotiations with an outside trading partner seriously. Cameron Kerry (2016), the key official liaising with the European Union on privacy-related issues during the initial period, complained that "blinkered decision making" by national security officials prevented a broad spectrum response to the Snowden revelations, which might have incorporated trade and other concerns. Interviews with US officials confirm that interactions between the US Department of Commerce and the US intelligence community over Safe Harbor and related issues were often frustrating for the former.[57] As a result, EU negotiators had little success in pressing the United States to make any explicit commitments on the national security aspects of Safe Harbor, let alone provide mechanisms of accountability.

Soon after the Commission's report, the United States released a Presidential Policy Directive, PPD-28, that was widely interpreted as an effort to soothe the anger of allies in the European Union and elsewhere at indiscriminate US surveillance. The directive stated that "privacy and civil liberties shall be integral considerations in the planning of U.S. signals intelligence activities." It further mandated that US signals intelligence must "include appropriate safeguards for the personal information of all individuals, regardless of the nationality of the individual to whom the information pertains or where that individual resides," and laid out restrictions on the ways in which data collected through bulk surveillance could be used.[58] PPD-28 was intended to reassure allies, most notably within the European Union, whose populations were unhappy at the revelations that they had likely been subjected to mass surveillance.

From the US perspective, and especially from the perspective of the US intelligence community, PPD-28 marked a significant and indeed unprecedented concession. US intelligence agencies were not used to having their activities trammeled by foreign privacy sensitivities. Nonetheless, it took the form of a unilateral US policy document, which could be revoked by future administrations and did not provide any mechanisms for external actors to exercise accountability. Moreover, "bulk" surveillance was a term of art, which excluded "targeted" forms of surveillance where the targeting could be broad indeed.[59] This meant that European privacy officials and activists were sure to be dissatisfied with it. Some European data officials wanted a more radical approach. When the European Parliament's Committee on Civil Liberties, Justice, and Home Affairs held an inquiry into the revelations, then European Data Protection Supervisor Peter Hustinx argued that

> we have the chance to turn a crisis into opportunity and use it to our advantage. E.U. Data Protection Regulation has to be stronger and applicable to all companies processing data of E.U. citizens. . . . All data flows must be aligned with E.U. law; we cannot accept a distinction between U.S. and non-U.S. citizens which leaves the latter without any legal protections. It is a "now or never" time to make a stand.[60]

European parliamentarian Jan Philipp Albrecht put it even more bluntly: "The EU cannot continue to remain silent in the face of these ongoing revelations: it gives the impression we are little more than a lap dog of the United States."[61]

The United States furthermore made concessions to the European Union on the stalled question of judicial redress under the Umbrella Agreement. In March 2015, bipartisan bills were introduced in both the House and Senate to implement legislation that would extend the judicial redress provisions enjoyed by US citizens under the 1974 Privacy Act so that they covered citizens of countries or regional organizations such as the European Union, where the United States had entered into relevant agreements.

The Schrems Case and the Unraveling of the Transnational Agreement

While negotiations were taking place between the European Union and United States on security data, a different and ultimately highly consequential legal process was getting under way in Ireland. In the wake of Safe Harbor, Ireland had established a comfortable economic niche hosting the European operations of major US e-commerce and online platform companies like Google, Facebook, and Microsoft. Ireland offered significant tax advantages for US businesses that wanted to keep their profits overseas. Moreover, it provided a highly flexible interpretation of EU privacy rules, taking advantage of the directive to attract US businesses that wanted to locate in Europe but were unenthused by the prospect of overly vigorous enforcement of privacy law. The Irish Data Protection Commissioner was notoriously underfunded (its office was located in a provincial town where it shared a building with a supermarket) and complaisant. While favorable tax treatment was important to attracting businesses, flexibility on privacy was too; Google, for example, privately told Irish officials that "the strength of a country's competent authority for data privacy was now as important an issue for a country's competitive edge as its competent authority for taxation."[62]

This meant that Ireland became critical for political battles over how US e-commerce businesses, which for legal purposes were usually based in Ireland, were gathering personal information on EU citizens. Schrems, a young Austrian lawyer and privacy advocate, made a particular practice of using European data privacy law to make life difficult both for Facebook and for the Irish data privacy authority that supposedly oversaw it.[63] Like many other European privacy activists, Max Schrems saw US e-commerce firms as undermining European privacy law. He was committed to pushing back against them so as to restore the existing institutional balance. As Schrems described it, the fundamental problem was that a clash between European and US laws meant that the latter were undermining the former:

> We have two jurisdictions that are in part not compatible with each other. The solution up to now has been that Europe didn't enforce its fundamental rights. It's as if the U.S. said we're not going to enforce our law anymore. If you're an international company, you just have to deal with it somehow. It's going to be hard. It would be wonderful to have an agreement between the two parties to resolve the situation, but I'm fed up with the solution being just sticking to U.S. law and ignoring European law. If you're doing business in a different country, you have to follow the law, just as Volkswagen is facing huge issues in the U.S. with its emissions scandal.[64]

Hence Schrems's primary goal was to find ways to insulate European institutions against the encroachment of US rules and practices through the Trojan horse of the Safe Harbor Agreement, even when this involved attacking and weakening the accommodations that the European Union and United States had previously reached.

When Schrems heard about the Snowden revelations, he quickly realized that he could make a plausible case that Facebook, by transporting users' information from the European Union to the United States, was in violation of European law. He could use the information provided by Snowden to link the commercial and security debates, and hence gain access to legal and regulatory opportunity structures that had hitherto been closed off. The

European legal system provides ample opportunities for private actors to pursue litigation as a means toward policy change.[65]

> I thought that's actually something where Europe has jurisdiction, since this mass surveillance only works in public-private partnership, because the NSA's not going to be in every phone. . . . [Y]ou actually have a point where you can actually hit them, where you have jurisdiction and at least a remote possibility that someone could possible care about it.[66]

Schrems initially sought relief from Ireland's data privacy agency, which supervised Facebook and other major US e-commerce firms, expecting a lengthy investigation and drawn-out battle in the Irish system. In July 2013, the Irish Data Protection Commissioner declined to open an investigation, stating that Facebook had met its obligations for data export since it was registered under the Safe Harbor Agreement and noting that there were political efforts under way to resolve the surveillance issue.[67] Schrems then applied to the Irish High Court for adjudication on the question of whether or not the Irish Data Protection Commissioner was obliged to open an investigation into the possibility that Facebook was exposing EU citizens to a privacy breach by exporting their data through Safe Harbor to a jurisdiction where it could be readily accessed by the NSA. This allowed him to open a line of attack on the Commission's ability to make political deals that undermined European privacy law. Since the Irish data privacy authority claimed that its freedom of action was preempted by the Commission's adequacy finding on Safe Harbor, Schrems could challenge the status of the adequacy ruling and of the Commission's competence to make determinations that arguably watered down EU privacy laws.

Notably, both Facebook and the US government declined to state any interest in the proceedings.[68] This had crucial consequences; it meant that the eventual ruling reflected Schrems's and other privacy advocates' understanding of the factual record of surveillance. Justice Gerard Hogan, the presiding judge, noted that the accuracy of many of the Snowden revelations were "not in dispute" and stated that

> I will therefore proceed on the basis that personal data transferred by companies such as Facebook Ireland to its parent company in the United States is thereafter capable of being accessed by the NSA in the course of a mass and indiscriminate surveillance of such data. Indeed, in the wake

of the Snowden revelations, the available evidence presently admits of no other realistic conclusion. . . . [Furthermore, the] Snowden revelations demonstrate a massive overreach of the security authorities, with an almost studied indifference to the interests of ordinary citizens. Their data protection rights have been seriously compromised by mass and largely unsupervised surveillance programmes.

Hogan then referred to the specific matter under dispute: whether the Irish Data Privacy Commissioner was bound by the Commission's adequacy ruling that Safe Harbor was working as designed or alternatively should open an investigation as Schrems requested to the European Court of Justice, which serves as the final arbiter on how European law ought to be interpreted. He suggested to the European Court of Justice that it should consider the matter in light of the European Union's Charter of Fundamental Rights and specifically its provision protecting privacy, noting that it was "not immediately apparent" how the Safe Harbor Agreement could satisfy the requirements of this article, especially given a recent European Court of Justice ruling (known as *Digital Rights Ireland*).[69]

The European Court of Justice Steps In

The European Court of Justice responded to the Irish court's request for a clarification of EU law on privacy and the Commission's responsibilities with remarkable alacrity. In initial hearings in March 2015, the Irish data privacy authority argued that the Commission's Safe Harbor decision should be allowed to stand, receiving support from the European Commission and United Kingdom, but encountering opposition from Belgium, Austria, Poland, Slovenia, and the European Parliament and European Data Protection Supervisor. Questioning from the Court's Advocate General (who prepares an initial recommendation on cases) and the presiding judge revealed a considerable degree of skepticism about Ireland and the European Commission's position, in part because of uncertainty over whether the United States would indeed address the key flaws in Safe Harbor.[70] This skepticism informed both the Advocate General's initial recommendation, which made some strong and empirically questionable assertions about US surveillance, and the more carefully worded yet nearly equally stringent final ruling, which emerged a few weeks later.[71]

In its ruling, the Court found that Safe Harbor provided grossly inadequate protections for the privacy of European citizens given that national security, public interest and law enforcement requirements of the United States prevail over the safe harbour scheme, so that United States undertakings are bound to disregard, without limitation, the protective rules laid down by that scheme were they to conflict with such requirements. The United States safe harbour scheme enables interference, by United States public authorities, with the fundamental rights of persons.[72]

In other words, the protections apparently provided by Safe Harbor were irrelevant. US national security law obliged US businesses to provide information, even when supplying it interfered with the fundamental rights of European citizens, as laid out in the Charter that serves the European Union in lieu of a constitution. Importantly, the Court found that the oversight requirements agreed to in the Safe Harbor arrangement could not be met because of the institutional mismatch: the FTC lacks jurisdiction over the public sector actors conducting the surveillance.

Hence the European Court of Justice created additional hurdles for intelligence sharing. The original Safe Harbor Agreement contained standard language that exempted "necessary" law enforcement and intelligence-sharing activity. In the decision, the Court ruled that this exemption did not trump European law or fundamental rights. In particular, it stressed that third countries must guarantee that they have equivalent data privacy policies in place through their domestic law. More specifically, exemptions for national security must still meet key privacy principles such as the proportionality of data collected and the clear ability to remedy abuse. As the European Court of Justice (2015a, 25) concluded,

Protection of the fundamental right to respect for private life at EU level requires derogations and limitations in relation to the protection of personal data to apply only in so far as is strictly necessary. . . . [L]egislation permitting the public authorities to have access on a generalised basis to the content of electronic communications must be regarded as compromising the essence of the fundamental right to respect for private life, as guaranteed by Article 7 of the Charter. . . . Likewise, legislation not providing for any possibility for an individual to pursue legal remedies in order to have access to personal data relating to him, or to obtain the rectification or erasure of such data, does not respect the essence of the fundamental right to effective judicial protection, as enshrined in Article 47 of the Charter.

The court decision narrowed the window of acceptable exemptions for national security purposes and at the same time increased the scope of its own purview over such issues, ruling out international arrangements that trampled on the right to privacy and failed to provide any means for recourse or remedy for violation.

This further empowered the Court and European data privacy authorities to scrutinize adequacy decisions pertaining to third countries. Prior to the court decision, the Commission would evaluate the privacy protections of other countries, receive input from data privacy authorities, and make an adequacy decision. All actors had hitherto assumed that these decisions were binding and that other institutional actors could not challenge them. The Court ruled that even after the negotiation of such agreements, citizens can bring complaints to data privacy authorities regarding the legitimacy of international data transfers. In the European Court of Justice (2015b) press release's words, "The existence of a Commission decision finding that a third country ensures an adequate level of protection of the personal data transferred cannot eliminate or even reduce the powers available to the national supervisory authorities under the Charter of Fundamental Rights of the European Union and the directive." Moreover, the Court made it clear that the Court and not the Commission is the final arbiter of such decision: "It is thus ultimately the Court of Justice which has the task of deciding whether or not a Commission decision [concerning third-country adequacy] is valid."

This ruling completely changed the power relationship between actors arguing over EU privacy and the transatlantic agenda. Previously, the policy agenda had been dominated by the actors with access to transatlantic negotiation channels: the European Commission, and through the European Commission, the member states that it was responsible to under a so-called comitology procedure. Other actors—such as privacy activists, the data privacy authorities, and privacy friendly MEPs in the European Parliament—had only indirect influence, although the Parliament's influence had increased significantly as it acquired new veto powers. Now the Commission's ability to make binding decisions via adequacy determinations had been substantially undermined. Actors who wanted to insulate EU rules from outside influence—such as activists and activist data privacy authorities—could challenge Commission determinations in front of judges who appeared highly sympathetic to privacy concerns.

The Consequences of the Ruling for Transatlantic Relations

The European Court of Justice decision had dramatic consequences for transatlantic markets and politics, establishing a new reversion point for EU officials and rule makers, and creating radical uncertainty as to the legitimacy of data transfers outside the European Union absent some compromise. US Department of Commerce secretary Penny Pritzker (2015) warned that the dispute could "put at risk the thriving transatlantic digital economy," costing US firms billions. Microsoft president Brad Smith (2015) feared that such fragmentation of the internet threatened a "digital dark ages" that could undermine digital services ranging from payment systems to airline reservations. Alphabet (the parent company of Google) chair Eric Schmidt went so far as to claim that the dispute jeopardized "one of the greatest achievements of humanity."[73]

While these warnings were hyperbolic, they reflected a genuinely far-reaching change in the politics of transatlantic privacy. US officials were initially in shock. As described by one former official,

> Things went seriously backward with Snowden. They started gradually improving because of a variety of things—the passing of time, the realization of double standards that the Europeans were applying, the steps that the United States took to be more transparent about its surveillance, revealing more about the process and the limits that had been in place, as well as putting new limits in place, primarily through Presidential Policy Directive 28. All of that was moving things back in a more positive direction, getting them to where they were. I think that the atmosphere in the wake of Schrems has been at least as bad as the atmosphere in the wake of Snowden. I think that it was probably not as widespread in the headlines and popular outrage, but it has a far more direct and immediate impact.[74]

US officials believed that the European Court of Justice had gotten the facts wrong, and was basing its ruling on an understanding of US privacy law and practice that was both incorrect and badly out of date, given post-Snowden reforms. A variety of prominent US actors had already complained that the Advocate General's opinion rested on what the US Mission to the European Union (2015) described as "numerous inaccurate assertions about intelligence practices of the United States."[75] Given that the European Court of Justice does not rule on findings of fact (leaving those to lower courts) but rather only on interpretation of EU law, the United States had missed its opportunity to engage in debate over what the United States did or did not do by declining to intervene in the Irish High Court action.

The Department of Commerce, anxious to address business fears of legal uncertainty, announced immediately that it would work with the European Commission to reach a revised Safe Harbor deal as soon as possible.[76] It was initially unclear how a deal might be achieved. The European Court of Justice appeared to be demanding a radical change in how US surveillance and intelligence dealt with data on European citizens, obliging US practices to conform to EU standards of accountability and transparency. The US intelligence community was unenthused at this prospect.

Early US efforts focused on trying to persuade the European Union that the court ruling was incorrect and that existing US efforts were in fact sufficient to provide adequate protection to European citizens. Former administration privacy official Peter Swire (2015), working with the Future of Privacy Forum, a transatlantic group that had already sought to reconcile European and US approaches, released a white paper arguing that US laws indeed provided "fundamentally equivalent" privacy protections to those offered by Europe. Daniel Sepulveda, the US coordinator for international communications and information policy, announced that there would be no change in US law, and that the "underlying evidence that [the Court used] to reach the conclusion that intelligence practices are excessive in the United States is fundamentally and demonstratively [*sic*] wrong."[77]

European negotiators swiftly made it clear that this was insufficient and that a deal that might have addressed the commercial aspects of Safe Harbor while leaving the national security questions for later discussion was politically impossible.[78] The Court decision created as many problems as it did opportunities for Commission negotiators, who now had to satisfy the requirements of a complex court decision, which furthermore empowered the more activist data privacy commissioners to take up actions before the Court. Indeed, in the short term, data privacy commissioners had considerable bargaining power vis-à-vis US firms since the Safe Harbor arrangement was no longer considered adequate. This meant that they could introduce enforcement actions at their discretion against US firms that had previously relied on Safe Harbor, and now were forced either to consider cumbersome and time-consuming alternative arrangements (which were themselves likely also vulnerable to challenges in the European Court of Justice), or to continue carrying out data transfers without any legal basis and just hope for the best. In any event, the Article 29 Working Party of data privacy commissioners agreed to hold off on regulatory action to allow negotiators a chance to come up with an alternative arrangement— but only until the end of January 2016. Although US negotiators publicly claimed that this deadline was "meaningless," they recognized that data privacy authorities could make life uncomfortable for US companies if negotiators ignored it.[79]

On the European side, the most important consequence of the Schrems ruling was to increase the clout of national-level privacy actors who had previously often not had a seat at the table. In the description of one commission negotiator,

> There was clearly a pre- and post-Schrems judgment. I felt as a negotiator, that there was much more solidarity and cohesion amongst the EU after the Schrems judgment. That's not because people all of a sudden fell in love with data protection. But it was objectivized in a certain sense. There were requirements, criteria to meet. . . . What also had an important role to play was public opinion. I think that these issues in the last 2, 3, 4 years became much more relevant and could not only be approached from an economic trade point of view. That also has an impact on governments and that is also probably why in the national decision making process, other views such as the views of the ministry of justice, the views from the DPAs, came probably to have more weight.[80]

Notably, the European Court of Justice ruling required that any arrangement provide roughly "equivalent" protections to European privacy rules. This resulted in both a high benchmark and opportunities for data privacy authorities, as the expert actors charged with interpreting and administering European privacy rules, to interpret how that benchmark should be administered.

For the US side, the most important consequence was to render the European Union's position more inflexible on just the points that Department of Commerce negotiators were least capable of making concessions on. New actors, most prominently involving Robert Litt, the general counsel for the Director of National Intelligence, became directly involved in negotiations. In later comments, Litt (2016) acknowledged that it was odd for a national security official to be involved in negotiations over a commercial agreement and depicted his role as enabling a "process of education" in which he helped EU officials learn about the legal regime that governs the US collection of surveillance data.[81]

Forging the Privacy Shield

A replacement for Safe Harbor, the so-called Privacy Shield, was announced on February 2, 2016, even though the text was not fully agreed on until some weeks later, prompting the accusation from some EU-based privacy activists that the Commission had caved in and accepted a vaguely worded deal because it needed the negotiations to appear successful.[82] The final arrangement was, like the original deal, an exchange of letters based primarily on political commitments and the implicit threat that if the deal did not work out, it could be revoked by either side. The new agreement involved some concessions from the United States. It provided a more transparent and robust monitoring and enforcement regime for transatlantic data transfers, gave European data privacy authorities the authority to follow up on unresolved complaints with the FTC and the Department of Commerce, and put in place clear sanctions for noncompliance as well as a dispute settlement mechanism. On questions of national security, the United States made fewer concessions, instead incorporating a letter in which Litt laid out the protections that the United States already provided to EU citizens. Nearly simultaneously with the deal, the US Congress passed the Judicial Redress Act, which was meant to provide the necessary redress to allow the parallel Umbrella Agreement to be ratified. Last-minute amendments meant that the act's protections were effectively made conditional on the European Union's agreement to and continued participation in a replacement for Safe Harbor.

The most important security innovation was the introduction of an ombudsman position, thus allowing EU citizens who felt that their privacy had been compromised by US intelligence measures to complain to an official. While the European Union had strongly pressed for the ombudsman position to be held by a representative of EU intelligence services, whom commission negotiators argued would both have the necessary independence and be trusted by both sides, the US side refused to provide foreign officials with any oversight role over sensitive US intelligence operations, leaving the definition of the ombudsman's role and office vague in the initial text.[83]

The deal—or more precisely, the fact that there was a deal, regardless of its specific implications for intelligence relations—prompted considerable relief within the US business community, although that relief was dampened by fears that the deal might not prove politically viable over the longer term.[84] As the details of the arrangement became more apparent, it became obvious that the business community's nervousness was justified.

European data privacy officials and the European Parliament were far less enthusiastic about the agreement. German data privacy officials in particular were quite skeptical about the deal, suggesting that it needed to be sent back to the drawing board.[85] In April 2016, the Article 29 Working Party released a statement regarding the deficiencies of the proposed Privacy Shield.[86] On the one hand, the group criticized the proposed redress and transparency mechanisms for the private sector as too vague, putting pressure on the Commission to further strengthen the monitoring and enforcement of the private sector over and above the original Safe Harbor. On the other hand, it cast doubt on the new safeguards against security abuses. Here the Article 29 Working Party focused on the fact that the commitments offered by national security officials were voluntary rather than legally binding (e.g., the director of national intelligence's pledge to limit mass surveillance) and that the independence of the proposed ombudsperson was questionable.

On May 30, European Data Protection Supervisor (2016) Giovanni Buttarelli concluded, "The Privacy Shield as it stands is not robust enough to withstand future legal scrutiny before the Court. Significant improvements are needed should the European Commission wish to adopt an adequacy decision, to respect the essence of key data privacy principles with particular regard to necessity, proportionality and redress mechanisms. Moreover, it's time to develop a longer term solution in the transatlantic dialogue."

Also in May, the European Parliament (2016) adopted a resolution by 501 to 119 votes, with 31 abstentions, claiming that the agreement was deficient because it did not properly address bulk surveillance, failed to provide for a truly independent ombudsman, and had an overly complicated mechanism for redress.[87] Some member states—most prominently Austria—were also quite skeptical of the deal, leading to delays in member state approval as commission negotiators sought further concessions from the US side.[88] Much of the skepticism focused on the independence of the proposed ombudsman mechanism.[89] Although the United States was unwilling to make large concessions, it offered a compromise under which the ombudsman would be a high official within the US Department of State and would not be a member of the intelligence community. This official would work with existing protective institutions within the US intelligence community—e.g., inspectors general and the like—to resolve problems and to report back in extremely nonspecific terms. This proved sufficient for the member states to approve the deal, with Austria, Bulgaria, Croatia, and Slovenia abstaining. The member states in their deliberations also fixed on the idea of a centralized EU arrangement for dealing with complaints to the ombudsman, perhaps linked to the European Data Protection Board, which was to be set up under new data privacy regulations.[90]

The Commission officials who negotiated the Privacy Shield defended it as protecting the privacy of European citizens in general and in particular as having set up a genuinely novel institutional mechanism for providing accountability for international surveillance. In the words of Commission negotiators,

> This goes far beyond what PPD-28 has foreseen because that was exactly the idea that one would only have this government-to-government exchange, and this goes far beyond that, and only for our context, which needs to be better appreciated by some people in Europe. . . . It is something that over time hopefully will develop into something through the constant contact. It will probably create on our end a centralized body. The complaints will be received in a decentralized way but centralized in a body that the text foresees as a probability and that will probably happen. That body will be the interlocutor of the ombudsperson and over time will hopefully develop a certain working relationship.[91]

Critics of the deal continue to believe that it does not go nearly far enough in insulating US citizens from the surveillance of US intelligence agencies. One NGO began a court action before the European Court of Justice pressing for the arrangement to be declared invalid, while Johannes Caspar, the data privacy commissioner for Hamburg and a persistent critic of transatlantic data exchanges, threatened a challenge under forthcoming German legislation.[92]

The failure of the United States fully to comply with the terms of Privacy Shield is creating further pressures on the agreement.[93] As of September 2018, the Trump administration has failed to appoint an ombudsperson, and has left vacancies on the Privacy and Civil Liberties Oversight Board, leading the European Commission to threaten to suspend the agreement in the wake of pressure from the European Parliament. The unwillingness of the United States to deliver on its side of the bargain, together with general European distrust of and hostility toward the Trump administration, adds to the controversy surrounding an already-unpopular agreement.

Most worrying for firms dependent on transatlantic data exchange, Schrems filed a second complaint against Facebook with the Irish Data Protection Commissioner. This compliant shifted the focus from the Safe Harbor Agreement to standard contractual clauses, a core legal instrument that multinational firms frequently employ to transfer data into and out of the European Union.

This court action seems likely to provoke a second wave of crisis and response. The Irish Data Privacy Commissioner found in early 2018 that the standard contractual clauses used by Facebook do not adequately protect European citizens, owing to the limits of US privacy and national security law.[94] Rather than invalidating such clauses outright, the Irish Data Privacy Commissioner referred the case to the Irish High Court, which in turn has referred the case to the European Court of Justice.[95] In doing so, the Irish High Court laid out eleven questions regarding the legality of transatlantic data sharing, thereby indicating a high bar for arrangements such as the Privacy Shield. Notably, the Irish Court suggested that the "mass, indiscriminate processing of data" was taking place in the United States, and specifically asked the European Court of Justice to rule on whether the Privacy Shield was binding under EU law and whether the Privacy Shield's ombudsperson system was sufficient. While the outcome of the case is still uncertain, it highlights how rule overlap opened up domestic institutional possibilities to privacy actors as they seek to use domestic political institutions to insulate themselves from transnational strategies.[96]

Conclusions

The transatlantic struggle over privacy and commercial data transfers has changed dramatically since the Snowden revelations of 2013. The first Safe Harbor was built by EU and US negotiators, who sought to use transatlantic negotiations to defend and, if possible, extend their respective domestic arrangements. They did this by creating a new kind of international institution that would serve as an interface between two different national privacy systems. Each side saw the Safe Harbor as a means to mitigate the pressure stemming from the other jurisdiction's rules and effectively placed a bet: that the Safe Harbor Agreement would, over time, undermine domestic practices and institutions in the other's jurisdiction rather than in theirs.

While Safe Harbor did not directly threaten European privacy rules, it opened a channel through which US platform companies dominated European markets and began to build their own transatlantic standards. For years, civil liberties advocates had little recourse as they watched US companies engage in business practices that they viewed as threatening basic European rights. The Snowden revelations upended the dynamic as they exposed and made politically salient the rule overlap between rules governing commercial data sharing and security data sharing. The

Schrems case weaponized this clash in an effort to insulate European privacy protections from continuing encroachment by US firms and US surveillance practices.

Now, US and EU negotiators are not the only important actors. They face pushback from different actors—NGOs, privacy advocates, and data privacy authorities—with different goals and different access to the international arena. European privacy activists not only have no direct access to transatlantic negotiations but are primarily organized at the national level.[97] This is why they are less interested in a strategy of defend and extend than in one of insulating European (and sometimes national) institutional arrangements from transnational pressures. The same is true of data privacy commissioners, whose mandate in their individual capacity is to protect the citizens of specific EU countries or (in Germany) federal states, and in their collective capacity is to interpret and protect the European privacy regime.

The Schrems case has substantially strengthened activists and data privacy authorities at the expense of the Commission and state ministries that might have preferred to reach deals with the United States. By allowing activists and data privacy authorities to challenge the Commission's adequacy determinations in court, the case makes it much easier for these activists and officials to insulate European arrangements from external pressure. Over time, privacy advocates in Europe are likely to target transnational arrangements beyond Safe Harbor and its successor(s). On July 26, 2017, the European Court of Justice ruled that a PNR data agreement with Canada violated key provisions of European law.[98] It is highly likely that activists will look to build on this precedent by challenging the EU-US PNR and SWIFT agreements, and perhaps the Umbrella Agreement too.

The Schrems case also demonstrates the importance of other political transformations associated with the age of interdependence. Snowden used global information channels to ensure general distribution for the documents that he accessed, also leveraging different jurisdictions to make it impossible for any one government to block publication. This information created the basis for the Schrems case, by showing how commercial privacy issues could be linked to those of domestic security.

As the second part of this chapter described, civil-liberties-oriented actors are using opportunity structures such as the European Court of Justice to insulate domestic rules that they favored, limiting and disrupting transnational data-sharing agreements. Their ability to engage and take advantage of transnational opportunity structures themselves has been comparatively limited.

This may be starting to change. In the wake of the 2018 Cambridge An-alytica scandal, where a company used Facebook data to secretly build up extensive profiles for political purposes, privacy actors too may be seeking to exploit interdependence to press their case. Cambridge Analytica ac-cessed hundreds of millions of US consumers' data without explicit con-sent. Because the company was based in Britain, the processing of these data falls under European law. US professor of media design David Carroll has thus sought to use UK and European law to find out what Cambridge Analytica was doing with these data of US citizens, who have little effective recourse against commercial data use in their own jurisdiction. In May 2018, the UK Information Commissioner ruled that Cambridge Analytica, under UK data privacy law, had to comply with the information request by US citizens, opening up a historic legal precedent for US consumers.[99] As interdependence increases, it may also be possible for actors who are denied access to the usual venues of cross-national negotiation to exploit interdependence for their political advantage. We return to this question in the final chapter.

The long-term trajectory of the transatlantic commercial data ex-change is again uncertain. Many legal observers—including some in the Commission—predicted from the beginning that the Privacy Shield was unlikely to survive legal challenge before the European Court of Justice. A ruling against the Privacy Shield would lead to renewed turmoil, in which, again, activists and privacy officials would plausibly play a leading role in shaping the EU response.

This nicely illustrates the ways in which the most crucial causal mecha-nism described in our book has come to change the world. The debate over privacy and security has been interpreted by many as a fight between Europe and the United States, but has in fact not been contained within national borders. Europe is not a monolithic entity dedicated to protecting privacy. Instead, there is an ongoing struggle within Europe between more privacy- and more security-oriented actors, each looking to take advantage of the political opportunity structures generated by economic interdependence to press their objectives or blunt the efforts of their opponents. As this chapter demonstrates, privacy actors increasingly understand the limits of fighting only national battles and are now turning to domestic political institutions to shield European privacy rules against the transatlantic campaign of those seeking to press for greater security.

Conclusion

INFORMATION, POWER, AND WORLD POLITICS

On April 10, 2018, Facebook CEO Mark Zuckerberg was forced to defend the firm's reputation before the US Senate. The company had rapidly and unexpectedly found itself ensnared in two apparently distinct but mutually reinforcing scandals that entwined US national security with the fundamental privacy rights of citizens. Both resulted from novel uses of Facebook's platform by foreign third parties in the run-up to the 2016 presidential election. Russian operatives used fake accounts, Facebook groups, and advertising to try to spread rumors as well as foster political and social division. While it is unclear how well they succeeded, successive revelations about their efforts (and Facebook's lethargic-to-nonexistent response) stirred up political furor.[1] Cambridge Analytica, a consulting firm based in the United Kingdom, and partly owned and backed by US billionaire Robert Mercer, took advantage of social media platforms to try to manipulate the information environment in the run-up to the 2016 presidential election, accessing the personal data of over fifty million US voters.[2]

These controversies illustrate two things. First, the cross-national information economy has become a crucial part of modern politics. For a long time, companies like Facebook or Google presented themselves as drifting high above the sordid realities of fights in Washington, Brussels, or Berlin. Yet pretty well every aspect of traditional politics—campaigning, lobbying, and efforts to shape public opinion—and of political economy is being profoundly reshaped by information technology.

Nor are the consequences of technology confined by national borders. Instead, these technologies are used within a complex system of global interactions in which companies, politicians, and privacy advocates engage in rule arbitrage. These actors exploit domestic laws when they can, but also take advantage of differences between national systems when they present themselves, lobbying and applying pressure to shape both domestic and international regulations, and exploiting the gaps between rules when it is to their advantage.

Second, the dynamics unleashed by cross-border information flows are radically redefining security, and sometimes in uncomfortable ways. For example, the US Department of Defense's (2017, 9) Task Force for Cyber Deterrence recently recommended that the United States should seek to deter "sustained campaigns to undermine U.S. . . . political institutions (e.g., elections), and social cohesion." This recommendation, presumably spurred by Russian influence campaigns, treats such campaigns as a traditional security threat. More or less the same tools and methods, however, could be employed by a domestic actor, and possibly were deployed by Cambridge Analytica and other such firms during the US general election. Are influence campaigns only a national security threat to be deterred when they are being run by adversarial states? Are they still a national security threat when they are mounted by private companies in allied countries? Are they a national security threat when they are deployed by US billionaires (and if so, how should they be distinguished from other forms of spending to influence the public)? What are the security implications for the transatlantic partners, for instance, if the Chinese firm Alibaba comes to dominate facial recognition software? Simultaneous rapid changes in information technology, combined with the ability of businesses to operate and transport personal data across national borders, are creating new and very difficult policy challenges. Many of these challenges involve the kind of internationalization of domestic security that the book focuses on.

The global nature of the information economy means that privacy policy faces similar dilemmas. What obligations, if any, do states have to protect the citizens of other countries? How do individuals get redress against foreign firms or national authorities that abuse their data? Should national governments or regulators that want to protect the privacy of their citizens be able to apply their rules extraterritorially? What happens when the firms holding vast amounts of data are located in authoritarian countries, which place less value on notions of privacy? In the wake of Zuckerberg's US testimony, he testified before the European Parliament. Facebook officials are being called to account as well before the UK Parliament. The information commissioner in the United Kingdom has ordered Cambridge Analytica to provide detailed data to a US citizen, who filed a complaint under UK data privacy laws.[3] And large US companies including Facebook and Microsoft have publicly stated that they will extend European-style privacy protections to US customers while quietly looking to maintain as much free action as they can.[4] Both privacy problems and proposed policy solutions have been transnationalized.

Questions of privacy, security, and information will be at the heart of many political battles over the next century as information has at last been politicized. Security officials, regulators, politicians, interest groups, NGOs, and citizens are increasingly engaged in controversies that will have enormous long-term implications for national and domestic security, the ability to enforce rules and to make them, the economic viability of entire industries, and the civil rights and personal interests of citizens.

Unfortunately, the political science discipline is poorly positioned to contribute to these debates. International relations scholars have paid remarkably little sustained attention to the international politics of information. While there is a somewhat-larger literature in comparative politics, it tends to emphasize the public policy aspects of governance more than it stresses the political controversies.[5]

A major finding of the book is that information technology is not a self-contained issue that can be consigned to a quiet backwater of interest only to specialists.[6] Instead, the proliferation of data, information exchange, and information processing are crucial to central scholarly debates, including those over the coercive power of the state, the management of terrorist threats, and the key conditions of economic development. *Of Privacy and Power*, then, calls scholars of political science to refocus their attention on the politics of information as core to the world order challenges that the discipline is meant to address.

Policy experts are more concerned with the urgent and topical, and hence more directly engaged with these issues. They too, however, lack road maps to guide them, let alone policy paradigms to provide them with actionable policy recommendations. It is increasingly clear that the anti-regulation approach of the United States and some other states is no longer politically viable, but no coherent alternative has succeeded in replacing it.

Transatlantic battles over security and privacy provide a microcosm of these broader tensions as well as a set of guidelines for how to study them. As we have argued, these battles were not simply a story of systems clash between Europe and the United States. Instead, they offer a window into an alternative framework for understanding international affairs under the banner of the NIA. Our account offers a detailed history of the struggle between security-oriented actors located across a range of government agencies (e.g., finance, interior, and foreign ministries) and more civil-liberties-oriented actors in NGOs, privacy regulation agencies, and courts. Before globalization, these struggles were largely contained within national borders. Now economic interdependence has generated political opportunities for these actors to reach out to allies across the Atlantic and press their interests. In the main body of *Of Privacy and Power*, we described and explained the specific actor strategies—defend and extend, cross-national layering, and insulation—that actors employed, given the varying opportunities open to them to influence transatlantic battles over freedom and security. We now devote the remaining pages of the book to thinking more broadly about the evolving nature of privacy challenges, information as a source of power, and how the NIA is transforming world politics.

Of Privacy . . .

The long-enduring political conflict over privacy has been transformed. Conventional fears of loss of privacy typically focus on the government. The state appears in these imaginings as long gray corridors of closed doors, behind each of which sits an anonymous bureaucrat surrounded by rows of filing cabinets, containing manila folders of documents on people's most intimate personal and political secrets. Such images and fears stemmed from the totalitarian experiences of the 1930s, and were the motor driving many of the post–World War II public policy responses. National laws focus on national government intrusions and national government data collection efforts. The US Privacy Act, which is limited to federal government data processing, offers the most extreme case, but many other privacy regulations across the globe implicitly concentrate on this threat rather than on others.

One central implication of our argument is that these Orwellian fears, while not exactly wrong, are grossly simplistic. We do not face any threat as specific as a Big Brother with centralized systems for listening to us through our television screens. Instead, we face something more complex and pervasive: an entire decentralized architecture of systems, some private, some public, some domestic, and some international, all gathering data on us, and intersecting in murky, complex, and sometimes-invisible ways.[7] The state is not gone; it still uses data to rationalize services, target political opponents, and go after criminals. But the world around the state has been radically transformed by the decentralized monitoring of internet browsing, the ubiquity of cell phones with altitude sensors and GPS that endlessly whisper information back to the mothership, vast banks of commercially available data, and machine-learning processes collating it all to search for traces and patterns that can be used to categorize information and predict behavior.[8] As governments across the Atlantic seek to globalize domestic security issues in this new world, they do not simply re-create the old fears but also transform them. They rent—or steal—commercial data, combining it with their own, and putting out large-scale analysis to for-profit firms such as Palantir. They surveil each others' citizens and their own, and share the resulting information with each other through publicly invisible channels of information exchange that often accidentally or deliberately circumvent mechanisms supposed to provide federal-level responsibility and account-ability. Academics and policy makers concerned with surveillance and pri-vacy must learn how to map this shifting transnational environment if they hope to engage with its consequences for politics. Political scientists working on the state need to understand how its basic functions from census taking to policing are being transformed as the line between public and private is washed away.

These transformations are the product of economic changes. Until the end of the 1970s, surveillance data were generated primarily by state service provision—welfare benefits, pensions, and health care—or state control—passports, drivers licenses, and criminal records—and were kept in paper files. With the advent of revolving consumer credit and credit cards, how-ever, individuals started leaving far richer traces of data about their everyday activities, which were visible to those with the right tools, like the trails of particle collisions in a cloud chamber.[9] As citizens have embraced social media and other platform economy applications, the data have gotten im-measurably better. The "likes," photos, and updates on health status that people provide as part of their social lives along with the data that they leave behind in the course of their everyday activities provide information that can be fed to the maws of the machine-learning systems that both analyze behavior and help companies manipulate it.[10] Whereas states used to have to demand that people provide data, consumers now voluntarily update and publicize risky behavior, including even highly intimate sexual encounters.

New forms of personally linked information are being collected, includ-ing both biometric and location data. Fingerprints and retina scans are in-creasingly being used by companies and governments to replace numerical identification systems. The Indian government biometric state ID, known as Aadhaar, covers over one billion people.[11] Smartphones and smart-tracking systems generate constant streams of precisely coded GPS data, which detail individual movements at specific points in time. Radio-frequency identification provides information about the movement of things. As facial recognition technology is layered on top of biometric and location information, surveillance is reaching new levels of sophistication. Machine-learning techniques feed on all these rich data and take advantage of new kinds of networked analysis, using the information to try to shape behavior, and learning more from how people do or do not respond to their manipulations.

While states still look to exploit information sharing for surveillance and control, they rely on private sector data collection efforts to do so. Political campaigns from Obama to Trump use microtargeting tactics based on merging commercially available consumer behavior information with voter and party behavior records. Banks, online retailers, and airline companies hold and process far more and better data today than governments could have possibly imagined having access to in a previous generation, potentially transforming the mandate of those who provide quantitative information for the government, such as its statistical agencies. The terms of privacy, then, often shift from managing state databases to managing state access to private sector databases. Additionally, the privatization of many state functions means that privacy risks including discrimination or manipulation can no longer be easily quarantined within the public sector, or treated as issues of "constitutional" privacy. This is compounded by the increasing role that business plays in modern politics whether because of the weakening of campaign financing laws in the United States, or the dominance of powerful commercial conglomerates in states ranging from Hungary to Russia.

As public and private surveillance have blurred into each other, so has the national and the global. While privacy policy debates in the 1970s and the 1980s considered data to be an important aspect of international trade, they could have hardly imagined how companies like Amazon, Apple, Facebook, and Google would dominate international markets. Increasingly, the most consequential and seemingly mundane information about a society and its governance, from traffic patterns to consumer spending, is kept by foreign companies.[12] As the book demonstrates, states do not simply look to domestic data sources to achieve surveillance goals. Instead, they reach out across jurisdictional borders to access data troves held by companies and governments in other countries. And increasingly, consumers turn to foreign courts and regulators to remedy abuse and fraud. The case of Cambridge

Analytica and the UK Information Commissioner is just one recent example of the growing push toward transnational and extraterritorial enforcement for the implementation of domestic data privacy rules.[13]

This is why this book sets out to spark conversation over how best to safeguard privacy in the context of global domestic security demands. We stress that we see much value in information sharing and government efforts to suppress criminal activity. We have also deliberately written the book to be useful to people with a wide variety of perspectives on these questions, including people who disagree with our priors (our analysis in the main part of the book asks why actors did one thing and not another rather than making assumptions about what they ought to have done, given some external set of ethical or political principles). We do have our own views, however; specifically, we believe that current private and public sector data collection and sharing practices grossly underestimate the downside risks of mass state and capitalist surveillance.

As Facebook's experience with Russian manipulators and Cambridge Analytica illustrates, data can be employed as a sword as well as a shield. Adversaries may use personal information to manipulate or confuse domestic populations for profit or power. Although we are still learning the extent of such interference in the 2016 election, we know that actors from Russia as well as private companies sought to influence the results. This could provide the foundation for a radically different notion of robust privacy protection: not as weakening national security, but instead providing its necessary foundations.[14] If personal data can be exploited to undermine the very nature of democratic governance and the freedom to choose one's own government, then it is hard to imagine how democracy can be secure so long as it does not place strict limits on the abuse of personal information.

These concerns become all the more urgent when we look at how the rules of information collection and sharing may be compromised in a world where personal data moves readily back and forth across national borders. Policy debate needs to transcend nationally tailored legislation toward regional and international efforts. At the same time, there must be a concerted effort to break down artificial distinctions between private and public sector data use, and examine and better understand how the two fade into each other.

The fight between US security agencies and multinational corporations, which hold data in data centers in other countries, exemplifies this dynamic. The US CLOUD Act of 2018 provides US legal authorities a means to access data held abroad by US-based companies and creates incentives for other jurisdictions to make executive agreements with the United States over data transfer.[15] The legislation was written in response to a case in which Microsoft refused government data requests as the data were held offshore. The European Union is now moving ahead with its "E-Evidence Regulation," which would provide for similar transfers of evidence within the European Union. In combination, these two are building the foundations of a possible EU-US framework agreement, which would extend the precedent of the Umbrella Agreement, facilitating the reciprocal transfer of criminal data between the two jurisdictions.[16] This has led privacy advocates, such as the Electronic Privacy Information Center, based in Washington, DC, to oppose the EU proposal, warning about how the existing US law and similar EU proposal "raise concerns about the protection of fundamental rights." On the one hand, EU and US security officials continue to work across jurisdictions to try to achieve their goals. On the other hand, privacy actors are increasingly willing to do the same—and to exploit the possibilities of legal action in other jurisdictions—in pursuit of their quite-different objectives.[17]

One transnational effort to address these problems is only mentioned in passing in the main body of the book: the European Union's General Data Protection Regulation, which entered into force on May 25, 2018.[18] Updating the 1995 Privacy Directive described earlier in the book, this law creates a single data privacy architecture for the entire continent. In contrast to the 1995 directive, which effectively provided a model law to each member state, the GDPR is standardized legislation. It further empowers data privacy regulators by supplying them with real enforcement powers. They can fine companies up to 4 percent of their global revenue or twenty million euros, whichever is higher. The GDPR attempts to minimize unwanted or unnecessary data collection and processing through privacy-by-design initiatives, opt-in requirements, and a right to data erasure (often referred to as the right to be forgotten). At the same time, it explicitly recognizes the transnational nature of data sharing, extending the legislation's scope to data concerning individuals based in the European Union regardless of whether or not data collection or processing occurs within the European Union. In other words, individuals based in the European Union enjoy extraterritorial protection of their rights.

The GDPR does include a national security provision (Article 23) that allows member state governments the ability to carve out derogations to the legislation for national security concerns, but even these must meet legal scrutiny as necessary and proportionate. These same balancing tests have been used in court by privacy activists to promote privacy safeguards within state surveillance architectures.

There is no magical solution that would resolve the struggle between privacy and security. That said, the discussion on how best to balance competing interests through policy has hardly begun. The GDPR starts a global conversation on the appropriate defaults for data collection, encouraging firms and governments to minimize unnecessary data collection, to delete unneeded data, and to secure the data that are kept. We sincerely hope that such a conversation will open up the space for policy makers to see the reinforcing benefits of privacy policies for security. A continuing Wild West approach to privacy, in contrast, will expose democratic societies to further attacks by those seeking to exploit information manipulation.

We expect that the GDPR, as it is implemented, will give rise to new transatlantic disputes as well as disputes with other third states. As we write, in May 2018, a second case taken on by Max Schrems has been referred to the European Court of Justice, threatening yet again to upset efforts by EU and US negotiators to contain politics within narrow interstate agreements. Social media companies such as Facebook are newly controversial in both the European Union and United States, generating political opportunities. Vera Jourova, the European Union's justice commissioner, has suggested that the Cambridge Analytica saga shows that Facebook is in breach of its obligations under Privacy Shield, and has pushed the United States to investigate Facebook's behavior and possibly suspend it from the program.[19] This action aims both to persuade European Court of Justice judges that Privacy Shield is not a set of empty promises and to press US regulators to make US companies more responsive to European privacy concerns.

Six minutes after the GDPR entered into force, Schrems's advocacy organization (None of Your Business) filed four more cases with data privacy authorities; three were aimed at Facebook and its subsidiaries, and the fourth was aimed at Google's Android operating system. Schrems argues that Facebook cannot require its customers to consent to their personal data being used to target advertising at them. If he succeeds in convincing data privacy authorities and courts of this claim, he may make it effectively impossible for Facebook and Google to continue operating their current business model by driving a wedge between the users whom these companies provide services to and their real customers—the advertisers to whom they serve up the segmented and categorized attention of their users.

As the GDPR establishes a new field of battle, and the European Court of Justice issues further rulings, we may expect many other efforts by EU privacy actors to insulate the GDPR from transnational processes, and defend and extend their approach to privacy globally, and by US privacy actors to use the European Union as leverage to achieve their own domestic aims.[20] The changes described in *Of Privacy and Power*, then, are iterations of an ongoing fight over security and freedom that will continue well into the future.

And Power

The substance of the book describes the specific policy challenges around privacy and domestic security in transatlantic relations. The broader argument of the book has important implications for global politics more generally. Ultimately, the book recasts the notion of power.

Comparative political economy scholars have many important things to say about the relationship between institutions and power, but they focus their attention nearly exclusively on power relations within borders. The international relations scholarship on institutions, in contrast, has relatively little to say about institutions and power, both because of its reliance on efficiency arguments from the new institutional economics and because it emerged in competition with realist scholarship that saw power relations as the fundamental engine of global politics.[21]

Our account shows how institutions shape power relations across borders. Specifically, it identifies the ways in which transnational and international institutions are not simply sites of coordination but generate asymmetrical influence too. Standard rationalist accounts of institutional politics focus on how institutions resolve coordination problems associated with insufficient information or the threat of cheating. Institutions, in their view, provide information that helps boundedly rational and imperfectly informed actors make decisions.

We start from a different set of assumptions, developed by sociologists and scholars of comparative politics among others, and apply them to the rich space of transnational institutions that emerged after globalization. Here, institutions do not solve distributional issues in which some win and some lose. Instead, they generate power asymmetries.[22] Access to transatlantic interactions, soft law, or international organizations is not equally distributed, and those actors who gain access to them stand ready to reopen previously settled bargains. The politics of globalization, then, is not only about mitigating the frictions generated by international exchange but also about leveraging the institutions created to facilitate those exchanges for particular advantage.

To study power in a globalized world, we need not only to understand its sources but also the actors who draw on it. Thus, another major lesson of the book is that power is not solely exercised by traditional international actors. Governments and their executives still matter in world affairs, but they no longer enjoy a monopoly over diplomatic interactions. Rather, they find themselves jostling against a host of nonstate and substate actors, including firms, regulators, and foreign and interior ministries, which compete with and against each other to set the terms of global interactions. As was made painfully clear by the Russian influence operation within the United States in the run-up to the 2016 election, there are powerful internal tensions and divisions within societies. Transnational politics underscores how these divisions are not locked within national borders but instead span them.

Our findings also push scholars of the transatlantic relationship to reconsider its distributional implications for groups within and across it. This relationship is often framed as a common project animated by the West's postwar resistance to the Soviet Union. The book, however, highlights the significant disagreements that simmer inside each jurisdiction and across them. In other words, the book reminds readers that the transatlantic relationship is not a moribund talking point in speeches given by leaders visiting each others' capitals but rather a living, breathing set of interactions. And like most relationships, they express and contain real points of asymmetry and power, particularly for those actors who have access to it.

As the main body of the book shows, a community of security-minded actors have used transnational interactions to alter both domestic and global policy. They have faced off against another group of actors that seek to promote and defend civil-liberties-oriented policies. The book's major innovation is not to expand the set of actors that international relations scholars should study in world politics—a task that other scholars have done before us. It is to open up a new, more systematic research agenda that may start to answer a key question about these actors' efforts to exercise power: why they choose some strategies rather than others in order to try to achieve specific goals under specific sets of circumstances.

This points the way toward a new way of thinking about international politics, and a new set of debates that highlight aspects of international and domestic politics that are obscured or entirely occluded by existing approaches. In previous work, we have dubbed this way of thinking the NIA, providing a theoretical promissory note that the book now looks to deliver on, showing how the NIA offers insight into disputes and bargaining processes that have substantial consequences for the world economy.[23] We do not, of course, suggest that our approach provides a complete understanding of the dynamics of power in a global setting. Indeed, we hope to produce as much fruitful disagreement as agreement with our arguments. To both ends, we offer a specific set of claims, ideas, and arguments that appear to have purchase, and that others can fruitfully debate.

Specifically, we set out a historical institutionalist account of power in international politics, showing how it highlights far-greater dynamism in power relations than traditional bargaining approaches.[24] As we demonstrate over the course of the book, EU-US interactions over privacy and security have never reached a stable equilibrium, where all parties are better off with the particular institutional setup than a feasible alternative given everyone else's actions, and surely never will. Instead of discrete bargaining outcomes, in which one side can be coded as the winner and the other as the loser, or efficiency-enhancing durable compromises, we see ongoing and heated contestation.

In part, this reflects the transnational nature of political interactions. We live in a time of upheaval, where domestic, transatlantic, and global interactions disturb seemingly settled bargains, and open up political opportunities for dissatisfied actors to relitigate their concerns and overturn status quo rules. In part, it reflects the inability of the "state" to control the agenda for international negotiations.[25]

The dynamics of power that we identify will be strongest in the areas where interdependence has progressed furthest—that is, in economic interactions among the advanced industrialized economies. Here, actors who are best able to take advantage of transnational alliance building, and who have easiest access to the relevant transnational opportunity structures will be greatly advantaged over those who do not. As we have already noted, this is likely to be especially true of the new information economy. Yet we may also expect similar dynamics across other economic sectors and geographic areas (e.g. global value chains and production networks), where there is deep cross-border exchange, and strong resulting pressures for rule alignment.

This also implies clear scope conditions for our arguments. In sectors or policy areas where there is relatively little exchange and rule alignment, there will be correspondingly little room for the dynamics we identify. Many areas of global politics and indeed of global exchange involve relatively rudimentary cross border interdependence. These relationships are likely to involve more traditional bargaining dynamics based on raw power, market size and other factors sketched out in more traditional comparative politics approaches.

Are the dynamics that we identify the ephemeral side effect of a brief global moment when globalization went too far? Globalization has left a sour taste in the mouths of publics within the advanced industrialized democracies. The United States—once the guarantor of the soi-disant 'liberal order' that underpinned interdependence seems now to prefer once-off mercantilist bargains to long term institution building. Britain has chosen through a democratic referendum to withdraw from the European Union, while some other member states appear increasingly to want European rules only on an a-la-carte basis. The global supply chains on which globalized production depended may be starting to unravel, as countries start to fear in earnest that they are creating security and economic vulnerabilities that can easily be exploited by adversaries.

We are no better prophets than the rest of our profession. However, we believe that the intricate threads that have woven together the advanced industrialized economies over the last twenty years will prove immensely difficult to unravel, since they are now warp and woof of the fabric of the countries that might want to unravel them. The difficulties that Britain faces in withdrawing from the European Union provide a particularly stark reminder of how deep integration can go. Indeed, we expect that exactly the kinds of dynamics we have written about—conflict between overlapping rules; struggles among competing actors; access or lack of access to the relevant opportunity structures—will characterize and often stymie efforts to withdraw from this system just as much as they characterize the current struggles within it.[26]

Finally, our book points toward a new set of debates about power: how information and information technology has become a locus of power, which scholars and policy makers can ignore only if they are willing to risk failing to understand the dynamics of global politics. Information has joined oil, tanks, and money as a key currency of international affairs. States, firms, and substate actors among others leverage it to influence economic interactions and coerce adversaries. It provides the basis for business models that drive economies. The largest publicly valued companies in the United States include Apple, Google, Microsoft, Facebook, and Amazon. If data are the key input of the future economy, then, the concentration of such resources will benefit some states over others. Just as many Middle Eastern societies grew rich from their control over oil and gas deposits, the United States stands to benefit from the fact that US firms have a monopoly over US and European data.[27] This will further propel advances in a host of economic sectors from artificial intelligence to driverless cars. Governments in Europe and Asia view the economic development of these sectors along with the dominance of overseas (mostly US) multinationals as a major challenge for their economic and strategic futures. The US government, for its part, fears that it is losing dominance over artificial intelligence to China and other competitors, with major economic and strategic consequences.

As firms like Google, Facebook, and Amazon went global, they reshaped the domestic economies and political environments of the countries that they did business in, often pressing for rules that were to their advantage and to the disadvantage of potential competitors. What is less appreciated is how these firms also became potential "points of control" for governments and nonstate actors that could use them as leverage.[28] As the Snowden revelations demonstrate, the US and UK agencies employed their privileged access to data held by these companies and the internet backbone to track terrorists and other criminals. Sanctions regimes used to primarily involve denial of access to domestic markets. Now they leverage access to global information networks as a powerful incentive. US and European governments, for example, delinked Iranian and North Korean banks from the SWIFT network. This effectively cut those countries' financial services sectors out of international financial markets. Such effects can be mobilized against dominant states such as the United States as well as by them. Russian disinformation campaigns in Europe and the United States demonstrate how information manipulation turn the internet and social media into a weapon of hybrid warfare. Information, then, is not simply a fight over competitive advantage but also a source of asymmetrical power.

As the information economy becomes a greater point of disagreement among democracies as well as between democracies and nondemocracies, and as governments abandon their initial hesitancy to regulate the information economy, we may expect further transatlantic disputes—and for that matter, transpacific disputes—to break out over whose rules should prevail and when.[29]

The European Union is now engaged in a major reconsideration of its approach to information in the wake of the GDPR. As described by one participant in these debates,

> Together with the GDPR, Facebook now faces fines of up to 1.6 billion dollars . . . and people really [want] to use the GDPR against these big American monopolies. Together with the revelations on Cambridge Analytica, this has created a new momentum, I think. Europe really wants to take its role seriously and become the global gold standard setter and also the global regulator for these issues on monopoly. And in a way, to find a

European way. The Silicon Valley or Washington approach is that they do what they want and then move fast and break things and then see what happens, and if they make money it's fine. The Chinese approach, on the other side, they basically control everything, including the content, and have the social rating system and stuff like that. We don't want that. We are having much broader support for a European approach, that tries to regulate technology, to regulate technology companies, to regulate the platform and what have you, based on our European values, on privacy, on freedom of information and the rule of law. This is very vague, very abstract. It still hasn't been translated into specific policy decisions in each field and dossier. But this is the understanding of what Europe's role is in this digital world, that I see in the last weeks and months has found support.[30]

New regulatory powers and the traditional antitrust clout of the European Commission are coming to reinforce each other:

Silicon Valley Wild West digital capitalism has really gone out of control and we have to do something. The GDPR is a big first step of course, but we need to do more. We need to address it in terms of competition power and monopoly regulation. . . . This has been growing for two or three years and now with the Facebook scandal it has become much more vivid. This is our role and we have to do it. We have shown that we can do it. . . . People from all different corners in Brussels and on the national level are trying to think about how to get it under control. Getting it under control that is still guided by our European fundamental rights and rule of law values. . . . One institutional aspect . . . that hasn't become very public but may have been important in our institutional environment [is that] the European Data Protection Supervisor, BEUC, [which is] the consumer groups umbrella organization and the Competition Commissioner held a conference two years ago on how data protection, consumer protection and competition law can agree and reinforce each other, and work hand-in-hand, so to speak. I think that was a really interesting point, where also Margrethe Vestager [European Commissioner for Competition] really understood that if she talked about competition, you also need to address the amount of data the company has.[31]

This new willingness of the European Union to use its regulatory powers to shape international data flows is causing alarm among US commentators, and is likely to lead to new cross-national alliances, spurring further conflicts over privacy and power.[32]

Understanding these complex and crucially important dynamics of power will require new theories of international politics. This book provides a set of arguments that help to capture some significant aspects of these dynamics, but surely not all of them. It also offers a challenge to other scholars: to begin properly to grapple with changes spawned by economic interdependence and propelled by information technology that is transforming international relations and comparative politics alike.

NOTES

Preface

1. We thank Cambridge University Press, Taylor & Francis, and Sage for permission to reprint portions of the articles (Farrell and Newman 2014, 2015, 2016, 2018; Newman 2011).

Introduction

1. Although like other aspects of policy, they have stuttered in the early months of the Trump administration due to unfilled diplomatic vacancies.

2. Kagan 2002, 2007.

3. Farrell and Newman 2014, 2016.

4. Barnett and Coleman 2005; Deflem 2004; Lefebvre 2003; Efrat and Newman 2017; Hameiri and Jones 2013.

5. Pawlak 2010; Brimmer 2006.

6. Efrat and Newman 2017.

7. Andreas and Nadelmann 2006.

8. De Goede 2012b.

9. Donohue 2016; Scheppele 2010; Newman 2008a.

10. Argomaniz 2009b; Pawlak 2009a; Suda 2013.

11. Newman 2008b.

12. Honig 2009; Scheppele 2006; Beckman 2016.

13. Privacy International 2004.

14. MacDonald 2004.

15. Baker 2010.

16. Ibid.

17. Drezner 2007.

18. Berger 2000.

19. Braun and Gilardi 2006; Baccini and Dür 2012; Keohane and Nye 1977.

20. Richards 1999; Gruber 2000.

21. Slaughter 2004; Cerny 2010; Green 2013.

22. Schickler 2001; Thelen 2003; Mahoney and Thelen 2009; Hacker 2004.

23. Tarrow 2001; Callaghan 2010.

24. Hameiri and Jones 2013; Kelley and Simmons 2015; Dalgaard-Nielsen and Hamilton 2006.

25. The member states of the European Union are more interdependent, but also share a common jurisdictional space.

26. Drezner 2007; Simmons 2001; Posner 2009a; Young 2003.

27. Mahoney 2003; George and Bennett 2005.

28. Callaghan 2010; Cerny 2010; Oatley 2011; Weinberg 2016.

29. Putnam 1988; Mansfield, Milner, and Pevehouse 2007.

30. For a brief discussion of reverberation, see Evans, Jacobson, and Putnam 1993.

31. Kahler 2016.

32. Farrell and Héritier 2003; Helmke and Levitsky 2004.

33. Johnson 2014; Alter 2008; Newman 2010.

34. Tarrow 2001; Moe 2005; Della Porta and Tarrow 2005; Sikkink 2005; Zürn 2018.

35. Büthe 2002; Posner 2010.

36. Andreas and Nadelmann 2006; Barnett and Coleman 2005; Efrat 2015.

Chapter 1: Politics in an Age of Interdependence

1. Kahler and Lake 2003; Cerny 2010; Castells 1996; Locke, Amengual, and Mangla 2009.

2. Kahler 2009; Büthe and Mattli 2011; Green 2013.

3. Bartley 2018.

4. Braun and Gilardi 2006.

5. Mattli and Woods 2009.

6. Kagan 2002, 2007; Hall and Soskice 2001.

7. Sassen 2006; Newman and Posner 2011.

8. Cerny 2010; Tarrow 2001.

9. Sinha 2007; Murillo and Schrank 2005; Djelic and Quack 2010; Shaffer 2012; Andonova and Tuta 2014.

10. Berger 2000.

11. Andrews 1994; Mosley 2003; Garrett and Lange 1991; Ahlquist 2006; Culpepper 2015.

12. Tonnelson 2000.

13. Martin and Swank 2004; Mosley 2003; Rudra 2008; Culpepper and Reinke 2014.

14. Milner 1997; Rogowski 1989; Milner and Tingley 2011.

15. Mansfield, Milner, and Pevehouse 2007; Mansfield, Milner, and Rosendorff 2002.

16. Koremenos, Lipson, and Snidal 2001.

17. Simmons and Danner 2010; Simmons 2000; Carnegie 2014; Bearce, Eldredge, and Jolliff 2016.

18. Raustiala 2004; Keohane and Victor 2011.

19. Bach and Newman 2007; Drezner 2007; Posner 2009a.

20. Vogel 1995.

21. There is controversy over whether the European Union should be considered a state. While there are complex relations between the EU level and the politics of its individual member states, the EU level is important for most areas of regulation and considered as a polity. See Majone 1996; McNamara 2018.

22. Fioretos 2009, 2010; Drezner 2007.

23. Lake 2009; Keohane 2009.

24. Callaghan 2010; Oatley 2011; Chaudoin, Milner, and Pang 2015.

25. Brooks and Kurtz 2012.

26. Campbell 2004.

27. Colgan 2014; Alter 1998; Jabko 2006; Johnson 2013; Kalyanpur and Newman 2019.

28. Keohane 2009.

29. Kahler and Lake 2003; Mattli and Woods 2009.

30. Hameiri and Jones 2013; Andreas and Nadelmann 2006.

31. Keohane and Nye 1977; Vernon 1971; Rosenau 1990; Kaiser 1971.

32. Keohane and Nye 1977; Kaiser 1971; Vernon 1971.

33. Hopkins 1976; Burley 1993.

34. Slaughter 2004; Cerny 2010; Djelic and Quack 2010.

35. Farrell and Newman 2014.

36. Mattli and Büthe 2003; Büthe and Mattli 2011.

37. Braun and Gilardi 2006; Brooks and Kurtz 2012.

38. Simmons, Dobbin, and Garrett 2006.

39. Mosley 2010; Halliday and Carruthers 2009.

40. Risse-Kappan 1995; Andonova 2004; Green 2013; Roger and Dauvergne 2016.

41. Nye and Keohane 1971.

42. Knight 1992; Schickler 2001; Mahoney and Thelen 2009.

43. Putnam 2016; Raustiala 2009; Kaczmarek and Newman 2011.

44. Putnam 1988; Evans, Jacobson, and Putnam 1993; Meunier 2005.

45. Newman and Posner 2011; Whytock 2009.

46. Putnam 2009; Raustiala 2009; Kaczmarek and Newman 2011; Crasnic, Kalyanpur, and Newman 2017.

47. Mattli and Woods 2009; Newman 2008b; Putnam 2016; Arel-Bundock 2017.

48. Richards 1999; Gruber 2000.

49. Tarrow 2001; Della Porta and Tarrow 2005; Tarrow 2005.

50. Börzel and Risse 2003; Joachim 2003; Della Porta and Tarrow 2005; Sikkink 2005; Tarrow 2005.

51. Dobusch and Quack 2013; Bruszt and McDermott 2012; Bartley 2011; Shaffer 2012; Goldstein 1996; Newman and Posner 2018.

52. Moe 2005.

53. Lall 2012; Dobusch and Quack 2013; Newman and Posner 2018.

54. Quack 2010; Newman 2008a.

55. Knight 1992; Krasner 1991; Moe 2005; Hall and Thelen 2009.

56. Berger 2000; Schickler 2001; Hacker 2004; Mahoney and Thelen 2009.

57. Raustiala 2002; Bach and Newman 2010.

58. Mattli and Büthe 2003; Woll 2008; Freyburg, Lavenex, and Schimmelfennig 2009.

59. Dreher, Sturm, and Vreeland 2009.

60. Newman 2008a.

61. Ibid.

62. Schickler 2001; Thelen 2004; Hacker 2004.

63. Moe 2005; Fox and Stephenson 2015.

64. Young 2011.

65. Botzem and Quack 2009; Botzem 2012.

66. Raustiala 2009; Putnam 2009; Kaczmarek and Newman 2011; Crasnic, Kalyanpur, and Newman 2017. For a transnational analogue, see Moschella 2016.

67. Drezner 2007; Krasner 1991.

68. Allen, Farrell, and Shalizi 2017.

69. Jackson and Nexon 1999.

70. Blyth 2002; Woll 2008.

Chapter 2: Domestic Security and Privacy in the Transatlantic Space

1. Andreas and Nadelmann 2006; Barnett and Coleman 2005; Regan 1995.
2. Dalgaard-Nielsen and Hamilton 2006; Barnett and Coleman 2005.
3. Rees 2006; Dalgaard-Nielsen and Hamilton 2006.
4. Pawlak 2009b; Jančić 2016.
5. Newman 2008a; Bennett 2008.
6. Beckman 2016; Brimmer 2006.
7. Beckman 2016; Dalgaard-Nielsen and Hamilton 2006.
8. Horowitz and Potter 2014.
9. Barnett and Coleman 2005; Deflem 2004.
10. Deflem 2004.
11. Szumski 2016.
12. Efrat 2015.
13. Nadelmann 1993.
14. Clinton 1997; Hameiri and Jones 2013.
15. Nadelmann 1993; Beckman 2016.
16. Roxborough 2001.
17. Ibid., viii.
18. Lefebvre 2003.
19. Smith and Lippman 1996; Efrat 2015.
20. Zegart 2009; Jervis 2011.
21. Sandler, Arce, and Enders 2011.
22. Ryder 2015.
23. The following discussion of MLATs draws on and summarizes the introductory material in Efrat and Newman 2017.
24. Ellis and Pisani 1985; Zagaris and Resnick 1997; Bassiouni 2008.
25. Efrat and Newman 2017.
26. Weber 2003.
27. Goldsmith and Wu 2006.
28. See http://www.oas.org/juridico/english/cyb_pry_G8_network.pdf, accessed March 1, 2016.
29. Lander 2004, 487.
30. Sloan 2001.
31. Loeb 1999; Norton-Taylor and Black 2001; Wright 2002.
32. Walsh 2009; Jervis 2011.
33. A prime example is the EU-US MLAT, which entered into force in 2003. Agreement on Mutual Legal Assistance between the European Union and the United States of America, OJ L 181/34, July 19, 2003; Brimmer 2006.
34. Farrell and Newman 2010; Kalyanpur and Newman 2017.
35. Occhipinti 2003; Monar 2007.
36. Bures 2006; Keohane 2008.
37. Bures 2013.
38. Lander 2004.
39. Müller-Wille 2008.
40. Coolsaet 2010.
41. "Common Market in Pact on Terror" 1986.
42. Kaunert 2010; Den Boer, Hillebrand, and Nolke, 2008.

43. Zaiotti 2011.

44. Lodge 1989.

45. Monar 2001.

46. Monar 2004, 2014; Kaunert 2010.

47. Kaunert 2010.

48. Monar 2015.

49. Leonard 2009.

50. Landale and Fletcher 1999; Rees 2008. Section D of the agreement reads,

> 59. The European Council underlines that all competences and instruments at the disposal of the Union, and in particular, in external relations must be used in an integrated and consistent way to build the area of freedom, security and justice. Justice and Home Affairs concerns must be integrated in the definition and implementation of other Union policies and activities.
>
> 60. Full use must be made of the new possibilities offered by the Treaty of Amsterdam for external action and in particular of Common Strategies as well as Community agreements and agreements based on Article 38 TEU.
>
> 61. Clear priorities, policy objectives and measures for the Union's external action in Justice and Home Affairs should be defined. Specific recommendations should be drawn up by the Council in close co-operation with the Commission on policy objectives and measures for the Union's external action in Justice and Home Affairs, including questions of working structure, prior to the European Council in June 2000.
>
> 62. The European Council expresses its support for regional co-operation against organised crime involving the Member States and third countries bordering on the Union. In this context it notes with satisfaction the concrete and practical results obtained by the surrounding countries in the Baltic Sea region. The European Council attaches particular importance to regional co-operation and development in the Balkan region. The European Union welcomes and intends to participate in a European Conference on Development and Security in the Adriatic and Ionian area, to be organised by the Italian Government in Italy in the first half of the year 2000. This initiative will provide valuable support in the context of the South Eastern Europe Stability Pact.

51. Balzacq 2008. Created as the Europol Drug Unit in 1994, Europol became fully active in 1999. Europol differs starkly from, for example, the FBI in the United States. It does not have independent police powers, and cannot make arrests or hold criminals on its own. Instead, its competences involve information sharing and coordination for domestic intelligence. It runs an alert system, disseminating local warrants to other intelligence services, and conducts limited investigation. Europol's substantive and institutional mandate has grown considerable in the last decade. In 1999, it gained jurisdiction over terrorism issues, and in 2009 was transitioned into a formal EU agency. See Occhipinti 2003; Kaunert 2010. Eurojust, which has been less important to disputes over privacy and domestic security, is intended to provide a European prosecutorial service. It was established in 2002 to increase cooperation and information exchange among European prosecutors (Souminen 2008; Bures 2010), and consists of member state representatives who can be judges, prosecutors, or police officers. Its role is to strengthen cooperation rather than to undertake independent actions or investigations.

52. Maricut 2016.

53. Monar 2014.

54. Carrera 2016.

55. Bennett 1992; Schwartz and Peifer 2017. We use the term *data privacy* rather than *data protection* whenever possible as we find it more intuitive. In European policy debates, however,

the issue is often referred to as data protection, and some policy makers and documents in the book use the term. They can be understood as synonyms.

56. The exact regulatory authority of each agency varies based on the original legislative proposals. Some regulators enjoy more centralized authority and investigatory powers while others serve more as ombudsmen. The 1995 Privacy Directive harmonized many of these powers, thus mitigating many distinctions across the national authorities. Nevertheless, some administrative and enforcement differences persist.

57. OECD 1980.

58. Bennett 1992.

59. Newman 2008b.

60. Newman 2008a.

61. Ibid.

62. Regulation (EU) 2016/679; Kalyanpur and Newman 2019.

63. Swire and Litan 1998; Shaffer 2000.

64. Farrell 2003.

65. Scott 2016.

66. Bach and Newman 2007.

67. Jančić 2016.

68. Dimitrova and Brkan 2017.

69. Simitis 2003.

70. Kokott and Sobotta 2013.

71. Bennett 2008.

72. For more details, see https://edri.org/about/, accessed August 6, 2018.

73. For more details, see http://www.statewatch.org/, accessed August 6, 2018.

74. Albrecht 2015.

75. See DeSimmone 2010.

76. Waxman 2009, 388.

77. Kessler 2016.

78. Stuart 2009; Gregory 2016.

79. Troy 1981.

80. Bamford 1983; Gregory 2016.

81. Stuart 2009, 292.

82. Gregory 2016.

83. Donohue 2016.

84. Ibid.

85. Zegart 2009; Jervis 2011.

86. Zegart 2009.

87. Ibid., 66.

88. Zegart 2009; Jervis 2011.

89. Cohen, Cuéllar, and Weingast 2006.

90. Regan 1995.

91. Solove and Hartzog 2014.

92. https://epic.org, accessed August 6, 2018.

93. Bennett 2008.

94. Cronin 2003.

95. Scheppele 2010.

96. Talmon 2005.

97. Ryder 2015.

98. Scheppele 2010; Bianchi 2007.

99. Zegart 2009; Cohen, Cuéllar, and Weingast 2006.

100. Jervis 2011.

101. Zegart 2009.

102. Cohen, Cuéllar, and Weingast 2006.

103. Jones 2002.

104. Cohen, Cuéllar, and Weingast 2006.

105. May, Jochim, and Sapotichne 2011.

106. Dalgaard-Nielsen and Hamilton 2006; Beckman 2016. Other EU member states like Belgium have highly decentralized policing systems too.

107. Regan and Monahan 2013.

108. Donohue 2008.

109. Zarate 2013.

110. Donohue 2008.

111. Seamon and Gardner 2004.

112. Varghese 2003.

113. Savage 2011.

114. Landau 2013.

115. Greenwald 2013. For more on the Snowden leaks, see https://www.theguardian.com/us-news/the-nsa-files, accessed August 6, 2018.

116. Donohue 2016.

117. Landau 2014.

118. For a transcript, see https://www.nytimes.com/2014/01/18/us/politics/obamas-speech-on-nsa-phone-surveillance.html, accessed August 6, 2018.

119. Regan 1995.

120. See DHS Privacy Office Annual Reports, https://www.dhs.gov/publication/privacy-office-annual-reports, accessed August 6, 2018.

121. Kehaulani Goo and Hsu 2005.

122. Monar 2015.

123. Ibid.

124. Wennerholm, Brattberg, and Rhinard 2010 .

125. Whitlock 2008; Guild 2008.

126. Dempsey 2007.

127. Balzacq 2006.

128. Argomaniz 2009a; Bures 2013.

129. Argomaniz, Bures, and Kaunert 2015.

130. See https://www.europol.europa.eu/about-europol/statistics-data, accessed August 7, 2018.

131. EU Anti-Terrorism Coordinator 2015.

132. Monar 2014

133. Interview with European business representative, Brussels, May 12, 2004; Bignami 2007.

134. Digital Rights Ireland and Seitlinger v Minister for Communications, Marine and Natural Resources (C-293/12and C-594/12) [2014] E.C.R. I-238; Lillington 2014; Bignami and Resta 2015.

135. Dimitrova and Brkan 2018.

136. Borger 2013.

137. Baker 2010.

Chapter 3: Competing Atlantic Alliances and the Fight over Airline Passenger Data Sharing

1. Rees and Aldrich 2005; Argomaniz 2009b; Aldrich 2009.

2. Beckman 2016; Dalgaard-Nielsen and Hamilton 2006; Brimmer 2006; Lehrke and Scho-maker 2014; Porter and Bendiek 2012.

3. Salter 2008.

4. Fisher 2007; Kite 2004.

5. Government Accountability Office 2004.

6. Quoted in Singel 2004.

7. Trento and Trento 2006; Hoff 2014.

8. Baker 2010.

9. For a clear description of Advanced Passenger Information versus PNR, see http://www.iata.org/publications/Pages/api-pnr-toolkit.aspx, accessed August 7, 2018.

10. Salter 2008.

11. Lyon 2003.

12. In a letter dated October 16, 2001, President Bush had already urged the European Union to change various internal laws, to expedite cooperation with the United States on antiterrorism, border control, and aviation issues, and more generally to "consider data protection issues in the context of law enforcement and counterterrorism imperatives." US Mission to the European Union 2001.

13. Article 29 Data Protection Working Party 2002, 2003.

14. Interview with European Commission official, Brussels, 2004.

15. Ibid.

16. "Decimated Airlines Seek Solution to Passenger Data Feud" 2003.

17. Friedman et al., 2010.

18. Baker 2010.

19. Pawlak 2009b.

20. European Commission 2003.

21. Baker 2010.

22. Interview with Parliament official, Brussels, 2004.

23. European Parliament 2004.

24. Article 29 Data Protection Working Party 2002, 2003.

25. Ibid.

26. The sharing of sensitive data had previously been a point of contention between EU and US negotiators during the Safe Harbor talks. Interview with US Department of Commerce official, September 18, 2000, Washington, DC.

27. Rodotà 2003.

28. Alitalia, however, did not comply with the commissioner's demands, providing PNR data "quickly and smoothly, even over the objections of Italy's national privacy authority," thereby creating considerable goodwill with US authorities. When Alitalia was later fined $75,000 for accidentally not supplying the full names of the Italian Navy traveling band to US authorities, the US embassy in Italy requested the waiving of the fine, citing its past cooperation. See Wikileaks cable 03ROME5654, https://wikileaks.org/plusd/cables/03ROME5654_a.html, accessed July 23, 2017.

29. See, for example, the decision of the Belgian data privacy authority on January 19, 2004, http://www.radicalparty.org/privacy/etats_un.pdf, accessed August 8, 2018.

30. Ludford 2003. Rodotà's deputy, Butarelli, told US diplomats directly that the agreement violated national law. See Wikileaks Cable 03ROME2436, http://wikileaks.redfoxcenter.org/cable/2003/06/03ROME2436.html, accessed July 23, 2017.

31. Several years after the United States and European Union reached their deal, the European Court of Justice ruled that the Canada agreement required additional privacy safeguards. While this ruling did not invalidate the US agreement, it places a much higher burden on any future negotiations. Carson 2017.

32. Interview with European Parliament party leader, Brussels, October 2004.

33. Bolkestein 2003.

34. "The Europeans should put it in the win column. . . . The Europeans, it turned out, couldn't let it go because they didn't see it as a win." Baker 2010, 104.

35. Interview with European Parliament party leader, Brussels, October 2004.

36. The European Court of Justice (2003), in the 2003 Lindqvist case, ruled that the European Convention on Human Rights protects individual privacy within Europe.

37. The role of the European Court of Justice in the external affairs of the European Union has not yet been adequately studied. In issue areas ranging from competition policy to trade, the European Court has defined the international authority of the European Union. PNR is an important case as it demonstrates an instance when the European Court rejected a broad interpretation of the Commission's authority in external relations.

38. See European Court of Justice 2006. See also Clark 2006.

39. In a subsequently leaked cable, a US diplomat in Brussels described Jonathan Faull, director-general of justice and home affairs, as both "the power behind the throne on JHA matters" and a "key player in moving forward our agenda." See https://wikileaks.org/plusd/cables/04BRUSSELS1997_a.html, accessed July 11, 2017.

40. UK House of Lords European Union Committee 2008.

41. "EU Privacy Ruling Threatens Chaos on Flights to US" 2006.

42. Quoted in Clark 2006.

43. Field 2003, 8.

44. Watt and Clark 2006.

45. Quoted in "European Airlines in Legal Limbo" 2006.

46. Interview with European Parliament official, Brussels, 2004.

47. Pawlak 2009b.

48. Baker 2010.

49. "US Embassy Cables" 2010.

50. Friedman et al. 2010.

51. Ibid

52. Solms-Laubach 2007.

53. Pawlak 2009a.

54. Council 2007.

55. Interview with European Parliament official, Brussels, October 2004.

56. Article 29 Data Protection Working Party 2007.

57. Quoted in Cody 2010.

58. Romaniello 2013.

59. Kanter 2012.

60. Ibid.

61. "EU MPs Back Passenger Data Sharing Deal with US" 2012.

62. Quoted in Taylor 2015.

63. de Capitani 2013.

64. Nahashima 2007; Bossong 2008.

65. European Commission 2004.

66. Bossong 2008.

67. Quoted in Nielsen 2014.

68. As Tusk asserted, "If we do not manage to establish a single European PNR, we will end up with 28 national systems." Quoted in White 2015.

69. Quoted in Tomik 2007.

70. Schiltz 2006.

71. Traynor 2008.

72. Melander 2008.

73. Mahony 2013.

74. European Data Protection Supervisor 2015.

75. Maurice 2015.

76. Telephone interview with European Parliament official, June 15, 2018.

77. Quoted in Robert 2016.

78. Quoted in Nielsen 2016b.

79. Pop 2011b.

80. Fleming 2015.

81. Nielsen 2016b.

82. Rettman 2017; European Court of Justice 2017.

83. Telephone interview with Ralf Bendrath, former senior policy adviser for Jan Philipp Albrecht, June 6, 2018.

84. Pawlak 2009a.

Chapter 4: Cross-National Layering and the Regulation of Terrorist Financial Tracking

1. Lichtblau and Risen 2006.

2. Pollack and Shaffer 2009; Vogel 2012; Kelemen 2010; Büthe and Mattli 2011; Farrell and Newman 2010.

3. Mattli and Woods 2009; Krasner 1991; Posner 2009b. Adapting the work of Walter Mattli and Ngaire Woods (2009), we define economic regulation as the organization and control of market activity through rules promulgated by public or private entities, which are recognized by market actors as the authoritative rule setters in the relevant area.

4. Drezner 2007; Büthe and Mattli 2011.

5. Hall and Soskice 2001; Gourevitch and Shinn 2005; Fioretos 2009, 2010.

6. Drezner 2007, 40; Büthe and Mattli 2011, 57; Lake 2009, 229.

7. Tsebelis 2002; Mansfield, Milner, and Rosendorff 2002; Mansfield, Milner, and Pevehouse 2007; Lake 2009.

8. Bach and Newman 2007; Drezner 2007; Posner 2009b.

9. Vogel 1995; Young 2003.

10. Berger 2000; Young 2011; Posner 2009b. Drezner (2007) argues that sometimes with high switching costs, states can coordinate on "sham" standards that have little or no substantive content. The agreements identified in this research, however, are real and substantial. We are grateful to an anonymous reviewer for *Comparative Political Studies* for pressing us to elucidate on this point.

11. Here we treat this distribution as a given. For a more detailed discussion about how opportunity structures might be generated, see Farrell and Newman 2014.

12. Servent 2013; Suda 2013; Servent and MacKenzie 2011; Romaniello 2013.

13. Oatley et al. 2013.

14. De Goede 2012a.

15. Rees and Aldrich 2005.

16. Levey 2016; Obama 2010. See also Zarate 2013.

17. https://www.swift.com/, accessed August 8, 2018.

18. Scott and Zachariadis 2017.

19. Commission de la Protection de la Vie Privee 2006.

20. Lichtblau and Risen 2006; Levey 2016.

21. Zarate 2013.

22. Quoted in Scott and Zachariadis 2014, 128.

23. Ibid.

24. SWIFT 2006.

25. Ibid.

26. Each of these subpoenas could provide data for a much larger number of searches. See de Bruguiere 2010.

27. Schwartz and Reidenberg 1996; Swire and Litan 1998; Newman 2008a.

28. Lichtblau and Risen 2006; Commission de la Protection de la Vie Privee 2006.

29. de Bruguiere 2010.

30. Commission de la Protection de la Vie Privee 2006.

31. Zarate 2013.

32. Commission de la Protection de la Vie Privee 2006.

33. Article 29 Data Protection Working Party 2006b.

34. US Embassy to Germany 2006.

35. US Mission to the European Union 2007.

36. US Embassy to France 2007.

37. Article 29 Data Protection Working Party 2006a.

38. US Department of the Treasury 2007.

39. US Embassy to Germany 2007a.

40. Newman 2008b.

41. US Embassy to Germany 2007b.

42. US Embassy to the Netherlands 2007.

43. US Mission to the European Union 2001.

44. US Embassy to the Netherlands 2007.

45. Farrell and Héritier 2003.

46. Pop 2010c.

47. Servent 2014.

48. Jupille 1999; Pollack 2003.

49. Pawlak 2009b.

50. Justice and Home Affairs DG 2005. Unverified rumors circulated within the Commission that the Commissioner for the Internal Market, Charlie McCreevey, a canny politician who was also well known for his conviviality, had agreed to the transfer at the end of a drinking session with his fellow Commissioner. While these rumors are unsubstantiated, their broad circulation testifies to the surprise that the transfer elicited among some observers.

51. Interview with Commission official, Brussels, December 2009.

52. Pawlak 2009b.

53. Council 2008.

54. Servent 2014.

55. European Union and United States of America 2010.

56. Pop 2009.

57. European Parliament 2010b.

58. Library of the European Parliament 2011.

59. Kanter 2010; Pop 2010b.

60. US Embassy to Germany 2010.

61. Quoted in Pignal 2009.

62. "EU to Launch Anti-Terror Finance Tracking Plan" 2010.

63. Servent and MacKenzie 2011; Pop 2010a.

64. European Parliament 2009.

65. European Commission 2010.

66. Ibid.

67. European Parliament 2010c.

68. European Parliament 2010a.

69. European Data Protection Supervisor 2010.

70. European Parliament 2010b.

71. Council 2010. See also "EU to Launch Anti-Terror Finance Tracking Plan" 2010.

72. Nielsen 2012

73. European Commission 2011, 2.

74. See European Commission 2013a, 10.

75. Directorate General for Internal Policies, 29.

76. European Commission 2017.

77. Wesseling 2016.

78. Goede and Wesseling 2017.

79. Nielsen 2015b.

80. Telephone interview with EU ombudsperson's office official, February 2016.

81. Pop 2011a.

82. "France Eyes European System to Track Terrorism Finance" 2015.

83. Nielsen 2016a.

84. EU Anti-Terrorism Coordinator 2016.

85. European Commission 2016.

86. Telephone Interview with Member of European Parliament, January 7, 2011.

Chapter 5: insulation and the Transformation of Commercial Privacy Disputes

1. Gidda 2013.

2. Farrell 2003; Newman 2008b; Kobrin 2004.

3. Hafner and Lyon 1998.

4. Swire and Litan 1998; Newman 2008b.

5. Newman 2008b.

6. Ibid.

7. Regan 1995; Newman 2008b.

8. Interview with Ira Magaziner, New York, September 2000.

9. Bureau of International Information Programs interview with Ira Magaziner, n.d. Available from authors on request.

10. Interview with Ira Magaziner, New York, September 2000.

11. Interview with EU official, Brussels, June 2000.

12. Newman 2008a.

13. Interview with US negotiator, Washington, DC, September 2000.

14. Quoted in Andrews 1999.

15. Interviews with EU and US negotiators, Brussels and Washington, DC, June and September 2000.

16. Interview with EU official, Brussels, June 2000.

17. Farrell 2003.

18. Interview with US negotiator, Washington, DC, September 2000.

19. Farrell 2002.

20. Farrell 2005.

21. Interview with Ira Magaziner, New York, September 2000.

22. Quoted in Macavinta 2002.

23. Interview with European negotiator, Brussels, January 2001.

24. Farrell 2003.

25. Hofheinz and Mandel 2015.

26. Bennett 2008; Farrell 2005a.

27. Dhont, Asinari, and Poullet 2004.

28. Ibid., 18.

29. https://epic.org/privacy/streetview/, accessed August 11, 2018.

30. Connolly 2008.

31. German Data Protection Commissioners 2010.

32. Kerry 2014.

33. Reding and Bryson 2012.

34. Quoted in Kerry 2014, 6.

35. Telephone interview with former Department of Commerce official, January 2016.

36. See, for example, the discussion in Brill 2015.

37. Dhont, Asinari, and Poullet 2004, 101.

38. Interview with European negotiator, Brussels, December 2009.

39. Interviews with US officials, Washington, DC, September 2009.

40. American Embassy in Brussels 2008.

41. Council 2008, 2009.

42. Council 2009.

43. Teufel 2014.

44. Interview with Commission official, Brussels, December 2009.

45. Council 2009.

46. Department of Homeland Security 2011.

47. http://www.statewatch.org/news/2014/feb/ep-nsa-surveillance-report-consolidated-21-2-14.pdf, accessed August 11, 2018.

48. Quoted in Kerry 2016, 1.

49. Email conversation with former US national security official, October 2016.

50. Interview with Max Schrems, privacy activist, Washington, DC, March 2016. Although in principle there are grounds for a court action at the European Court of Justice over whether, for instance, surveillance conducted by one member state on the citizens of another was "necessary and proportionate," there has been no real test to date within the European Court of Justice. As both the European Court of Justice and European Convention on Human Rights move toward a more proactive stance on surveillance issues, it is possible that this will change. For example, one interesting question involves whether the United Kingdom—which is suspected of carrying out wide-scale surveillance on the citizens of its allies and is due to leave the European Union following the Brexit referendum—will continue to be regarded as a safe destination for EU data. A court ruling on this question could plausibly set a significant precedent for intelligence gathering within the European Union too.

51. "Large-scale US intelligence collection programmes, such as PRISM, affect the fundamental rights of Europeans and, specifically, their right to privacy and to the protection of personal data. These programmes also point to a connection between Government surveillance

and the processing of data by private companies, notably by US internet companies." European Commission 2013b, 3.

52. Chaffin 2013. See also http://wikileaks.wikimee.org/cable/2008/11/08BRUSSELS1718.html, accessed August 11, 2018.

53. Interview with European Commission negotiators, September 2016.

54. European Commission 2000.

55. Interview with former US Department of Commerce official, January 2016.

56. Telephone interview with former US Department of Commerce official, January 2016.

57. Telephone interview with former US Department of Commerce official, January 2016.

58. White House 2014.

59. For a detailed discussion of the complexities of intelligence community terminology, and how many forms of intelligence collection that might appear to be quite indiscriminate to an ordinary observer would be classified as targeted not bulk, and hence not covered by the protections of PPD-28, see Granick 2017.

60. "LIBE Series 6" 2013.

61. Quoted in "Parliament Calls for Freezing Anti-Terror Banking Data Transfers with the US" 2013.

62. McCabe 2015.

63. Kuchler 2018.

64. Interview with Max Schrems, Washington, DC, March 2016.

65. Kelemen 2011.

66. Interview with Max Schrems, March 2016, Washington, DC.

67. For the relevant correspondence, see http://www.europe-v-facebook.org/DPC_PRISM_all.pdf, accessed October 10, 2016.

68. In subsequent and ongoing litigation surrounding the so-called Schrems II case, they have behaved quite differently. Obama administration officials strongly urged Facebook to take a position in the proceedings (private discussion with former US Department of Commerce official, March 2017). Indeed, Facebook's expert witnesses received detailed comments on their draft testimony from US government lawyers, apparently without being told that it was the US government, rather than Facebook counsel, that was providing the advice.

69. High Court of Ireland 2014.

70. For a précis of the arguments, see McGarr 2015.

71. European Court of Justice 2015b, 2015a.

72. European Court of Justice 2015.

73. Quoted in Price 2015.

74. Telephone interview with former US Department of Commerce official, January 2016.

75. See also Litt 2015.

76. Pritzker 2015.

77. "'Safe Harbour 2' Doesn't Need Change on Surveillance" 2015.

78. Interview with Commission negotiators, September 2016.

79. Nielsen 2015a. As described by Commission negotiators in a September 2016 interview, "Whether the DPAs wanted to do more, or would be driven by complaints, because certain DPAs have to act on complaints . . . there was a potential that they would have to do something. . . . That created a lot of pressure. I wouldn't say that we tried to exploit this, but it was clear in the background to everybody that we don't have ample time to do something. That is why our commissioner said early on that we wanted to have this done by February."

80. Interview with Commission negotiators, September 2016.

81. Based on contemporaneous notes on the presentation available from the authors on request.

82. Interview with European privacy activist, Brussels, September 2016.

83. Interview with European Commission official, Brussels, September 2016.

84. Sheftalovich 2016; Raul 2016.

85. Sheftalovich 2016.

86. http://www.pdpjournals.com/docs/88536.pdf, accessed August 12, 2018.

87. The European Ombudsman (2016) had already raised doubts over the proposed ombudsman mechanism, stating in February that EU citizens "have legitimate expectations of the credentials as to the impartiality and independence of such an office and I would be concerned if anything were done that might undermine those expectations and confidence generally in the Ombudsman as an instrument of democratic accountability."

88. See Cerulus 2016.

89. See Baker 2010.

90. Ibid.

91. Interview with Commission negotiators, Brussels, September 2016.

92. Ibramova and Buckwell 2016; Meyer 2016.

93. For an excellent summary, which we rely on below, see Evans and Mercer 2018.

94. https://dataprotection.ie/viewdoc.asp?DocID=1598&ad=1, accessed August 12, 2018.

95. http://www.europe-v-facebook.org/sh2/ref.pdf, accessed August 12, 2018.

96. On litigation strategies in the European Union, see Kelemen 2011.

97. Farrell 2005a.

98. Rettman 2017.

99. Cadwalladr 2018.

Conclusion

1. Shane and Mazzetti 2018.

2. Cadwalladr and Graham-Harrison 2018.

3. Cadwalladr 2018.

4. McCarthy 2018.

5. Bennett and Raab 2007.

6. Simmons 2013; Weber 2017; Zysman and Newman 2006.

7. Zuboff 2015.

8. Lyon 2001; O'Neil 2016.

9. Clarke 1988.

10. May 2018.

11. Malik and Basu 2017.

12. Weber 2017; Zysman and Newman 2006.

13. Newman 2008b.

14. Swire and Steinfeld 2001.

15. Brandon and Lecher 2018.

16. Daskal and Swire 2018.

17. Kyriakides 2018.

18. Kalyanpur and Newman 2019.

19. Nielsen 2018.

20. Other dynamics will be set in motion by Britain's exit from the European Union. Britain will surely try to preserve carve-outs from external enforcement while maximizing its own freedom of action, even as European activists and privacy officials are already quietly talking about possible actions against Britain's surveillance agency, the GCHQ. The UK government is

attempting to minimize the data flow disruption. See https://assets.publishing.service.gov.uk/government/uploads/system/uploads/attachment_data/file/710147/DATA_-_FINAL.pdf, accessed August 13, 2018.

21. Keohane 2009. For exceptions, see Krasner 1991; Ikenberry 2001; Büthe and Mattli 2011; Newman and Posner 2018.

22. Hall and Taylor 1996; McNamara 2018.

23. Farrell and Newman 2014, 2015, 2016.

24. Farrell and Newman 2010; Büthe and Mattli 2011; Fioretos 2011; Rixen, Viola, and Zürn 2016; Zürn 2018.

25. Farrell and Newman 2018.

26. Farrell and Newman 2017.

27. Weber 2017.

28. Farrell 2005.

29. Goldsmith and Wu 2006.

30. Telephone interview with Ralf Bendrath, former senior policy adviser for Jan Philipp Albrecht, June 2018.

31. Ibid.

32. See the foreign policy figures quoted in Geller 2018.

REFERENCES

ACLU. 2003. "CAPPS II Data Mining System Will Invade Privacy and Create Government Blacklist of Americans, ACLU Warns." February 27. https://www.aclu.org/news/capps-ii -data-mining-system-will-invade-privacy-and-create-government-blacklist-americans-aclu.

Ahlquist, John S. 2006. "Economic Policy, Institutions, and Capital Flows: Portfolio and Direct Investment Flows in Developing Countries." *International Studies Quarterly* 50 (3): 681 –704. https://doi.org/10.1111/j.1468–2478.2006.00420.x.

Albrecht, Jan. 2012. "EU Plans for Big Brother Data Analysis Must Be Nipped in the Bud." *EU Observer*, April 24.

———. 2015. "EU Police Cooperation and Information Sharing: More Influence for the European Parliament?" In *Police Cooperation in the European Union under the Treaty of Lisbon*, edited by Hartmut Aden, 223–34. Munich: Nomos Verlagsgesellschaft mbH and Co. KG.

Aldrich, Richard J. 2009. "US-European Intelligence Co-Operation on Counter-Terrorism: Low Politics and Compulsion." *British Journal of Politics and International Relations* 11 (1): 122–39. https://doi.org/10.1111/j.1467–856X.2008.00353.x.

Allen, Danielle, Henry Farrell, and Cosma Shalizi. 2017. "Evolution and Institutional Change." Unpublished paper.

Alter, Karen. 1998. "Who Are the 'Masters of the Treaty'?: European Governments and the European Court of Justice." *International Organization* 52 (1): 121–47. https://doi .org/10.1162/002081898550572.

———. 2008. "Agent or Trustee: International Courts in Their Political Context." *European Journal of International Relations* 14 (1): 33–63. http://journals.sagepub.com/doi /pdf/10.1177/1354066107087769.

American Embassy in Brussels. 2008. "Demarche Delivered regarding US-EU Data Protection Issue and HCLG." November 10. http://wikileaks.wikimee.org/cable/2008/11/08BRUSSELS1718 .html.

Andonova, Liliana B. 2004. *Transnational Politics of the Environment: The European Union and Environmental Policy in Central and Eastern Europe*. Cambridge, MA: MIT Press.

Andonova, Liliana B., and Ioana A. Tuta. 2014. "Transnational Networks and Paths to EU Environmental Compliance: Evidence from New Member States." *JCMS: Journal of Common Market Studies* 52 (4): 775–93. https://doi.org/10.1111/jcms.12126.

Andreas, Peter, and Ethan Nadelmann. 2006. *Policing the Globe: Criminalization and Crime Control in International Relations*. New York: Oxford University Press.

Andrew, Edmund. 1999. "Europe and U.S. Are Still at Odds over Privacy." *New York Times*, May 27.

Andrews, David M. 1994. "Capital Mobility and State Autonomy: Toward a Structural Theory of International Monetary Relations." *International Studies Quarterly* 38 (2): 193–218. https:// doi.org/10.2307/2600975.

Arel-Bundock, Vincent. 2017. "The Unintended Consequences of Bilateralism: Treaty Shopping and International Tax Policy." *International Organization* 71 (2): 349–71. https://doi.org/10.1017/S0020818317000108.

Argomaniz, Javier. 2009a. "Post-9/11 Institutionalisation of European Union Counter-Terrorism: Emergence, Acceleration, and Inertia." *European Security* 18 (2): 151–72. https://doi.org/10.1080/09662830903460103.

———. 2009b. "When the EU Is the 'Norm-Taker': The Passenger Name Records Agreement and the EU's Internalization of US Border Security Norms." *European Integration* 31 (1): 119–36. https://doi.org/10.1080/07036330802503981.

Argomaniz, Javier, Oldrich Bures, and Christian Kaunert. 2015. *A Decade of EU Counter-Terrorism and Intelligence: A Critical Assessment*. London: Routledge.

Article 29 Data Protection Working Party. 2002. "Opinion 6/2002 on Transmission of Passenger Manifest Information and Other Data from Airlines to the United States." October 24.

———. 2003. "Opinion 4/2003 on the Level of Protection Ensured in the US for the Transfer of Passengers' Data." June 13.

———. 2006a. "Opinion 10/2006 on the Processing of Personal Data by the Society for Worldwide Interbank Financial Telecommunication." October 2006. http://ec.europa.eu/justice_home/fsj/privacy/docs/wpdocs/2006/wp128_en.pdf.

———. 2006b. "Press Release on the SWIFT Case Following the Adoption of the Article 29 Working Party Opinion on the Processing of Personal Data by SWIFT." November 23.

———. 2007. "Joint Opinion on the Proposal for a Council Framework Decision on the Use of Passenger Name Record (PNR) for Law Enforcement Purposes." December 5.

Baccini, Leonardo, and Andreas Dür. 2012. "The New Regionalism and Policy Interdependence." *British Journal of Political Science* 42 (1): 57–79. https://doi.org/10.1017/S0007123411000238.

Bach, David, and Abraham Newman. 2007. "The European Regulatory State and Global Public Policy: Micro-Institutions and Macro-Influence." *Journal of European Public Policy* 16 (4): 827–46. https://doi.org/10.1080/13501760701497659.

———. 2010. "Transgovernmental Networks and Domestic Policy Convergence: Evidence from Insider Trading Regulation." *International Organization* 64 (3): 505–28. https://doi.org/10.1017/S0020818310000135.

Baker, Jennifer. 2016. "Don't Hold Your Breath on Privacy Shield Deal—It'll Be Last Minute, Insider Says." *Ars Technica*, June 9. http://arstechnica.co.uk/tech-policy/2016/06/privacy-shield-safe-harbour-article-31-not-seen-ec-text/.

Baker, Stewart A. 2010. *Skating on Stilts: Why We Aren't Stopping Tomorrow's Terrorism*. Palo Alto, CA: Hoover Press.

Balzacq, Thierry. 2006. *Security and the Two-Level Game: The Treaty of Prüm, the EU, and the Management of Threats*. Brussels: Centre for European Policy Studies.

———. 2008. "The Policy Tools of Securitization: Information Exchange, EU Foreign and Interior Policies." *JCMS: Journal of Common Market Studies* 46 (1): 75–100. https://doi.org/10.1111/j.1468-5965.2007.00768.x.

Bamford, James. 1983. *The Puzzle Palace: A Report on America's Most Secret Agency*. New York: Penguin Books.

Barnett, Michael, and Liv Coleman. 2005. "Designing Police: Interpol and the Study of Change in International Organizations." *International Studies Quarterly* 49 (4): 593–620. https://doi.org/10.1111/j.1468-2478.2005.00380.x.

Bartley, Timothy. 2011. "Transnational Governance as the Layering of Rules: Intersections of Public and Private Standards." *Theoretical Inquiries in Law* 12 (2): 517–42. https://doi.org/10.2202/1565-3404.1278.

————. 2018. *Rules without Rights: Land, Labor, and Private Authority in the Global Economy.* Oxford: Oxford University Press.

Bassiouni, M. Cherif. 2008. *International Criminal Law, Volume 2: Multilateral and Bilateral Enforcement Mechanisms.* Leiden: Brill.

Bearce, David H., Cody D. Eldredge, and Brandy J. Jolliff. 2016. "Does Institutional Design Matter?: A Study of Trade Effectiveness and PTA Flexibility/Rigidity." *International Studies Quarterly* 60 (2): 307–16. https://doi.org/10.1093/isq/sqw008.

Beckman, James. 2016. *Comparative Legal Approaches to Homeland Security and Anti-Terrorism.* London: Routledge.

Bennett, Colin J. 1992. *Regulating Privacy: Data Protection and Public Policy in Europe and the United States.* Ithaca, NY: Cornell University Press.

————. 2008. *Privacy Advocates.* Cambridge, MA: MIT Press.

Bennett, Colin, J., and D. Raab Charles. 2007. *The Governance of Privacy: Policy Instruments in a Global Perspective.* Cambridge, MA: MIT Press.

Berger, Suzanne. 2000. "Globalization and Politics." *Annual Review of Political Science* 3:43–62. https://doi.org/10.1146/annurev.polisci.3.1.43.

Bianchi, Andrea. 2007. "Assessing the Effectiveness of the UN Security Council's Anti-Terrorism Measures: The Quest for Legitimacy and Cohesion." *European Journal of International Law* 17 (5): 881–919. https://doi: 10.1093/ejil/chl032.

Bignami, Francesca. 2007. "Privacy and Law Enforcement in the European Union: The Data Retention Directive." *Chicago Journal of International Law* 8 (1): 233–55. http://chicago unbound.uchicago.edu/cjil/vol8/iss1/13.

Bignami, Francesca, and Giorgio Resta. 2015. "Transatlantic Privacy Regulation: Conflict and Cooperation." *Law and Contemporary Problems* 78:231–66. http://scholarship.law.duke .edu/lcp/vol78/iss4/10.

Blyth, Mark. 2002. *Great Transformations: Economic Ideas and Institutional Change in the Twentieth Century.* Cambridge: Cambridge University Press.

Bolkestein, Fritz. 2003. Letter from the European Commission to US Secretary of Homeland Security Tom Ridge. http://www.statewatch.org/news/2003/sep/Bolkestein-12JUN2003 .html.

Borger, Julian. 2013. "NSA Files: What's a Little Spying between Old Friends?" *Guardian*, December 2. https://www.theguardian.com/world/2013/dec/02/nsa-files-spying-allies-enemies -five-eyes-g8.

Börzel, Tanja A., and Thomas Risse. 2003. "Conceptualizing the Domestic Impact of Europe." In *The Politics of Europeanization*, edited by Kevin Featherstone and Claudio Maria Radaelli, 57–80. Oxford: Oxford University Press.

Bossong, Raphael. 2008. "The Action Plan on Combating Terrorism: A Flawed Instrument of EU Security Governance." *JCMS: Journal of Common Market Studies* 46 (1): 27–48. https:// doi/full/10.1111/j.1468-5965.2007.00766.x.

Botzem, Sebastian. 2012. *The Politics of Accounting Regulation: Organizing Transnational Standard Setting in Financial Reporting.* London: Edward Elgar Publishing.

Botzem, Sebastian, and Sigrid Quack. 2009. "(No) Limits to Anglo-American Accounting? Reconstructing the History of the International Accounting Standards Committee: A Review Article." *Accounting, Organizations, and Society* 34 (8): 988–98. https://doi.org/10.1016/j .aos.2009.07.001.

Bowden, Casper. 2014. "The Cloud Conspiracy, 2008–2014." Paper presented at the 31C3 conference, Hamburg, December 27.

Brandon, Russell, and Colin Lecher. 2018. "House Passes Controversial Legislation Giving the US Access to Overseas Data." *Verge*, March 22.

Braun, Dietmar, and Fabrizio Gilardi. 2006. "Taking 'Galton's Problem' Seriously towards a Theory of Policy Diffusion." *Journal of Theoretical Politics* 18 (3): 298–322. https://doi.org/10.1177/0951629806064351.

Brill, Julie. 2015. "Transatlantic Privacy after Schrems: Time for an Honest Conversation." Keynote address at the Amsterdam Privacy Conference, October 23. https://www.ftc.gov/system/files/documents/public_statements/836443/151023amsterdamprivacy1.pdf.

Brimmer, Esther. 2006. *Transforming Homeland Security: U.S. and European Approaches*. Washington, DC: Center for Transatlantic Relations.

Brooks, Sarah M., and Marcus J. Kurtz. 2012. "Paths to Financial Policy Diffusion: Statist Legacies in Latin America's Globalization." *International Organization* 66 (1): 95–128. https://doi.org/10.1017/S0020818311000385.

Bruguière, Jean-Louis. 2010. "Second Report on the Processing of EU-Originating Personal Data by the United States Treasury Department for Counter Terrorism Purposes: Terrorist Finance Tracking Programme." January.

Bruszt, Laszlo, and Gerald A. McDermott. 2012. "Integrating Rule Takers: Transnational Integration Regimes Shaping Institutional Change in Emerging Market Democracies." *Review of International Political Economy* 19 (5): 742–78. https://doi.org/10.1080/09692290.2011.619469.

Bures, Oldrich. 2006. "EU Counterterrorism Policy: A Paper Tiger?" *Terrorism and Political Violence* 18 (1): 57–78. https://doi.org/10.1080/09546550500174905.

———. 2010. "Eurojust's Fledgling Counterterrorism Role." *Journal of Contemporary European Research* 6 (2): 236–56. http://www.jcer.myzen.co.uk/index.php/jcer/article/view/274.

———. 2013. *EU Counterterrorism Policy: A Paper Tiger?*. London: Ashgate Publishing, Ltd.

Burley, Anne-Marie. 1993. "Regulating the World: Multilateralism, International Law, and the Projection of the New Deal Regulatory State." In *Multilateralism Matters*, edited by John Ruggie, 125–56. New York: Columbia University Press.

Büthe, Tim. 2002. "Taking Temporality Seriously: Modeling History and the Use of Narratives as Evidence." *American Political Science Review* 96 (3): 481–93. https://doi.org/10.1017/S0003055402000278.

Büthe, Tim, and Walter Mattli. 2011. *The New Global Rulers: The Privatization of Regulation in the World Economy*. Princeton, NJ: Princeton University Press.

Cadwalladr, Carole. 2018. "UKL Regulator Orders Cambridge Analytica to Release Data on US Voters." *Guardian*, May 5. https://ico.org.uk/media/action-weve-taken/enforcement-notices/2258812/en-scl-elections-20180504.pdf.

Cadwalladr, Carole, and Emma Graham-Harrison. 2018. "50 Million Facebook Profiles Harvested for Cambridge Analytica in Major Data Breach." *Guardian*, March 17.

Callaghan, Helen. 2010. "Beyond Methodological Nationalism: How Multilevel Governance Affects the Clash of Capitalisms." *Journal of European Public Policy* 17 (4): 564–80. https://doi.org/10.1080/13501761003673351.

Campbell, John L. 2004. *Institutional Change and Globalization*. Princeton, NJ: Princeton University Press.

Carnegie, Allison. 2014. "States Held Hostage: Political Hold-Up Problems and the Effects of International Institutions." *American Political Science Review* 108 (1): 54–70. https://doi.org/10.1017/S003055413000646.

Carrera, Sergio. 2016. *Implementing the Lisbon Treaty: Improving the Functioning of the EU on Justice and Home Affairs*. Brussels: Centre for European Policy Studies.

Carson, Angelique. 2017. "MEPs Discuss Next Steps for EU-Canada PNR Agreement." IAAP, September 7.

Castells, Manuel. 1996. *The Rise of the Network Society*. Oxford: Blackwell.

Cerny, Philip G. 2010. *Rethinking World Politics: A Theory of Transnational Neopluralism*. Oxford: Oxford University Press.

Cerulus, Laurens. 2016. "Companies Get Data Transfer Safety Net—For Now." *Politico EU*, July 8. http://www.politico.eu/article/privacy-shield-adoption-eu-countries-national-experts-safe-harbor-data-transfers/.

Chaffin, Joshua. 2013. "EU to Review 'Safe Harbour' Data Privacy Rule for US Companies." *Financial Times*, July 19.

Chadoin, Stephen, Helen V. Milner, and Xun Pang. 2015. "International Systems and Domestic Politics: Linking Complex Interactions with Empirical Models in International Relations." *International Organization* 69 (2): 275–309. https://doi.org/10.1017/S0020818314000356.

Chertoff, Michael. 2006. "A Tool We Need to Stop the Next Airline Plot." *Washington Post*, August 29. http://www.washingtonpost.com/wp-dyn/content/article/2006/08/28/AR2006082800849.html.

Clark, Nicola. 2006. "EU Court Bars Giving Passenger Data to US." *International Herald Tribune*, May 31.

Clarke, Roger. 1988. "Information Technology and Dataveillance." *Communications of the ACM* 31 (5): 498–512.

Clinton, William Jefferson. 1997. Commencement address at the US Military Academy at West Point, May 31. http://www.presidency.ucsb.edu/ws/index.php?pid=54210.

Cody, Edward. 2010. "Europe Amplifies Objections to US Data-Sharing System." *Washington Post*, October 27. http://www.washingtonpost.com/wpdyn/content/article/2010/10/26/AR20101 02603612.html.

Cohen, Dara Kay, Mariano-Florentino Cuéllar, and Barry R. Weingast. 2006. "Crisis Bureaucracy: Homeland Security and the Political Design of Legal Mandates." *Stanford Law Review* 59 (3): 673–759.

Colgan, Jeff D. 2014. "The Emperor Has No Clothes: The Limits of OPEC in the Global Oil Market." *International Organization* 68 (3): 599–632. https://doi.org/10.1017/S0020818313000489.

Colgan, Jeff D., and Robert O. Keohane. 2017. "The Liberal Order Is Rigged." *Foreign Affairs* (May–June). https://www.foreignaffairs.com/articles/world/2017-04-17/liberal-order-rigged.

Commission de la Protection de la Vie Privee. 2006. *Opinion on the Transfer of Personal Data by the CSLR Swift by Virtue of UST (OFAC) Subpoenas*. Brussels: Commission de la Protection de la Vie Privee.

"Common Market in Pact on Terror." 1986. *New York Times*, April 25.

Connolly, Chris. 2008. "The US Safe Harbor—Fact or Fiction." Galexia. http://www.galexia.com/public/research/assets/safe_harbor_fact_or_fiction_2008/safe_harbor_fact_or_fiction.pdf.

Coolsaet, Rik. 2010. "EU Counterterrorism Strategy: Value Added or Chimera?" *International Affairs* 86 (4): 857–73. https://doi.org/10.1111/j.1468-2346.2010.00916.x.

Council. 2007. Council Decision 2007/551/CFSP/JHA of 23 July 2007 on the Signing, on behalf of the European Union, of an Agreement between the European Union and the United States of America on the Processing and Transfer of Passenger Name Record (PNR) Data by Air Carriers to the United States Department of Homeland Security (DHS) (2007 PNR Agreement). Official Journal of the European Union. L 204/16.

———. 2008. "Final Report by EU-US High Level Contact Group on Information Sharing and Privacy and Personal Data Protection." Brussels, May 28. https://www.dhs.gov/xlibrary/assets/privacy/privacy_intl_hlcg_report_02_07_08_en.pdf.

———. 2009. "EU-US High Level Contact Group on Data Protection and Data Sharing (HLCG)." Brussels, October 16.

————. 2010. "Declarations to Be Adopted upon the Adoption of the Council Decision on Signature of the TFTP Agreement 11350/2/10 REV 2 JAI 570 USA 92 RELEX 576 DAT-APROTECT 54." June 24. http://register.consilium.europa.eu/doc/srv?l=EN&f=ST%20 11350%202010%20REV%202.

Crasnic, Lori, Nikhil Kalyanpur, and Abraham Newman. 2017. "Networked Liabilities: Transnational Authority in a World of Transnational Business." *European Journal of International Relations* 23 (4): 906–29. https://doi.org/10.1177/1354066116679245.

Cronin, Audrey Kurth. 2003. "Behind the Curve: Globalization and International Terrorism." *International Security* 27 (3): 30–58. https://doi.org/10.1162/01622880260553624.

Culpepper, Pepper. 2015. "Structural Power and Political Science in the Post-Crisis Era." *Business and Politics* 17 (3): 391–409. https://doi.org/10.1515/bad-2015-0031.

Culpepper, Pepper D., and Raphael Reinke. 2014. "Structural Power and Bank Bailouts in the United Kingdom and the United States." *Politics and Society* 42 (4): 427–54. https://doi .org/10.1177/0032329214547342.

Dalgaard-Nielsen, Anja, and Daniel Hamilton. 2006. *Transatlantic Homeland Security: Protecting Society in the Age of Catastrophic Terrorism.* London: Routledge.

Daskal, Jennifer, and Peter P. Swire. 2018. "A Possible EU-US Agreement on Law Enforcement Access to Data?" *Lawfare*, May 21. https://lawfareblog.com/possible-eu-us-agreement-law -enforcement-access-data.

de Capitani, Emilio. 2013. "The EP Committee Rejects the Proposal for an European Passenger Name Record System (PNR). European Area of Freedom, Security, and Justice. https://free- group.eu/2013/05/01/the-ep-committee-rejects-the-proposal-for-an-european-passenger -name-record-system-pnr/.

De Goede, Marieke. 2012a. *Speculative Security: The Politics of Pursuing Terrorist Monies.* Minneapolis: University of Minnesota Press.

————. 2012b. "The SWIFT Affair and the Global Politics of European Security." *JCMS: Journal of Common Market Studies* 50 (2): 214–30. https://doi.org/10.1111/j.1468-5965.2011.02219.x.

"Decimated Airlines Seek Solution to Passenger Data Feud." 2003. *EU Observer*, March 26.

Deflem, Mathieu. 2004. *Policing World Society.* Oxford: Oxford University Press.

Della Porta, Donatella, and Sidney G. Tarrow. 2005. *Transnational Protest and Global Activism.* Lanham, MD: Rowman and Littlefield.

Dempsey, Judy. 2007. "Berlin Aims to Upgrade EU Policing," *International Herald Tribune*, January 16.

Den Boer, Monica, Claudia Hillebrand, and Andreas Nolke. 2008. "Legitimacy under Pressure: The European Web of Counter-Terrorism Networks." *JCMS: Journal of Common Market Studies* 46 (1): 101–24. https://doi.org/10.1111/j.1468-5965.2007.00769.x.

Department of Homeland Security. 2008. "Final Report by EU-US High Level Contact Group on Information Sharing and Privacy and Personal Data Protection." June 12. https://www.dhs .gov/xlibrary/assets/privacy/privacy_intl_hlcg_report_02_07_08_en.pdf.

————. 2011. "Statement on Information Sharing and Privacy and Personal Data Protection between the European Union and United States of America." February 9. https://www .dhs.gov/news/2011/02/09/statement-information-sharing-and-privacy-and-personal-data -protection-between.

DeSimmone, Christian. 2010. "Pitting Karlsruhe against Luxembourg-German Data Protection and the Contested Implementation of the EU Data Retention Directive." *German Law Journal* 11 (3): 291–318.

Dhont, Jan, Maria Asinari, and Yves Poullet. 2004. "Safe Harbor Decision Implementation Study." European Commission.

Dimitrova, Anna, and Maja Brkan. 2018. "Balancing National Security and Data Protection: The Role of EU and US Policy-Makers and Courts before and after the NSA Affair." *JCMS: Journal of Common Market Studies* 56 (4): 751–67. https://doi.org/10.1111/jcms.12634.

Directorate General for Internal Policies, Policy Department C: Citizens' Rights and Constitutional Affairs. 2014. "Evaluation of EU Measures to Combat Terrorist Financing: In-Depth Analysis for the LIBE Committee."

Djelic, Marie-Laure, and Sigrid Quack. 2007. "Overcoming Path Dependency: Path Generation in Open Systems." *Theory and Society* 36 (2): 161–86. https://doi.org/10.1007/s11186-007-9026-0.

———. 2010. *Transnational Communities: Shaping Global Economic Governance*. Cambridge: Cambridge University Press.

Dobusch, Leonhard, and Sigrid Quack. 2013. "Framing Standards, Mobilizing Users: Copyright versus Fair Use in Transnational Regulation." *Review of International Political Economy* 20 (1): 52–88. https://doi.org/10.1080/09692290.2012.662909.

Donohue, Laura K. 2008. *The Cost of Counterterrorism: Power, Politics, and Liberty*. Cambridge: Cambridge University Press.

———. 2016. *The Future of Foreign Intelligence: Privacy and Surveillance in a Digital Age*. Oxford: Oxford University Press.

Dreher, Axel, J. E. Sturm, and James Vreeland. 2009. "Development Aid and International Politics: Does Membership on the UN Security Council Influence World Bank Decisions?" *Journal of Development Economics* 88 (1): 1–18. https://doi.org/10.1016/j.eurocorev.2009.03.002.

Drezner, Daniel. 2007. *All Politics Is Global: Explaining International Regulatory Regimes*. Princeton, NJ: Princeton University Press.

Efrat, Asif. 2015. "Do Human Rights Violations Hinder Counterterrorism Cooperation? Evidence from the FBI's Deployment Abroad." *Review of International Organizations* 10 (3): 329–49. https://doi.org/10.1007/s11558-014-9202-8.

Efrat, Asif, and Abraham Newman. 2017. "Divulging Data: Domestic Determinants of International Information Sharing." *Review of International Organizations* (June): 1–25. https://doi.org/10.1007/s11558-017-9284-1.

Ellis, Alan, and Robert L. Pisani. 1985. "The United States Treaties on Mutual Assistance in Criminal Matters: A Comparative Analysis." *International Lawyer* 19 (1): 189–223.

EU Anti-Terrorism Coordinator. 2016. "State of Play on Implementation of the Statement of the Members of the European Council of 12 February 2015, the JHA Council Conclusions of 20 November 2015, and the Conclusions of the European Council of 18 December 2015." March 4.

"EU MPs Back Passenger Data Sharing Deal with US." 2012. *Agence France Presse*, March 27.

"EU Privacy Ruling Threatens Chaos on Flights to US." 2006. *Daily Telegraph*, May 31.

"EU to Launch Anti-Terror Finance Tracking Plan." 2010. *Euractiv*, March 15.

"European Airlines in Legal Limbo." 2006. *European Report*, October 3.

European Commission. 2000. Commission Decision of 26 July 2000 Pursuant to Directive 95/46/EC of the European Parliament and of the Council on the Adequacy of the Protection Provided by the Safe Harbour Privacy Principles and Related Frequently Asked Questions Issued by the US Department of Commerce. Brussels. July 26.

———. 2003. "Joint Statement." February 17. Brussels.

———. 2004. Transfer of Air Passenger Name Record Data: A Global EU Approach. Brussels.

———. 2010. "European Commission Prepares New Negotiations with US on Transfer of Bank Data for Counter-Terrorism Purposes." Brussels. March 24. http://europa.eu/rapid/press-release_IP-10–348_en.htm.

———. 2011. "Communication from the Commission to the European Parliament, the Council, the European Economic and Social Committee and the Committee of the Regions:

A European Terrorist Finance Tracking System: Available Options." (COM(2011) 429 final).

———. 2013a. "Communication from the Commission to the European Parliament and the Council: A European Terrorist Finance Tracking System (EU TFTS) (SWD (2013) Final). See also "Commission Staff Working Document. Impact Assessment: Accompanying the Document Communication from the European Commission to the European Parliament and the Council on a European Terrorist Financing Tracking System (TFTS)." (COM(2013) 842 Final/SWD(2013) 489 Final).

———. 2013b. "Rebuilding Trust in EU-US Data Flows, COM/2013/0846 Final." http://eur-lex.europa.eu/legal-content/EN/TXT/?uri=celex:52013DC0846.

———. 2016. "Remarks by Commissioners Avramopoulos, Jourová, and King at the Press Conference on Terrorism Financing, the Schengen Information System, and Visa Reciprocity." December 21. https://ec.europa.eu/commission/commissioners/2014-2019/king/announcements/remarks-commissioners-avramopoulos-jourova-and-king-press-conference-terrorism-financing-schengen_en.

———. 2017. "Commission Staff Working Document. Joint Review of the iImplementation of the Agreement between the European Union and the United States of America on the Processing and Transfer of Financial Messaging Data from the European Union to the United States for the Purposes of the Terrorist Finance Tracking Program. SWD/2017/017 Final. http://eur-lex.europa.eu/legal-content/en/TXT/?uri=CELEX:52017SC0017.

European Court of Justice. 2003. "C-101/01: Bodil Lindqvist." November 6.

———. 2006. "Parliament v Council of the European Union (C-317/04) and Commission of the European Communities (C-318/04). Protection of Individuals with regard to the Processing of Personal Data—Air Transport—Decision 2004/496/EC—Agreement between the European Community and the United States of America—Passenger Name Records of Air Passengers Transferred to the United States Bureau of Customs and Border Protection—Directive 95/46/EC—Article 25—Third Countries—Decision 2004/535/EC—Adequate Level of Protection.

———. 2015a. "C-362/14: Maximillian Schrems v Data Protection Commissioner." Brussels: European Court of Justice.

———. 2015b. "Factsheet: Advocate General's Opinion in Case C-362/14, Maximillian Schrems v Data Protection Commission." Brussels: European Court of Justice.

———. 2017. "Opinion 1/15 on the Draft Agreement between Canada and the European Union." July 26.

European Data Protection Supervisor. 2010. "Proposal for a Council Decision on the Conclusion of the Agreement between the European Union and the United States of America on the Processing and Transfer of Financial Messaging Data from the European Union to the United States for Purposes of the Terrorist Finance Tracking Program." Brussels, June 22.

———. 2015. "Second Opinion on the Proposal for a Directive of the European Parliament and of the Council on the Use of Passenger Name Record Data for the Prevention, Detection, Investigation, and Prosecution of Terrorist Offences and Serious Crime." Brussels, September 24, 1–16.

———. 2016. "Privacy Shield: More Robust and Sustainable Solution Needed." May 30. https://edps.europa.eu/sites/edp/files/edpsweb_press_releases/edps-2016-11-privacyshield_en.pdf.

European Ombudsman. 2016. "Use of the Title 'Ombudsman' in the 'EU-U Privacy Shield' Agreement." October 6.

European Parliament. 2004. "Report on the Initiative of the Kingdom of Spain with a View to the Adoption of a Council Directive on the Obligation of Carriers to Communicate Passenger Data. A5–0211/2004." Brussels: European Parliament.

———. 2009. "Recommendation on the Proposal for a Council Decision on the Conclusion of the Agreement between the European Union and the United States of America on the Processing and Transfer of Financial Messaging Data from the European Union to the United States for Purposes of the Terrorist Finance Tracking Program (05305/1/2010REV—C7–0004/2010–2009/0190(NLE))." February 5. http://www.europarl.europa.eu/sides/getDoc.do?language=EN&reference=A7–0013/2010.

———. 2010a. "European Parliament Resolution of 5 May 2010 on the Recommendation from the Commission to the Council to Authorise the Opening of Negotiations for an Agreement between the European Union and the United States of America to Make Available to the United States Treasury Department Financial Messaging Data to Prevent and Combat Terrorism and Terrorist Financing." May 5. http://www.europarl.europa.eu/sides/getDoc.do?pubRef=-//EP//TEXT+TA+P7-TA-2010–0143+0+DOC+XML+V0//EN.

———. 2010b. "Parliament's Rejection of the SWIFT Agreement." Brussels: European Parliament Press Office.

———. 2010c. "Recommendation on the Draft Council Decision on the Conclusion of the Agreement between the European Union and the United States of America on the Processing and Transfer of Financial Messaging Data from the European Union to the United States for the Purposes of the Terrorist Finance Tracking Program (11222/1/2010/REV 1 and COR 1—C7–0158/2010–2010/0178(NLE))." July 5. http://www.europarl.europa.eu/sides/getDoc.do?pubRef=-//EP//TEXT+REPORT+A7-2010–0224+0+DOC+XML+V0//EN&language=en.

———. 2016. European Parliament Resolution of 26 May 2016 on Transatlantic Data Flows. May 26.

European Union and United States of America. 2010. Agreement on the Processing and Transfer of Financial Messaging Data from the European to the United States for the Purposes of the Terrorist Finance Tracking Program.

Evans, Peter, Harold Jacobson, and Robert Putnam. 1993. *Double-Edged Diplomacy: International Bargaining and Domestic Politics*. Berkeley: University of California Press.

Evans, Hayley, and Shannon Togawa Mercer. 2018. "Privacy Shield on Shaky Ground: What's Up with EU-U.S. Data Privacy Regulations." *Lawfare*, September 2.

Farrell, Henry. 2002. "Negotiating Privacy across Arenas—The EU-US 'Safe Harbor' Discussions." In *Common Goods: Reinventing European and International Governance*, edited by Adrienne Héritier and Dominik Bölhoff, 105–26. Lanham, MD: Rowman and Littlefield.

———. 2003. "Constructing the International Foundations of E-Commerce: The EU-US Safe Harbor Arrangement." *International Organization* 57 (2): 277–306. https://doi.org/10.1017/S0020818303572022.

———. 2005. "Transnational Actors and the Transatlantic Relationship in E-Commerce—The Negotiation of the Safe Harbor Arrangement." In *Creating a Transatlantic Marketplace*, edited by Michelle Egan, 112–33. Manchester: Manchester University Press.

———. 2016. Here's Why the Activist Who Started the Safe Harbor Fight Thinks That Negotiations Won't Work (Interview with Max Schrems). *Washington Post*, January 31. https://www.washingtonpost.com/news/monkey-cage/wp/2016/01/31/heres-why-the-activist-who-started-the-safe-harbor-fight-thinks-that-negotiations-wont-work/.

Farrell, Henry, and Adrienne Héritier. 2003. "Formal and Informal Institutions under Codecision: Continuous Constitution-Building in Europe." *Governance* 16 (4): 577–600. https://doi.org/10.1111/1468-0491.00229.

Farrell, Henry, and Abraham Newman. 2010. "Making Global Markets: Historical Institutionalism in International Political Economy." *Review of International Political Economy* 17 (4): 609–38. https://doi.org/10.1080/09692291003723672.

———. 2014. "Domestic Institutions beyond the Nation-State: Charting the New Interdependence Approach." *World Politics* 66 (2): 331–63. https://doi.org/10.1017/S0043887114000057.

———. 2015. "The New Politics of Interdependence: Cross-National Layering in Trans-Atlantic Regulatory Disputes." *Comparative Political Studies* 48 (4): 497–526. https://doi.org/10.1177/0010414014542330.

———. 2016. "The New Interdependence Approach: Theoretical Development and Empirical Demonstration." *Review of International Political Economy* 23 (5): 713–36. https://doi.org/10.1080/09692290.2016.1247009.

———. 2017. "BREXIT, Voice, and Loyalty: Rethinking Electoral Politics in an Age of Interdependence." *Review of International Political Economy* 24 (2): 232–47. https://doi.org/10.1080/09692290.2017.1281831.

———. 2018. "Linkage Politics and Complex Governance in Transatlantic Surveillance." *World Politics* (October): 1–40. doi: 10.1017/s0043887118000114.

Field, C. 2003. "Wrangling over Passenger Lists: Transatlantic Tensions." *International Herald Tribune*, September 19.

Fioretos, Orfeo. 2009. "The Regulation of Transnational Corporate Identity in Europe." *Comparative Political Studies* 42 (9): 1167–92. https://doi.org/10.1177/0010414009331725.

———. 2010. "Capitalist Diversity and the International Regulation of Hedge Funds." *Review of International Political Economy* 17 (4): 696–723. https://doi.org/10.1080/09692291003723789.

———. 2011. "Historical Institutionalism in International Relations." *International Organization* 65 (2): 367–99. https://doi.org/10.1017/S002818311000002.

Fisher, James. 2007. "What Price Does Society Have to Pay for Security—A Look at the Aviation Watch Lists." *Willamette Law Review* 44 (1): 573–614.

Fleming, Jeremy. 2015. "Parliament's Alliance against Passenger Data Provisions Crumbles." *Euractiv*, February 12. https://www.euractiv.com/section/digital/news/parliament-s-alliance-against-passenger-data-provisions-crumbles/.

Fox, Justin, and Matthew Stephenson. 2015. "The Constraining, Liberating, and Informational Effects of Nonbinding Law." *Journal of Law, Economics, and Organization* 31 (2): 320–46. https://doi.org/10.1093/jleo/ewu013.

"France Eyes European System to Track Terrorism Finance." 2015. Euractiv, December 17. https://www.euractiv.com/section/justice-home-affairs/news/france-eyes-european-system-to-track-terrorism-finance/.

Freyburg, Tina, Sandra Lavenex, Frank Schimmelfennig, Tatiana Skripka, and Anne Wetzel. 2009. "EU Promotion of Democratic Governance in the Neighbourhood." *Journal of European Public Policy* 16 (6): 916–34. https://doi.org/10.1080/13501760903088405.

Friedman, Jan, John Goetz, Ralf Neukirch, Marcel Rosenbach, and Holger Stark. 2010. "America's Trojan Horse in Europe." *Der Spiegel*, November 30.

Garrett, Geoffrey, and Peter Lange. 1991. "Political Responses to Interdependence: What's 'Left' for the Left?" *International Organization* 45 (4): 539–64. https://doi.org/10.1017/S0020818300033208.

Geller, Eric. 2018. "China, EU Seize Control of the World Cyber Agenda." *Politico*, July 24.

George, Alexander, and Andrew Bennett. 2005. *Case Studies and Theory Development in the Social Sciences*. Cambridge, MA: MIT Press.

German Data Protection Commissioners. 2010. "Decision by the Supreme Supervisory Authorities for Data Protection in the Nonpublic Sector on 28/29 April 2010 in Hannover: Examination of the Data Importer's Self-Certification according to the Safe Harbor Agreement by the Company Exporting Data." April.

———. 2013. "Conference of Data Protection Commissioners Says That Intelligence Services Constitute a Massive Threat to Data Traffic between Germany and Countries outside Europe." https://www.datenschutz.bremen.de/detail.php?gsid=bremen236.c.9285.de.

Gidda, Mirren. 2013. "Edward Snowden and the NSA Files—Timeline." *Guardian*, August 21.

Goede, Marieke de, and Mara Wesseling. 2017. "Secrecy and Security in Transatlantic Terrorism Finance Tracking." *Journal of European Integration* 39 (3): 253–69. https://doi.org/10.1080/07036337.2016.1263624.

Goldsmith, Jack, and Tim Wu. 2006. *Who Controls the Internet?: Illusions of a Borderless World.* Oxford: Oxford University Press.

Goldstein, Herman. 1977. *Policing a Free Society.* Cambridge, MA: Ballinger Publishing.

Goldstein, Judith. 1996. "International Law and Domestic Institutions: Reconciling North American 'Unfair' Trade Laws." *International Organization* 50 (4): 541–64. https://doi.org/10.1017/S0020818300033506.

Gourevitch, Peter Alexis, and James Shinn. 2005. *Political Power and Corporate Control: The New Global Politics of Corporate Governance.* Princeton, NJ: Princeton University Press.

Government Accountability Office. 2004. *Computer-Assisted Passenger Prescreening System Faces Significant Implementation Challenges.* Washington, DC: Government Accountability Office.

Granick, Jennifer. 2017. *American Spies: Modern Surveillance, Why You Should Care, and What to Do about It.* Cambridge: Cambridge University Press.

Green, Jessica F. 2013. *Rethinking Private Authority: Agents and Entrepreneurs in Global Environmental Governance.* Princeton, NJ: Princeton University Press.

Greenwald, Glenn. 2013. "NSA Collecting Phone Records of Millions of Verizon Customers Daily." *Guardian*, June 6.

Gregory, Anthony. 2016. *American Surveillance: Intelligence, Privacy, and the Fourth Amendment.* Madison: University of Wisconsin Press.

Gruber, Lloyd. 2000. *Ruling the World: Power Politics and the Rise of Supranational Institutions.* Princeton, NJ: Princeton University Press.

Guild, Elspeth. 2008. "The Uses and Abuses of Counter-Terrorism Policies in Europe: The Case of the 'Terrorist Lists.'" *JCMS: Journal of Common Market Studies* 46 (1): 173–93. https://doi.org/10.1111/j.1468–5965.2007.00772.x.

Hacker, Jacob S. 2004. "Privatizing Risk without Privatizing the Welfare State: The Hidden Politics of Social Policy Retrenchment in the United States." *American Political Science Review* 98 (2): 243–60. https://doi.org/10.1017/S0003055404001121.

Hafner, Katie, and Matthew Lyon. 1998. *Where Wizards Stay up Late: The Origins of the Internet.* New York: Simon and Schuster.

Hall, Peter A., and David Soskice. 2001. *Varieties of Capitalism.* Oxford: Oxford University Press.

Hall, Peter A., and Rosemary C. R. Taylor. 1996. "Political Science and the Three New Institutionalisms." *Political Studies* 44: (5): 936–57. doi/pdf/10.1111/j.1467- 9248.1996.tb00343.x.

Hall, Peter A., and Kathleen Thelen. 2009. "Institutional Change in Varieties of Capitalism." *Socio-Economic Review* 7 (1): 7–34. https://doi.org/10.1093/ser/mwn020.

Halliday, Terence, and Bruce Carruthers. 2009. *Bankrupt: Global Lawmaking and Systemic Financial Crisis.* Palo Alto, CA: Stanford University Press.

Hameiri, Shahar, and Lee Jones. 2013. "The Politics and Governance of Non-Traditional Security." *International Studies Quarterly* 57 (3): 462–73. https://doi.org/10.1111/isqu.12014.

Helmke, Gretchen, and Steven Levitsky. 2004. "Informal Institutions and Comparative Politics: A Research Agenda." *Perspectives on Politics* 2 (4): 725–40. https://doi.org/10.1017/S1537592704040472.

High Court of Ireland. 2014. Schrems v Data Protection Commissioner. 2013 765 JR. June 18.

Hoff, Jessica. 2014. "Enhancing Security while Protecting Privacy: The Rights Implicated by Supposedly Heightened Airport Security." *Michigan State Law Review* 2014 (5): 1609–55.

Hofheinz, Paul, and Michael Mandel. 2015. "Uncovering the Hidden Value of Digital Trade." Progressive Policy Institute 19, 1–12. Lisbon: Lisbon Council.

Honig, Bonnie. 2009. *Emergency Politics: Paradox, Law, Democracy.* Princeton, NJ: Princeton University Press.

Hooghe, Lisebet, and Gary Marks. 2003. "Unraveling the Central State, but How?: Types of Multi-Level Governance." *American Political Science Review* 97 (2): 233–43. https://doi.org/10.1017/S0003055403000649.

Hopkins, Raymond 1976. "The International Role of 'Domestic' Bureaucracy." *International Organization* 30 (3): 405–32. https://doi.org/10.1017/S002081830001835X.

Horowitz, Michael C., and Philip B. K. Potter. 2014. "Allying to Kill: Terrorist Intergroup Cooperation and the Consequences for Lethality." *Journal of Conflict Resolution* 58 (2): 199–225. https://doi.org/10.1177/0022002712468726.

Ibramova, Isel, and Matt Buckwell. 2016. "Legal Challenge to EU-US Privacy Shield Framework." *National Law Journal,* October 31. http://www.natlawreview.com/article/legal-challenge-to-eu-us-privacy-shield-framework.

Ikenberry, G. John. 2009. *After Victory: Institutions, Strategic Restraint, and the Rebuilding of Order after Major Wars.* Princeton, NJ: Princeton University Press.

Jackson, Patrick, and Dan Nexon. 1999. "Relations before States: Substance, Process, and the Study of World Politics." *European Journal of International Relations* 5 (3): 291–332. https://doi.org/10.1177/1354066199005003002.

Jabko, Nicolas. 2006. *Playing the Market: A Political Strategy for Uniting Europe.* Ithaca, NY: Cornell University Press.

Jančić, Davor. 2016. "The Role of the European Parliament and the US Congress in Shaping Transatlantic Relations: TTIP, NSA Surveillance, and CIA Renditions." *JCMS: Journal of Common Market Studies* 54 (4): 896–912. https://doi.org/10.1111/jcms.12345.

Jervis, Robert. 2011. *Why Intelligence Fails: Lessons from the Iranian Revolution and the Iraq War.* Ithaca, NY: Cornell University Press.

Joachim, Jutta. 2003. "Framing Issues and Seizing Opportunities: The UN, NGOs, and Women's Rights." *International Studies Quarterly* 47 (2): 247–74. https://doi.org/10.1111/1468-2478.4702005.

Johnson, Tana. 2013. "Institutional Design and Bureaucrats' Impact on Political Control." *Journal of Politics* 75 (1): 183–97. https://doi.org/10.1017/S0022381612000953.

———. 2014. *Organizational Progeny: Why Governments Are Losing Control over the Proliferating Structures of Global Governance.* Oxford: Oxford University Press.

Jones, Del. 2002. "Homeland Security: A Tough Merger," *USA Today,* June 11.

Jupille, Joseph. 1999. "The European Union and International Outcomes." *International Organization* 53 (2): 409–21. https://doi.org/10.1162/002081899550922.

Justice and Home Affairs DG. 2005. "Press Release: Vice-President Franco Frattini and JLS in Charge of Data Protection." 16-03-2005. Brussels: European Commission.

Kaczmarek, Sarah C., and Abraham Newman. 2011. "The Long Arm of the Law: Extraterritoriality and the National Implementation of Foreign Bribery Legislation." *International Organization* 65 (4): 745–70. https://doi.org/10.1017/S0020818311000270.

Kagan, Robert. 2002. "Power and Weakness: Why the United States and Europe See the World Differently." *Policy Review* 113:3–28.

———. 2007. *Of Paradise and Power: America and Europe in the New World Order.* New York: Knopf Doubleday Publishing Group.

Kahler, Miles. 2009. *Networked Politics: Agency, Power, and Governance*. Ithaca, NY: Cornell University Press.

———. 2016. "Complex Governance and the New Interdependence Approach (NIA)." *Review of International Political Economy* 23 (5): 825–39. https://doi.org/10.1080/09692290.2016. 1251481.

Kahler, Miles, and David Lake. 2003. *Governance in a Global Economy: A Political Authority in Transition*. Princeton, NJ: Princeton University Press.

Kaiser, Karl. 1971. "Transnational Politics: Toward a Theory of Multinational Politics." *International Organization* 25 (4): 790–817. https://doi.org/10.1017/S0020818300017732.

Kalyanpur, Nikhil, and Abraham Newman. 2017. "Form over Function in Finance: International Institutional Design by Bricolage." *Review of International Political Economy* 24 (3): 363–92. https://doi.org/10.1080/09692290.2017.1307777.

———. 2019. "The MNC-Coalition Paradox: Issue Salience, Foreign Firms, and the General Data Protection Regulation." *JCMS: Journal of Common Market Studies*.

Kanter, James. 2010. "EU Blocks US Efforts to Track Terrorist Funding." *International Herald Tribune*, February 12.

Kaunert, Christian. 2010. "The External Dimension of EU-Counter-Terrorism Relations: Competences, Interests, and Institutions." *Terrorism and Political Violence* 22 (1): 41–61. https://doi.org/10.1080/09546550903409551.

Kehaulani Goo, Sara, and Spencer Hsu. 2005. "First Privacy Officer Calls 'Experiment' a Success." *Washington Post*, September 29.

Kelemen, Daniel. 2011. *Eurolegalism: The Transformation of Law and Regulation in the European Union*. Cambridge, MA: Harvard University Press.

Kelley, Judith G., and Beth A. Simmons. 2015. "Politics by Number: Indicators as Social Pressure in International Relations." *American Journal of Political Science* 59 (1): 55–70. https://doi.org/10.1111/ajps.12119.

Keohane, Daniel. 2008. "The Absent Friend: EU Foreign Policy and Counter-Terrorism." *JCMS: Journal of Common Market Studies* 46 (1): 125–46. https://doi/full/10.1111/j.1468 -5965.2007.00770.x.

Kelemen, R.D., 2010. *Globalizing European union environmental policy*. Journal of European Public Policy, 17(3), pp. 335-349. doi.org/10.1080/13501761003662065

Keohane, Robert O. 2009. "The Old IPE and the New." *Review of International Political Economy* 16 (1): 34–46. https://doi.org/10.1080/09692290802524059.

Keohane, Robert O., and Joseph Nye. 1977. *Power and Interdependence: World Politics in Transition*. Boston: Little, Brown.

Keohane, Robert O., and David G. Victor. 2011. "The Regime Complex for Climate Change." *Perspectives on Politics* 9 (1): 7–23. https://doi.org/10.1017/S1537592710004068.

Kerry, Cameron. 2014. *Missed Connections: Talking with Europe about Data, Privacy, and Surveillance*. Washington, DC: Brookings Institution. https://www.brookings.edu/wp-content /uploads/2016/06/Kerry_EuropeFreeTradePrivacy.pdf.

———. 2016. *Bridging the Internet-Cyber Gap: Digital Policy Lessons for the Next Administration*. Washington, DC: Brookings Institution. https://www.brookings.edu/wp-content /uploads/2016/10/internet-cyber-gap-final.pdf.

Kessler, Ronald. 2016. *The Bureau: The Secret History of the FBI*. London: Macmillan.

Kite, Leigh A. 2004. "Red Flagging Civil Liberties and Due Process Rights of Airline Passengers: Will a Redesigned CAPPS II System Meet the Constitutional Challenge." *Washington and Lee Law Review* 61:1385–436.

Knight, Jack. 1992. *Institutions and Social Conflict*. Cambridge: Cambridge University Press.

Kobrin, Stephen. 2004. "Safe Harbours Are Hard to Find: The Trans-Atlantic Data Privacy Dispute, Territorial Jurisdiction, and Global Governance." *Review of International Studies* 30: 111–31. https://doi.org/10.1017/S0260210504005856.

Kokott, Juliane, and Christoph Sobotta. 2013. "The Distinction between Privacy and Data Protection in the Jurisprudence of the CJEU and the ECtHR." *International Data Privacy Law* 3 (4): 222–28. https://doi.org/10.1093/idpl/ipt017.

Koremenos, Barbara, Charles Lipson, and Duncan Snidal. 2001. "The Rational Design of International Institutions." *International Organization* 55 (4): 761–99. https://doi.org/10.1162/002081801317193592.

Krasner, Stephen. 1976. "State Power and the Structure of International Trade." *World Politics* 28 (2): 317–47. https://doi.org/10.2307/2009974.

———. 1991. "Global Communications and National Power: Life on the Pareto Frontier." *World Politics* 43 (3): 336–66. https://doi.org/10.2307/2010398.

Kuchler, Hannah. 2018. "Max Schrems: The Man Who Took on Facebook—and Won." *Financial Times*, April 5. https://www.ft.com/content/86d1ce50-3799-11e8-8eee-e06bde01c544.

Kyriakides, Eleni. 2018. "Digital Free for All Part Deux: European Commission Proposal on E-Evidence." *Just Security*, May 17. https://www.justsecurity.org/56408/digital-free-part-deux-european-commission-proposal-e-evidence/.

Lake, David A. 2009. "Open Economy Politics: A Critical Review." *Review of International Organizations* 4 (3): 219–44. https://doi.org/10.1007/s11558-009-9060-y.

Lall, Ranjit. 2012. "From Failure to Failure: The Politics of International Banking Regulation." *Review of International Political Economy* 19 (4): 609–38. https://doi.org/10.1080/09692290.2011.603669.

Landale, James, and Martin Fletcher. 1999. "Europe Plans Cross-Border Crime Fighters." *Times*, October 16.

Landau, Susan. 2013. "Making Sense from Snowden: What's Significant in the NSA Surveillance Revelations." *IEEE Security Privacy* 11 (4): 54–63. https://doi.org/10.1109/MSP.2013.90.

———. 2014. "Highlights from Making Sense of Snowden, Part II: What's Significant in the NSA Revelations." *IEEE Security Privacy* 12 (1): 62–64. https://doi.org/10.1109/MSP.2013.161.

Lander, Stephen. 2004. "International Intelligence Cooperation: An Inside Perspective." *Cambridge Review of International Affairs* 17 (3): 481–93. http://www.tandfonline.com/doi/full/10.1080/0955757042000296964.

Lefebvre, Stephanie. 2003. "The Difficulties and Dilemmas of International Intelligence Cooperation." *International Journal of Intelligence and Counterintelligence* 16 (4): 527–42. https://doi.org/10.1080/716100467.

Lehrke, Jesse Paul, and Rahel Schomaker. 2014. "Mechanisms of Convergence in Domestic Counterterrorism Regulations: American Influence, Domestic Needs, and International Networks." *Studies in Conflict and Terrorism* 37 (8): 689–712. https://doi.org/10.1080/1057610X.2014.921769.

Leonard, Sarah. 2009. "The Creation of FRONTEX and the Politics of Institutionalisation in the EU External Borders Policy." *Journal of Contemporary European Research* 5 (3): 371–88. http://www.jcer.net/index.php/jcer/article/view/239.

Levey, Stuart. 2016. "Testimony before the House Financial Services Subcommittee on Oversight and Investigations." Washington, DC: US House of Representatives.

"LIBE Series 6: Safe Harbor under Scrutiny by European Parliament." 2013. *Access Now*, October 15. https://www.accessnow.org/libe-series-6-safe-harbour-under-scrutiny-by-the-european-parliament/.

Library of the European Parliament. 2011. "EU Response to the Terrorist Finance Tracking Programme." http://www.europarl.europa.eu/RegData/bibliotheque/briefing/2011/110164 /LDM_BRI(2011)110164_REV1_EN.pdf.

Lichtblau, Eric, and James Risen. 2006. "Bank Data Is Sifted by US in Secret to Block Terror." *New York Times*, June 23.

Lillington, Karlin. 2014. "Striking a Blow for Data Rights in Europe." *Irish Times*, April 9.

Litt, Robert. 2015. "Europe's Court Should Know the Truth about US Intelligence." *Financial Times*.

———. 2016. "Remarks on Privacy Shield Negotiations." Paper presented at the SAIS Colloquium, February 11, Washington, DC.

Locke, Richard, Matthew Amengual, and Akshay Mangla. 2009. "Virtue out of Necessity? Compliance, Commitment, and the Improvement of Labor Conditions in Global Supply Chains." *Politics and Society* 37 (3): 319–51. https://doi.org/10.1177/0032329209338922.

Lodge, Juliet. 1989. "Terrorism and the European Community: Towards 1992." *Terrorism and Political Violence* 1 (1): 28–47. https://doi.org/10.1080/09546558908427012.

Loeb, Vernon. 1999. "Critics Questioning NSA Reading Habits," *Washington Post*, November 13.

Ludford, Sarah. 2003. "Debate on the Resolution concerning PNR." Plenary Session of the European Parliament. Brussels, March 12.

Lyon, David. 2001. *Surveillance Society: Monitoring Everyday Life*. London: McGraw-Hill Education.

———. 2003. "Airports as Data Filters: Converging Surveillance Systems after September 11th." *Journal of Information, Communication, and Ethics in Society* 1 (1): 13–20. https://doi .org/10.1108/14779960380000222.

Macavinta, Courtney. 2002. "BBB Privacy Project Faces Critics." CNET, January 2. https:// www.cnet.com/news/bbb-privacy-project-faces-critics/.

Mahoney, James, and Kathleen Thelen. 2009. *Explaining Institutional Change: Ambiguity, Agency, and Power*. Cambridge: Cambridge University Press.

Mahoney, Joseph. 2003. "Strategies of Causal Assessment in Comparative Historical Analysis." In *Comparative Historical Analysis in the Social Sciences*, edited by Joseph Mahoney and Dietrich Rueschemeyer, 337–72. Cambridge: Cambridge University Press.

Mahony, Honor. 2013. "MEPs Vote Down Air Passenger Data Scheme." *EU Observer*, April 24.

Majone, Giandomenico. 1996. *Regulating Europe*. New York: Routledge.

Malik, Rhyea, and Subhajit Basu. 2017. "India's Dodgy Mass Surveillance Project Should Concern Us All." *Wired*, August 25.

Mansfield, Edward D., Helen V. Milner, and Jon C. Pevehouse. 2007. "Vetoing Co-Operation: The Impact of Veto Players on Preferential Trading Arrangements." *British Journal of Political Science* 37 (3): 403–32. https://doi.org/10.1017/S0007123407000221.

Mansfield, Edward D., Helen V. Milner, and B. Peter Rosendorff. 2002. "Why Democracies Cooperate More: Electoral Control and International Trade Agreements." *International Organization* 56 (3): 477–513. https://doi.org/10.1162/002081802760199863.

Maricut, Adina. 2016. "With and without Supranationalisation: The Post-Lisbon Roles of the European Council and the Council in Justice and Home Affairs Governance." *Journal of European Integration* 38 (5): 541–55. https://doi.org/10.1080/07036337.2016.1178253.

Martin, Cathie Jo, and Duane Swank. 2004. "Does the Organization of Capital Matter?: Employers and Active Labor Market Policy at the National and Firm Levels." *American Political Science Review* 98 (4): 593–611. https://doi.org/10.1017/S0003055404041371.

Mattli, Walter, and Tim Büthe. 2003. "Setting International Standards: Technological Rationality or Primacy of Power." *World Politics* 56 (1): 1–42. https://doi.org/10.1353/wp.2004.0006.

Mattli, Walter, and Ngaire Woods. 2009. *The Politics of Global Regulation*. Princeton, NJ: Princeton University Press.

Maurice, Eric. 2015. "Terrorism Shakes Europe." *EU Observer*, December 24.

May, Ashley. 2018. "Dating App Grindr Says It Will Stop Sharing HIV Status, Profile Info with Other Companies." *USA Today*, April 3.

May, Peter J., Ashley E. Jochim, and Joshua Sapotichne. 2011. "Constructing Homeland Security: An Anemic Policy Regime." *Policy Studies Journal* 39 (2): 285–307. https://doi.org/10.1111/j.1541–0072.2011.00408.x.

McCabe, Sarah. 2015. "Data Privacy Is as Important as Tax, Google Exec Warns Noonan." *Irish Independent*, April 12. https://www.independent.ie/business/irish/data-privacy-is-as-important-as-tax-google-exec-warns-noonan-31134213.html.

McCarthy, Kieran. 2018. "GDPR for Everyone, Cries Microsoft. *Register*, May 22.

McDonald, Heather. 2004. "What We Don't Know Can Hurt Us." *City Journal* (Spring): 14–31.

McGarr, Simon. 2015. "Do Facebook and the USA Violate EU Data Protection Law? The CJEU Hearing in Schrems." *EU Law Analysis*, March 29. http://eulawanalysis.blogspot.co.uk/2015/03/does-facebook-and-usa-violate- eu-data.html.

McNamara, Kathleen. 2018. "Authority under Construction: The European Union in Comparative Political Perspective." *JCMS: Journal of Common Market Studies*. https://doi.org/10.1111/jcms.12784.

Melander, Ingrid. 2008. "EU Considers Air Passenger Profiling in 2009." *Gazette*, January 26.

Meunier, Sophie. 2005. *Trading Voices: The European Union in International Commercial Negotiations*. Princeton, NJ: Princeton University Press.

Meyer, David. 2016. "Hamburg's DPA Aiming to Challenge Privacy Shield." *IAPP News*, August 4. https://iapp.org/news/a/hamburgs-dpa-aiming-to-challenge-privacy-shield/.

Milner, Helen V. 1997. *Interests, Institutions, and Information*. Princeton, NJ: Princeton University Press.

Milner, Helen V., and Dustin H. Tingley. 2011. "Who Supports Global Economic Engagement?: The Sources of Preferences in American Foreign Economic Policy." *International Organization* 65 (1): 37–68. https://doi.org/10.1017/S0020818310000317.

Moe, Terry M. 2005. "Power and Political Institutions." *Perspectives on Politics* 3 (2): 215–33. https://doi.org/10.1017/S1537592705050176.

Monar, Jörg. 2001. "The Dynamics of Justice and Home Affairs: Laboratories, Driving Factors, and Costs." *JCMS: Journal of Common Market Studies* 39 (4): 747–64. https://doi.org/10.1111/1468–5965.00329.

———. 2004. "The EU as an International Actor in the Domain of Justice and Home Affairs." *European Foreign Affairs Review* 9:395–416. https://doi.org/10.1080/09557570701414633.

———. 2007. "The EU's Approach Post–September 11: Global Terrorism as a Multidimensional Law Enforcement Challenge." *Cambridge Review of International Affairs* 20 (2): 267–83. https://doi.org/10.1080/09662839.2013.856308.

———. 2014. "EU Internal Security Governance: The Case of Counter-Terrorism." *European Security* 23 (2): 195–209.

———. 2015. "The EU as an International Counter-Terrorism Actor: Progress and Constraints." *Intelligence and National Security* 30 (2–3): 333–56. https://doi.org/10.1080/02684527.2014.988448.

Moschella, Manuela. 2016. "Negotiating Greece. Layering, Insulation, and the Design of Adjustment Programs in the Eurozone." *Review of International Political Economy* 23 (5): 799–824. https://doi.org/10.1080/09692290.2016.1224770.

Mosley, Layna. 2003. *Global Capital and National Governments*. Cambridge: Cambridge University Press.

———. 2010. "Regulating Globally, Implementing Locally: The Financial Codes and Standards Effort." *Review of International Political Economy* 17 (4): 724–61. https://doi.org/10.1080/09692290903529817.

Müller-Wille, Björn. 2008. "The Effect of International Terrorism on EU Intelligence Co-Operation." *JCMS: Journal of Common Market Studies* 46 (1): 49–73. https://doi.org/10.1111/j.1468–5965.2007.00767.x.

Murillo, M. Victoria, and Andrew Schrank. 2005. "With a Little Help from My Friends: Partisan Politics, Transnational Alliances, and Labor Rights in Latin America." *Comparative Political Studies* 38 (8): 971–99. https://doi.org/10.1177/0010414004274402.

Nadelmann, Ethan. 1993. *Cops across Borders*. University Park: Penn State Press.

Nakashima, Ellen. 2007. "EU Satisfied with Data Sharing." *Washington Post*, January 12, D2.

Newman, Abraham. 2008a. "Building Transnational Civil Liberties: Transgovernmental Entrepreneurs and the European Data Privacy Directive." *International Organization* 62 (1): 103–30. https://doi.org/10.1017/S0020818308080041.

———. 2008b. *Protectors of Privacy: Regulating Personal Data in the Global Economy*. Ithaca, NY: Cornell University Press.

———. 2010. "International Organization Control under Conditions of Dual Delegation: A Transgovernmental Politics Approach." In *Who Governs the Globe*, edited by Deborah Avant, Martha Finnemore, and Susan Sell, 131–52. Cambridge: Cambridge University Press.

Newman, Abraham, and Elliot Posner. 2011. "International Interdependence and Regulatory Power: Authority, Mobility, and Markets." *European Journal of International Relations* 17 (4): 589–610. https://doi.org/10.1177/1354066110391306.

———. 2016. "Transnational Feedback, Soft Law, and Preferences in Global Financial Regulation." *Review of International Political Economy* 23 (1): 123–52. https://doi.org/10.1080/09692290.2015.1104375.

———. 2018. *Voluntary Disruptions: International Soft Law, Finance, and Power*. Oxford: Oxford University Press.

Nielsen, Nikolaj. 2012. "EU Hands Personal Data to US Authorities on a Daily Basis." *EU Observer*, June 22.

———. 2014. "Data Retention Issue Stymies EU Air Passenger Bill." *EU Observer*, November 11.

———. 2015a. "Deadline Uncertain for New EU-US Data Pact." *EU Observer*, December 11.

———. 2015b. "US Gag Order on EU Police Agency Stirs Controversy." *EU Observer*, January 8.

———. 2016a. "EU Wants to Give Police Greater Digital Access." *EU Observer*, March 10.

———. 2016b. "MEPs Set to Back Air-Passenger Data Sharing." *EU Observer*, April 14.

———. 2018. "Facebook Threatened with Removal from US-EU Pact." *EU Observer*, May 21.

Norton-Taylor, Richard, and Ian Black. 2001. "Leaked Spy Report Names UK: Privacy Warning across Europe." *Guardian*, May 26. https://www.theguardian.com/uk/2001/may/26/richardnortontaylor.ianblack1.

Nye, Joseph S., and Robert O. Keohane. 1971. "Transnational Relations and World Politics: An Introduction." *International Organization* 25 (3): 329–49. https://doi.org/10.1017/S0020818300026187.

Oatley, Thomas. 2011. "The Reductionist Gamble: Open Economy Politics in the Global Economy." *International Organization* 65 (2): 311–41. https://doi.org/10.1017/S002081831100004X.

Oatley, Thomas, W. Kindred Winecoff, Andrew Pennock, and Sarah Bauerle Danzman. 2013. "The Political Economy of Global Finance: A Network Model." *Perspectives on Politics* 11 (1): 133–53. https://doi.org/10.1017/S1537592712003593.

Obama, Barack. 2010. "US–European Union Agreement on the Terrorist Finance Tracking Program (TFTP)." Washington, DC: White House.

Occhipinti, John. 2003. *The Politics of EU Police Cooperation: Toward a European FBI*. Boulder, CO: Lynn Rienner.

OECD. 1980. *Guidelines on Trans-Border Data Flows and the Protection of Privacy*. Paris: OECD.

O'Neil, Cathy. 2016. *Weapons of Math Destruction: How Big Data Increases Inequality and Threatens Democracy*. New York: Broadway Books, 2016.

"Parliament Calls for Freezing Anti-Terror Banking Data Transfers with the US." 2013. *Euractiv*, October 24. https://www.euractiv.com/section/justice-home-affairs/news/parliament-calls-for-freezing-anti-terror-banking-data-transfers-with-the-us/.

Pawlak, Patryk. 2009a. "Made in the USA? The Influence of the US on the EU's Data Protection Regime." Brussels: Centre for European Policy Studies. http://www.ceps.eu/book/made-usa-influence-us-eu%E2%80%99s-data-protection-regime.

———. 2009b. "Network Politics in Transatlantic Homeland Security Cooperation." *Perspectives on European Politics and Society* 10 (4): 560–81. https://doi.org/10.1080/15705850903314833.

———. 2010. "Transatlantic Homeland Security Cooperation: The Promise of New Modes of Governance in Global Affairs." *Journal of Transatlantic Studies* 8 (2): 139–57. https:// doi .org/10.1080/14794011003760277.

Pignal, Stanley. 2009. "Brussels Outlines Plan to Give US Cross-Border Bank Data." *Financial Times*, November 12.

Pollack, Mark A. 2003. *The Engines of Integration? Delegation, Agency, and Agenda Setting in the European Union*. New York: Oxford University Press.

Pollack, Mark A., and Gregory C. Shaffer. 2009. *When Cooperation Fails: The International Law and Politics of Genetically Modified Foods*. New York: Oxford University Press.

Pop, Valentina. 2009. "EU Stalls Bank Data Deal with US Ahead of Lisbon Treaty." *EU Observer*, November.

———. 2010a. "Biden Sweet-Talks MEPs on Anti-Terrorism Deal." *EU Observer*, May 6.

———. 2010b. "Clinton Balls Parliament Chief over Bank Data Deal." *EU Observer*, February 4.

———. 2010c. "MEPs Look to New Data Protection Battle with US." *EU Observer*, July 7.

———. 2011a. "Court Only Option against Swift Agreement, Says MEP." *EU Observer*, March 17.

———. 2011b. "EU to Collect Data of International Air Travelers." *EU Observer*, February 1.

Porter, Andrew L., and Annegret Bendiek. 2012. "Counterterrorism Cooperation in the Transatlantic Security Community." *European Security* 21 (4): 497–517. https://doi.org/10.1080/09662839.2012.688811.

Posner, Elliot. 2009a. "Making Rules for Global Finance: Transatlantic Regulatory Cooperation at the Turn of the Millennium." *International Organization* 63 (4): 665–99. https://doi.org/10.1017/S0020818309990130.

———. 2009b. *The Origins of Europe's New Stock Markets*. Cambridge, MA: Harvard University Press.

———. 2010. "Sequence as Explanation: The International Politics of Accounting Standards." *Review of International Political Economy* 17 (4): 639–64. https://doi.org/10.1080/09692291003723748.

Price, Rob. 2015. "Eric Schmidt Thinks a Ruling by Europe's Top Court Threatens 'One of the Greatest Achievements of Humanity.'" *Business Insider*, October 15.

Privacy International. 2004. *Transferring Privacy: The Transfer of Passenger Records and the Abdication of Privacy Protection*. February. http://www.statewatch.org/news/2004/feb/transferringprivacy.pdf.

Putnam, Robert. 1988. "Diplomacy and Domestic Politics: The Logic of Two-Level Games." *International Organization* 42 (3): 427–60. https://doi.org/10.1017/S0020818300027697.

Putnam, Tonya L. 2009. "Courts without Borders: Domestic Sources of U.S. Extraterritoriality in the Regulatory Sphere." *International Organization* 63 (3): 459–90. https://doi.org/10.1017/S002081830909016X.

————. 2016. *Courts without Borders: Law, Politics, and U.S. Extraterritoriality.* New York: Cambridge University Press.

Pritzker Penny. 2015. "Statement from U.S. Secretary of Commerce Penny Pritzker on European Court of Justice Safe Harbor Framework Decision." Washington, DC: Department of Commerce.

Quack, Sigrid. 2010. "Law, Expertise, and Legitimacy in Transnational Economic Governance: An Introduction." *Socio-Economic Review* 8 (1): 3–16. https://doi.org/10.1093/ser/mwp029.

Raul, Alan Charles. 2016. "The EU-U.S. Privacy Shield Is a Victory for Common Sense and Transatlantic Good Will." *Net Politics*, March 1. http://blogs.cfr.org/cyber/2016/03/01/the-eu-u-s-privacy-shield-is-a-victory-for-common-sense-and-transatlantic-good-will/.

Raustiala, Kal. 2002. "The Architecture of International Cooperation: Transgovernmental Networks and the Future of International Law." *Virginia Journal of International Law* 43:1–92.

————. 2004. "The Regime Complex for Plant Genetic Resources." *International Organization* 58 (2): 277–309.

————. 2009. *Does the Constitution Follow the Flag?: The Evolution of Territoriality in American Law.* New York: Oxford University Press.

Reding, Viviane, and John Bryson. 2012. "U.S.-EU Joint Statement on Privacy from EU Commission Vice-President Viviane Reding and U.S. Commerce Secretary John Bryson."

Rees, Wyn. 2006. *Transatlantic Counter-Terrorism Cooperation: The New Imperative.* New York: Routledge.

————. 2008. "Inside Out: The External Face of EU Internal Security Policy." *Journal of European Integration* 30 (1): 97–111. https://doi.org/10.1080/07036330801959515.

Rees, Wyn, and Richard J. Aldrich. 2005. "Contending Cultures of Counterterrorism: Transatlantic Divergence or Convergence?" *International Affairs* 81 (5): 905–23. https://doi.org/10.1111/j.1468–2346.2005.00494.x.

Regan, Priscilla M. 1995. *Legislating Privacy: Technology, Social Values, and Public Policy.* Raleigh: University of North Carolina Press.

Regan, Priscilla M., and Torin Monahan. 2013. "Beyond Counterterrorism: Data Sharing, Privacy, and Organizational Histories of DHS Fusion Centers." *International Journal of E-Politics (IJEP)* 4 (3): 1–14. https://doi.org/10.4018/jep.2013070101.

Rettman, Andrew. 2017. "EU Defends Airline Data-Sharing after Court Ruling." *EU Observer*, July 26.

Richards, John. 1999. "Toward a Positive Theory of International Institutions: Regulating International Aviation Markets." *International Organization* 53 (1): 1–37. https://doi.org/10.1162/002081899550797.

Risse-Kappan, Thomas. 1995. Ed. *Bringing Transnational Actors Back In: Non-State Actors, Domestic Structures and International Institutions.* Cambridge: Cambridge University Press.

Rixen, Thomas, Lora Anne Viola, and Michael Zürn, eds. *Historical Institutionalism and International Relations: Explaining Institutional Development in World Politics.* Oxford: Oxford University Press, 2016.

Robert, Aline. 2016. "Hypocrisy at the Heart of the PNR Debate." *Euractiv*, March 29.

Rodotà, Stefano. 2003. Letter to European Parliament Committee on Citizens' Freedom and Rights. Brussels.

Roger, Charles, and Peter Dauvergne. 2016. "The Rise of Transnational Governance as a Field of Study." *International Studies Review* 18 (3): 415–37. https://doi.org/10.1093/isr/viw001.

Rogowski, Ronald. 1989. *Commerce and Coalitions: How Trade Affects Domestic Political Alignments.* Princeton, NJ: Princeton University Press.

Romaniello, Maria. 2013. "The International Role of the European Parliament: The SWIFT Affair and the 'Re-Assessed' European Institutional Balance of Power." *Perspectives on Federalism* 5 (1): 97–121. http://www.on-federalism.eu/attachments/156_download.pdf.

Rosenau, James N. 1990. *Turbulence in World Politics: A Theory of Change and Continuity*. Princeton, NJ: Princeton University Press.

Roxborough, Ian. 2001. *The Hart-Rudman Commission and the Homeland Defense*. Philadelphia: DIANE Publishing.

Rudra, Nita. 2008. *Globalization and the Race to the Bottom in Developing Countries: Who Really Gets Hurt?* Cambridge: Cambridge University Press.

Ryder, Nicholas. 2015. *The Financial War on Terrorism: A Review of Counter-Terrorist Financing Strategies since 2001*. London: Routledge.

"'Safe Harbour 2' Doesn't Need Change on Surveillance, Top US Official Insists." 2015. *Euractiv*, November 3. https://www.euractiv.com/section/digital/news/safe-harbour-2-doesn-t-need-change-on-surveillance-top-us-official-insists/.

Salter, Mark B. 2008. *Politics at the Airport*. Minneapolis: University of Minnesota Press.

Sandler, Todd, Daniel G. Arce, and Walter Enders. 2011. "An Evaluation of Interpol's Cooperative-Based Counterterrorism Linkages." *Journal of Law and Economics* 54 (1): 79–110. https://doi.org/10.1086/652422.

Sassen, Saskia. 2006. *Territory, Authority, Rights: From Medieval to Global Assemblages*. Princeton, NJ: Princeton University Press.

Savage, Charlie. 2011. "Public Said to Be Misled on Use of Patriot Act." *New York Times*, September 21.

Schäuble, Wolfgang. 2006. "Interview with Wolfgang Schäuble." *General Anzeiger*, August 24.

Scheppele, Kim Lane. 2006. "North American Emergencies: The Use of Emergency Powers in Canada and the United States." *International Journal of Constitutional Law* 4 (2): 213–43. https://doi.org/10.1093/icon/mo1003.

———. 2010. "The International Standardization of National Security Law." *Journal of National Security Law and Policy* 4:437–54.

Schickler, Eric. 2001. *Disjointed Pluralism*. Princeton, NJ: Princeton University Press.

Schiltz, Christoph. 2006. "Zypries will passagierdaten auch in der EU nutzen." *Die Welt*, October 7.

Schwartz, Paul M., and Karl-Nikolaus Peifer. 2017. "Transatlantic Data Privacy Law." *Georgetown Law Journal* 106:115–79.

Schwartz, Paul M., and Joel Reidenberg. 1996. *Data Privacy Law: A Study of United States Data Protection*. Charlottesville, VA: Michie.

Scott, Mark. 2016. "Europe Approves New Trans-Atlantic Data Transfer Deal." *New York Times*, July 13. https://www.nytimes.com/2016/07/13/technology/europe-eu-us-privacy-shield.html.

Scott, Suzan V., and Markos Zachariadis. 2014. *The Society for Worldwide Interbank Financial Telecommunication (SWIFT): Cooperative Governance for Network Innovation, Standards, and Community*. London: Routledge.

Seamon, Richard Henry, and William Dylan Gardner. 2004. "The Patriot Act and the Wall between Foreign Intelligence and Law Enforcement." *Harvard Journal of Law and Public Policy* 28:319–464.

Servent, Ariadna Ripoll. 2013. "Holding the European Parliament Responsible: Policy Shift in the Data Retention Directive from Consultation to Codecision." *Journal of European Public Policy* 20 (7): 972–87. https://doi.org/10.1080/13501763.2013.795380.

———. 2014. "The Role of the European Parliament in International Negotiations after Lisbon." *Journal of European Public Policy* 21 (4): 568–86.

Servent, Ariadna Ripoll, and Alex MacKenzie. 2011. "Is the EP Still a Data Protection Champion? The Case of SWIFT." *Perspectives on European Politics and Society* 12 (4): 390–406. https://doi.org/10.1080/15705854.2011.622957.

Shaffer, Gregory C. 2000. "Globalization and Social Protection: The Impact of EU and International Rules in the Ratcheting up of US Privacy Standards." *Yale Journal of International Law* 25 (1): 1–88. http://digitalcommons.law.yale.edu/cgi/viewcontent.cgi?article=1112& context=yjil.

Shaffer, Gregory C., ed. 2012. *Transnational Legal Ordering and State Change.* Cambridge: Cambridge University Press.

Shane, Scott, and Mark Mazzetti. 2018. "Inside a 3-Year Russian Campaign to Influence US Voters." *New York Times*, February 16.

———. 2012. *Transnational Legal Ordering and State Change.* Cambridge: Cambridge University Press.

Sheftalovich, Zoya. 2016. "Safe Harbor Deal Divides Opinion." *Politico EU*, February 2. http://www.politico.eu/article/political-handshake-on-safe-harbor-deal/.

Sikkink, Kathryn. 2005. "Patterns of Dynamic Multilevel Governance and the Insider-Outsider Coalition." In *Transnational Protest and Global Activism*, edited by Donatella Della Porta and Sidney Tarrow, 151–73. New York: Rowan and Littlefield.

Simitis, Spiros. 2003. *Kommentar zum Bundesdatenschutzgesetz.* Baden-Baden: Nomos.

Simmons, Beth. 2000. "International Law and State Behavior: Commitment and Compliance in International Monetary Affairs." *American Political Science Review* 94 (4): 819–35. https://doi.org/10.2307/2586210.

———. 2001. "The International Politics of Harmonization: The Case of Capital Market Regulation." *International Organization* 55 (3): 589–620. https://doi.org/10.1162/00208180152507560.

———. 2013. "Preface: International Relationships in the Information Age." *International Studies Review* 15 (1): 1–4.

Simmons, Beth, and Allison Danner. 2010. "Credible Commitments and the International Criminal Court." *International Organization* 64 (2): 225–56. https://doi.org/10.1017/S0020818310000044.

Simmons, Beth, Frank Dobbin, and Geoffrey Garrett. 2006. "Introduction: The International Diffusion of Liberalism." *International Organization* 60 (4): 781–810. https://doi.org/10.1017/S0020818306060267.

Singel, Ryan. 2004. "Life after Death for CAPPS II?" *Wired*, July 16.

Sinha, Aseema. 2007. "Global Linkages and Domestic Politics: Trade Reform and Institution Building in India in Comparative Perspective." *Comparative Political Studies* 40 (10): 1183–210. https://doi.org/10.1177/0010414007304669.

Slaughter, Anne-Marie. 2004. *A New World Order.* Princeton, NJ: Princeton University Press.

Sloan, Lawrence D. 2001. "ECHELON and the Legal Restraints on Signals Intelligence: A Need for Reevaluation." *Duke Law Journal* 50 (5): 1467–510. https://doi.org/10.2307/1373027.

Smith, Brad. 2015. "The Collapse of the US-EU Safe Harbor: Solving the New Privacy Rubik's Cube." *Microsoft Blog*, October 20. https://blogs.microsoft.com/on-the-issues/2015/10/20/the-collapse-of-the-us-eu-safe-harbor-solving-the-new-privacy-rubiks-cube/.

Smith, Jeffrey, and Thomas Lippman. 1996. "FBI Plans to Expand Overseas; 23 New Offices Slated, Raising Some Criticism at State Department and CIA." *Washington Post*, August 20.

Solms-Laubach, Franz. 2007. "Vorbild USA." *Berliner Morgenpost*, June 30.

Solove, Daniel J., and Woodrow Hartzog. 2014. "The FTC and the New Common Law of Privacy." *Columbia Law Review* 114:583–676. https://papers.ssrn.com/sol3/papers.cfm?abstract_id=2312913.

Souminen, Annika. 2008. "The Past, Present, and the Future of Eurojust." *Maastricht Journal of European and Comparative Law* 15 (2): 217–34.

Stuart, Douglas T. 2009. *Creating the National Security State: A History of the Law That Transformed America.* Princeton, NJ: Princeton University Press.

Suda, Yuko. 2013. "Transatlantic Politics of Data Transfer: Extraterritoriality, Counter-Extraterritoriality, and Counter-Terrorism." *JCMS: Journal of Common Market Studies* 51 (4): 772–88. https://doi.org/10.1111/jcms.12017.

SWIFT. 2006. *Executive Summary of SWIFT's Response to the Belgian Privacy Commission's Advisory Opinion.* Brussels: SWIFT.

Swire, Peter P. 2015. "US Surveillance Law, Safe Harbor, and Reforms since 2013." Future of Privacy Forum. https://papers.ssrn.com/sol3/papers.cfm?abstract_id=2709619.

Swire, Peter P., and Robert Litan. 1998. *None of Your Business: World Data Flows, Electronic Communication, and the European Privacy Directive.* Washington, DC: Brookings.

Swire, Peter P., and Lauren B. Steinfeld. 2001. "Security and Privacy after September 11: The Health Care Example." *Minnesota Law Review* 86:1515–40.

Szumski, Adrian. 2016. "Instruments Used by Interpol in the Fight against International Trafficking in Human Beings." *Internal Security* 8 (1): 59–68. https://doi.org/10.5604/20805268 .1231513.

Talmon, Stefan. 2005. "The Security Council as World Legislature." *American Journal of International Law* 99 (1): 175–93. https://doi.org/10.2307/3246097.

Tarrow, Sidney. 2001. "Transnational Politics: Contention and Institutions in International Politics." *Annual Review of Political Science* 4 (1): 1–20. https://doi.org/10.1146/annurev .polisci.4.1.1.

———. 2005. *The New Transnational Activism.* Cambridge: Cambridge University Press.

Taylor, Mistale. 2015. "Privacy and Data Protection in the European Parliament: An Interview with Sophie in't Veld." *Utrecht Journal of International and European Law* 31 (80): 141–44.

Teufel, Hugo. 2014. "An Explanation of the DHS Privacy Policy behind Review Group Recommendation #14." *Lawfare*, January 8. https://www.lawfareblog.com/explanation-dhs-privacy -policy-behind-review-group-recommendation-14.

Thelen, Kathleen. 2003. "How Institutions Evolve: Insights from Comparative Historical Analysis." In *Comparative Historical Analysis in the Social Sciences,* edited by Joseph Mahoney and Dietrich Rueschemeyer, 208–40. Cambridge: Cambridge University Press.

———. 2004. *How Institutions Evolve: The Political Economy of Skills in Germany, Britain, the United States, and Japan.* Cambridge: Cambridge University Press.

Tomik, Stefan. 2007. "Die EU will Fluggastdaten speichern—Eigentlich könnte sie das schon lange." *Frankfurter Allgemeine Zeitung,* July 7.

Tonnelson, Alan. 2000. *The Race to the Bottom.* Boulder, CO: Westview Press.

Traynor, Ian. 2008. "Government Wants Personal Details of Every Traveller." *Guardian,* February 23. https://www.theguardian.com/uk/2008/feb/23/uksecurity.terrorismandtravel.

Trento, Susan B., and Joseph J. Trento. 2006. *Unsafe at Any Altitude: Failed Terrorism Investigations, Scapegoating 9/11, and the Shocking Truth about Aviation Security Today.* Hanover, NH: Steerforth.

Troy, Thomas F. 1981. *Donovan and the CIA: A History of the Establishment of the Central Intelligence Agency.* Washington, DC: Center for the Study of Intelligence.

Tsebelis, George. 2002. *Veto Players: How Political Institutions Work.* Princeton, NJ: Princeton University Press.

UK House of Lords European Union Committee. 2008. "The Passenger Name Record Framework Decision." *Report with Evidence,* June 11.

US Department of Defense. 2017. *Task Force on Cyber Deterrence*. US Defense Science Board. https://www.hsdl.org/?abstract&did=799190.

US Department of the Treasury. 2007. "Letter from United States Department of the Treasury regarding SWIFT/Terrorist Finance Tracking Programme." July 20.

"US Embassy Cables: Madeleine McCann Case Pushes EU to Act on Child Abductions, 11 October 2007." 2010. *Guardian*, December 13. https://www.theguardian.com/world/us-embassy -cables-documents/125480.

US Embassy to France. 2007. "French Support for the Terror Finance Tracking Program." February 1. https://search.wikileaks.org/plusd/cables/07PARIS408_a.html.

US Embassy to Germany. 2006. "Treasury Officials Underscore Basis, Value of TFTP ("Swift" Program)." September 25. http://cables.mrkva.eu/cable.php?id=79611.

———. 2007a. "Chancellor Merkel Angered by Lack of German MEP Support for TFTP." February 12. https://wikileaks.org/plusd/cables/10BERLIN180_a.html.

———. 2007b. "Deputy Treasury Secretary Kimmitt Meets with German Interior Minister Wolfgang Schäuble." February 11.

———. 2010. "Chancellor Merkel Angered by Lack of German MEP Support for TFTP." Wikileaks Cables, February 12. https://search.wikileaks.org/plusd/cables/10BERLIN180 _a.html.

US Mission to the European Union. 2001. "Letter to President Prodi." October 16. http://www .statewatch.org/news/2001/nov/06Ausalet.htm.

———. 2007. "French Support for the Terror Finance

Tracking Program." February 1. https://search.wikileaks.org/plusd/cables/07PARIS408_a.html.

———. 2015. "Safe Harbor Protects Privacy and Provides Trust in Data Flows That Underpin Transatlantic Trade." Brussels.

US Embassy to the Netherlands. 2007. "SWIFT/TFTP: Treasury Explores Next Steps with the Dutch." January 29. http://wikileaks.ikiru.ch/cable/07THEHAGUE163/.

Varghese, George P. 2003. "A Sense of Purpose: The Role of Law Enforcement in Foreign Intelligence Surveillance." *University of Pennsylvania Law Review* 152 (1): 385–430. https://doi .org/10.2307/3313064.

Vernon, Raymond. 1971. *Sovereignty at Bay: The Multinational Spread of U.S. Enterprises*. Cambridge, MA: Harvard University Press.

Vogel, David. 1995. *Trading Up: Consumer and Environmental Regulation in a Global Economy*. Cambridge, MA: Harvard University Press.

———. 2012. *The Politics of Precaution: Regulating Health, Safety, and Environmental Risks in Europe and the United States*. Princeton, NJ: Princeton University Press.

Walsh, James. 2009. *The International Politics of Intelligence Sharing*. New York: Columbia University Press.

Waltz, Kenneth. 1979. *Theory of International Politics*. Reading, MA: Addison-Wesley

Watt, Nicholas, and Andrew Clark. 2006. "Airlines Alarmed as European Court Annuls Passenger Data Deal with US." *Guardian*, May 31.

Waxman, Matthew C. 2009. "Police and National Security: American Local Law Enforcement and Counterterrorism after 9/11." Journal of National Security Law and Policy 3:377–408. https://papers.ssrn.com/sol3/papers.cfm?abstract_id=1305268.

Weber, Amalie M. 2003. "The Council of Europe's Convention on Cybercrime." *Berkeley Technology Law Journal* 18 (1): 425–46. https://scholarship.law.berkeley.edu/cgi/viewcontent .cgi?article=1416&context=btlj.

Weber, Steven. 2017. "Data, Development, and Growth." *Business and Politics* 19 (3): 397–423. https://doi.org/10.1017/bap.2017.3.

Weinberg, Joe. 2016. "European Union Member States in Cross-National Analyses: The Dangers of Neglecting Supranational Policymaking." *International Studies Quarterly* 60 (1): 98–106. https://doi.org/10.1093/isq/sqv009.

Wennerholm, Peter, Erik Brattberg, and Mark Rhinard. 2010. "The EU as a Counter-Terrorism Actor Abroad: Finding Opportunities, Overcoming Constraints." European Policy Centre Issue Paper #60. Brussels: European Policy Centre.

Wesseling, Mara. 2016. *An EU Terrorist Finance Tracking System.* London: Royal United Services Institute.

White, Samuel. 2015. "Donald Tusk Urges Parliament to Accept European PNR." *Euractiv,* January 14.

White House. 2014. Presidential Policy Directive—Signals Intelligence Activities (PPD-28). January 17.

Whitlock, Craig. 2008. "Terrorism Financing Blacklists at Risk." *Washington Post,* November 2, A1.

Whytock, Christopher A. 2009. "Domestic Courts and Global Governance." *Tulane Law Review* 84:67–123. http://papers.ssrn.com/sol3/papers.cfm?abstract_id=923907.

Woll, Cornelia. 2008. *Firm Interests: How Governments Shape Business Lobbying on Global Trade.* Ithaca, NY: Cornell University Press.

Wright, Steve. 2002. "The ECHELON Trail: An Illegal Vision." *Surveillance and Society* 3 (2–3): 198–215. http://www.statewatch.org/news/2006/mar/wright-echelon-s-and-sur.pdf.

Young, Alasdair R. 2003. "Political Transfer and 'Trading Up'? Transatlantic Trade in Genetically Modified Food and US Politics." *World Politics* 55 (4): 457–84. https://doi.org/10.1353/wp.2003.0026.

———. 2011. "Of Executive Preferences and Societal Constraints: The Domestic Politics of the Transatlantic GMO Dispute." *Review of International Political Economy* 18 (4): 506–29. https://doi.org/10.1080/09692290.2010.483885.

Zagaris, Bruce, and Jessica Resnick. 1997. "The Mexico-U.S. Mutual Legal Assistance in Criminal Matters Treaty: Another Step toward the Harmonization of International Law Enforcement." *Arizona Journal of International and Comparative Law* 14:1–96.

Zaiotti, Ruben. 2011. *Cultures of Border Control: Schengen and the Evolution of European Frontiers.* Chicago: University of Chicago Press.

Zarate, Juan. 2013. *Treasury's War: The Unleashing of a New Era of Financial Warfare.* New York: PublicAffairs.

Zegart, Amy B. 2009. *Spying Blind: The CIA, the FBI, and the Origins of 9/11.* Princeton, NJ: Princeton University Press.

Zuboff, Shoshana. 2015. "Big Other: Surveillance Capitalism and the Prospects of an Information Civilization." *Journal of Information Technology* 30 (1): 75–89. doi:10.1057/jit.2015.5.

Zürn, Michael. 2018. *A Theory of Global Governance: Authority, Legitimacy, and Contestation.* Oxford: Oxford University Press.

Zysman, John, and Abraham Newman. 2006. *How Revolutionary Was the Digital Revolution?* Stanford, CA: Stanford University Press.

INDEX

A NOTE ON THE TYPE

This book has been composed in Adobe Text and Gotham. Adobe Text, designed by Robert Slimbach for Adobe, bridges the gap between fifteenth- and sixteenth-century calligraphic and eighteenth-century Modern styles. Gotham, inspired by New York street signs, was designed by Tobias Frere-Jones for Hoefler & Co.